English Intonation

Intonation – the rise and fall of pitch in our voices – plays a crucial role in how we express meaning. This accessible introduction shows the student how to recognize and reproduce the intonation patterns of English, providing clear explanations of what they mean and how they are used. It looks in particular at three key functions of intonation – to express our attitude, to structure our messages to one another, and to focus attention on particular parts of what we are saying. An invaluable guide to how English intonation works, it is complete with extensive exercises, drills and practice material, encouraging students to produce and understand the intonation patterns for themselves. The accompanying CD contains a wealth of spoken examples, clearly demonstrating English intonation in context. Drawing on the perspectives of both language teaching and linguistics, this textbook will be welcomed by both learners of English and beginning undergraduates in phonetics and linguistics.

J. C. WELLS is Professor of Phonetics at University College, London. He has lectured in countries all over the world and makes regular appearances on BBC Radio and TV. He is author of the three-volume set *Accents of English* (Cambridge University Press, 1982).

English Intonation

An introduction

J. C. WELLS

Professor of Phonetics, UCL

CAMBRIDGE
UNIVERSITY PRESS

CAMBRIDGE UNIVERSITY PRESS
Cambridge, New York, Melbourne, Madrid, Cape Town, Singapore, São Paulo

Cambridge University Press
The Edinburgh Building, Cambridge CB2 2RU, UK

Published in the United States of America by Cambridge University Press, New York

www.cambridge.org
Information on this title: www.cambridge.org/9780521683807

First published 2006

Printed in the United Kingdom at the University Press, Cambridge

A catalogue record for this publication is available from the British Library

ISBN-13 978-0-521-86524-1 hardback
ISBN-10 0-521-86524-7 hardback
ISBN-13 978-0-521-68380-7 paperback
ISBN-10 0-521-68380-7 paperback

Contents

Preface

This book is written from a descriptive-linguistic and language-teaching perspective. It is intended both for native speakers and for learners of English at university level. My aim is to help the reader to recognize and reproduce the important intonation patterns of English and to understand what they mean and how they are used. The emphasis is on conversational English.

My debt to my teachers J. D. O'Connor and Michael Halliday will be evident. Among more recent writers on intonation I would particularly mention Paul Tench, to whom I owe the idea of devoting a separate chapter to each of the three Ts. My other main sources are listed in the References.

I have benefited from many discussions over the years with my colleagues Michael Ashby, Patricia Ashby, Jill House and John Maidment. Email discussions on the Supras list were stimulating, particularly the input from Tamikazu Date. Mercedes Cabrera offered useful comments on a draft version. Thanks to all.

Thanks, too, to those whose voices are heard, along with my own, on the accompanying CD: Michael Ashby, Patricia Ashby, Jill House, Alison Keable, Josette Lesser, Jane Setter and Matt Youens. And thanks to Masaki Taniguchi for help with proofreading.

1   Introduction

1.1   What is intonation?

Intonation is the melody of speech. In studying intonation we study how the pitch of the voice rises and falls, and how speakers use this pitch variation to convey linguistic and pragmatic meaning. It also involves the study of the rhythm of speech, and (in English, at any rate) the study of how the interplay of accented, stressed and unstressed syllables functions as a framework onto which the intonation patterns are attached.

If we had no intonation, our speech would be – in the literal sense of the word – monotonous. Either it would all remain on one pitch throughout, or every utterance would employ exactly the same stereotyped tune at all times. But speakers do neither of those things: they make the pitch of their voice rise, fall, jump and swoop, in all sorts of different ways. Even the most boring speaker has access to a considerable repertoire of tunes (intonation patterns) – though maybe some speakers are better than others at exploiting this. Lively speakers typically make good use of the wide repertoire of possible intonation patterns that English offers.

This is true both for the broadcaster, lecturer, preacher, politician, or business-man addressing a public audience and for the participant in an ordinary everyday conversational interchange or informal chat.

The purpose of this book is to show how intonation works in English, and to describe a selection of the intonation patterns of English from the point of view of English language teaching (ELT). The emphasis is on points that should be useful for those teaching or learning English as a non-native language. At the same time it will, I hope, enable native speakers of English to appreciate the functioning of English intonation.

Why is the study of English intonation useful for the student of English? The linguistic study of any language is of course academically valuable in itself. But for the learner of English there is also a very practical reason for making some attempt to acquire a command, both active and passive, of its intonation.

If they study pronunciation at all, learners of English usually concentrate on the segmental phonetics – the 'sounds' of the language (known technically as the **segments**). It is indeed important to learn to recognize and reproduce the consonant sounds and vowel sounds of English and the differences between them. Every learner of English should be taught to make the *th*-sounds of *thick* and *this*, the vowel sound of *nurse*, and the differences in sound between *leave* and *live*, *bet* and *bat*. Most learners also learn about word stress. They know that *happy* is stressed on the first syllable, but *regret* on the second. But intonation (also known as **prosody** or **suprasegmentals**) is mostly neglected. The teacher fails to teach it, and the learner fails to learn it. Like other elements of language, some gifted learners will pick it up more or less unconsciously; but many will not.

The problem is this: native speakers of English know that learners have difficulty with vowels and consonants. When interacting with someone who is not a native speaker of English, they make allowances for segmental errors, but they do not make allowances for errors of intonation. This is probably because they do not realize that intonation can be erroneous.

After all, almost any intonation pattern is *possible* in English; but different intonation patterns have different meanings. The difficulty is that the pattern the learner uses may not have the *meaning* he or she intends. Speakers of English assume that – when it comes to intonation – you mean what you say. This may not be the same as what you think you are saying.

Audio recordings of selected examples from the text and exercises are provided on the accompanying CD. The icon ๏ tells you which they are.

The intonation symbols used in this book are explained in appendix A1.

EXERCISES

E1.1.1 Listen to the following sentences spoken (i) normally and (ii) strictly on a monotone (= the pitch of the voice stays level, not going up and not going down). Repeat them aloud in the same way.

๏   I 'can't \stand it.
๏   'What do I do \now?
๏   O /Lord, | 'open thou our \lips!
๏   Are you 'ready to /answer?
๏   'Silly old \fool!

What do these sound like when spoken on a monotone? Would they ever be said like this in real life? (Singing? Chanted in a church service? In conversation, with some special meaning?)

E1.1.2 Pitch awareness exercise. ๏ Listen to the syllable *ma* said with high pitch (⁻*ma*) and then with low pitch (_*ma*). Imitate. Learn to produce high (H) or low (L) pitch at will.

⁻ma	⁻ma	⁻ma	_ma	_ma	_ma
H	H	H	L	L	L
_ma	⁻ma	⁻ma	_ma	_ma	⁻ma
L	H	H	L	L	H

E1.1.3 Repeat E1.1.2, but with English words.

⁻mine	_mine	_mine	⁻mine	⁻mine
H	L	L	H	H
_yours	⁻yours	⁻yours	_yours	_yours
L	H	H	L	L

1.2   Prosodic features

The **prosodic** (or suprasegmental) characteristics of speech are those of pitch, loudness and speed (or tempo, or speech rate; its inverse is the duration of the constituent segments). These combine together to make up the **rhythm** of speech, and are combined in turn with stretches of silence (pause) to break up the flow of speech.

To some extent prosodic characteristics are the same in all languages. It is probably true of all human societies that speakers speed up when they are excited or impatient and slow down when they are being thoughtful or weighty. We all speak more quietly than normal when we do not wish to be overheard. We all have to speak more loudly to be heard over a distance or in noisy conditions (unless, of course, we can use modern technology to transmit and amplify the signal for us).

But it is clear that different languages also regularly differ in their prosodic characteristics. Simply transferring the prosodic patterns of one's mother tongue or L1 to a foreign language or L2 (such as English) contributes to making you sound foreign, and may quite possibly lead to your being misunderstood by other speakers.

Stress is realized by a combination of loudness, pitch and duration. Some languages use stress placement **lexically** (= to distinguish between different words in the dictionary). For example, the Greek words πόλι ['poli] and πολύ [po'li] differ in meaning. The first means 'city', the second means 'much, very'. The difference of meaning depends entirely upon the location of the stress, and involves no difference in the consonant and vowel sounds. Other languages do not use stress lexically: in French there are no pairs of words of different meaning distinguished by stress placement.

In English there are a few pairs of words distinguished just by stress, for example '*billow* and *be'low* or '*import* (noun) and *im'port* (verb). However, the English habit of weakening unstressed vowels means that most pairs of words differing in stress often also have differences in their vowel sounds, so that the distinction is not carried by stress alone. Nevertheless, English is, like Greek, a stress language: stress is an important part of the spoken identity of an English word.

A complicating factor is that differences of stress in English are largely signalled by pitch movements, as discussed in chapters 2 and 5 below.

Tone is another prosodic characteristic, being realized mainly by differences in the pitch of the voice (e.g. high level, mid level, low level, rising or falling). A high pitch results from the relatively rapid vibration of the vocal folds in the larynx, a low pitch from a relatively slow vibration. An acceleration in the rate of vibration is heard as a rising pitch, a slowing down as a falling pitch. In a level pitch the vocal folds vibrate at a constant rate.

Some languages use tone lexically. For example, in Thai the syllable [kha:] has different meanings depending on the tone with which it is said. With tone 1 (a mid level tone) it means 'to be stuck'. With tone 2 (low level) it is the name of a plant, 'galingale'. With tone 3 (falling) it means 'value', with tone 4 (high level) 'to trade', and with tone 5 (rising) 'leg'. In Mandarin Chinese, [ma] with tone 1 (high) means 'mother', with tone 2 (rising) 'hemp', with tone 3 (low fall–rise) 'horse', and with tone 4 (falling) 'to scold'. In Zulu, [i'ɲaŋga] *inyanga* with high tones on the first and last syllables means 'moon, month', but with high tone only on the first syllable means 'traditional practitioner, herbalist'.

Some languages have tonal differences, but only on stressed syllables. In Norwegian, ['bønər] has two possible meanings. With one tone on the stressed syllable it means 'peasants' (*bønder*), but with another, 'beans' (*bønner*).

Tokyo Japanese makes lexical use of what is known as pitch accent, which is manifested as a sudden drop in pitch immediately after the place in the word where the accent (if any) is located. The segmental string [haɕi] *hashi* with no accent means 'end, edge'. With an accent on the first syllable it means 'chopsticks', and with an accent on the second syllable it means 'bridge'. For 'chopsticks' the second syllable is much lower pitched than the first, but the difference between 'bridge' and 'end, edge' is manifested in the pitch of the syllable at the beginning of the following particle, e.g. in the [ga] of *hashi-ga*, which is low pitched for 'bridge' but not for 'end, edge'.

EXERCISES

E1.2.1 Practise making and hearing sequences of high and low level tones.

‾ma_ma	_ma‾ma	_ma‾ma_ma	‾ma_ma‾ma	‾ma‾ma_ma
H L	L H	L H H	H L L	H H L

_one‾two	‾one‾two	_one_two	_one‾two‾one	‾one_two‾one
L H	H H	L L	L H H	H L H

E1.2.2 Practise hearing and produce falling and rising tones, in which there is a change of pitch on a single syllable.

🎧
\ma	/ma	\ma\ma	/ma/ma	\ma/ma	/ma\ma
HL	LH	HL HL	LH LH	HL LH	LH HL

🎧
\mine	/mine	/mine	\mine	/un\known	\un/known
HL	LH	LH	HL	LH HL	HL LH

1.3   Is English a tone language?

English has nothing like these prosodic characteristics of Thai, Mandarin, Zulu, Norwegian or Japanese. *English does not use tone lexically*: in this sense, it is not a tone language. But English does use tone for intonation.

We can say any English word with any of the intonational 'tones' identified in this book, but the choice of tone does not alter the lexical identity of the word. Whichever we say of

🎧   \chair
🎧   /chair
🎧   ∨chair

– the lexical meaning (= the meaning as shown in a dictionary) is still the same. The non-lexical meaning is different, as discussed in chapter 2, where we see that a fall may indicate definiteness, a rise may indicate incompleteness, and a fall–rise may indicate implications. But these intonational meanings apply equally to any other word:

🎧   \monkey
🎧   /monkey
🎧   ∨monkey

or, more usually, to a clause, sentence, or sentence fragment.

Thus English makes use of tone intonationally, but not lexically. In fact the intonation system of English constitutes the most important and complex part of English prosody. By combining different pitch levels (= unchanging pitch heights) and contours (= sequences of levels, changing pitch shapes) we express a range of intonational meanings: breaking the utterance into chunks, perhaps distinguishing between clause types (such as statement vs. question), focusing on some parts of the utterance and not on others, indicating which part of our message is background information and which is foreground, signalling our attitude to what we are saying.

Some of this intonational meaning is shown in writing, through the use of punctuation, but most of it is not. This is why spoken English, as spoken by native speakers, is richer in information content than written English. This is also why some non-native speakers, not being attuned to English intonation and what it means, may fail to catch a substantial part of the overall meaning of something spoken by a native speaker.

We complain, 'It's not what you said, it's the way that you said it', meaning that your words when written down appear innocuous – yet when spoken aloud they were offensive or insensitive. The same words in the same grammatical constructions may have different pragmatic effects. This is because they may differ in intonation, and perhaps also in other, paralinguistic, features (e.g. huskiness, breathiness, whisper, nasality, special voice qualities).

Like other prosodic characteristics, intonation is partly universal (= the same in all languages), but also partly language-specific (= differing from one language to another). Languages differ in the intonation patterns they use, and in the extent to which they rely on intonation to convey aspects of meaning. More importantly, the same physical pattern of rises and falls may have different meanings – different pragmatic implications – in different languages.

A low-rise tone pattern may signal a simple statement in Danish or Norwegian. But in most kinds of English it has implications of non-finality, or perhaps uncertainty or truculence. An accent on a pronoun (a high tone, say) may have a neutral meaning in many African languages, and indeed in French or some other European languages; but in English it highlights the pronoun, perhaps suggesting a contrast between its referent and some other person involved.

Between speakers of different languages, intonation patterns can be much more easily *misunderstood* than segmental patterns.

EXERCISES

E1.3.1 Practise making and hearing mixtures of level and moving tones on sequences of monosyllables.

⁻ma\ma	\ma‿ma	\ma⁻ma	/ma⁻ma	/ma‿ma	⁻ma/ma
H HL	HL L	HL H	LH H	LH L	H LH

‿no/no	⁻no\no	\no‿no	/no⁻no	⁻no/no	‿no\no
L LH	H HL	HL L	LH H	H LH	L HL

1.4   The three Ts: a quick overview of English intonation

As concerns intonation, speakers of English repeatedly face three types of decision as they speak. They are: how to break the material up into chunks, what is to be accented, and what tones are to be used. These linguistic intonation systems are known respectively as **t**onality, **t**onicity and **t**one. We refer to them as the three Ts.

Tonality. The first matter a speaker has to decide is the division of the spoken material into chunks. There will be an intonation pattern associated with each chunk. These chunks are known as **intonation phrases** or **IPs**. Each IP in an utterance has its own intonation pattern (or 'tune'). (Various authors use various other names for the IP, including 'word group', 'tone group' and 'intonation group'.) In general, we make each clause into a separate IP. (The symbols | and ‖ represent the boundaries between IPs.)

> Because I love languages | I'm studying intonation. ‖When I've finished this book, | I'll know a lot more about it.

However, the speaker does not inevitably have to follow the rule of an IP for each clause. There are many cases where different kinds of chunking are possible.

For example, if a speaker wants to say *We don't know who she is*, it is possible to say the whole utterance as a single IP (= one intonation pattern):

🎧   We don't know who she is.

But it is also possible to divide the material up, in at least the following possible ways:

🎧   We don't know | who she is.
🎧   We | don't know who she is.
🎧   We don't | know who she is.
🎧   We | don't know | who she is.

Thus the speaker may present the material as two, or three, pieces of information rather than as a single piece. This is **tonality** (or **chunking**), and is the topic of chapter 4.

Tonicity. Speakers use intonation to highlight some words as *important* for the meaning they wish to convey. These are the words on which the speaker **focuses** the hearer's attention. To highlight an important word we **accent** it. More precisely, we accent its stressed syllable (or one or both of its stressed syllables, if it has more than one). That is to say, we add pitch prominence (= a change in pitch, or the beginning of a pitch movement) to the rhythmic prominence that a stressed syllable bears. The accents that result are also the 'hooks' on which the intonation pattern is hung.

Which words are to have attention drawn to them by being accented? And which are not to be focused on in this way? In particular, where is the speaker to locate the last accent (the **nucleus**) within the intonation phrase? The nucleus is the most important accent in the IP. It indicates the end of the focused part of the material. In terms of pitch, it is marked out by being the place where the pitch change or pitch movement for the nuclear **tone** begins.

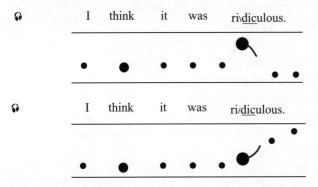

In this example the nucleus is the syllable *-dic-*. It does not matter what nuclear tone is used: the point is that the tone movement begins on this syllable. In this way both the syllable *-dic-* and the word *ridiculous* are accented. (Some authors call it the 'tonic' rather than the nucleus. Other names are 'intonation centre'

and 'sentence accent' or even 'sentence stress'.) The nucleus is usually placed at the end of the IP unless there are special reasons for it to go somewhere else.

At this point we need to consider the anatomy of the IP as a whole. The part of the IP that follows the nucleus is called the **tail**. By definition, the tail contains no accented syllables. If the nucleus is located on the last syllable in an IP, there is no tail:

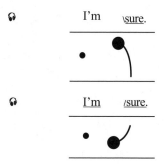

If an IP contains an accent in the part before the nucleus, the first (or only) such accent is called the **onset**. The part extending from the onset to the last syllable before the nucleus is called the **head**:

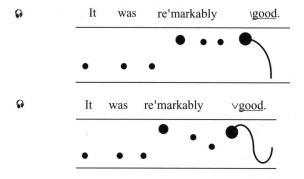

In this example the onset is the syllable *-mark-*. There is a pitch change there, making the syllable stand out. In this way the syllable, and therefore the word *remarkably*, are accented. The syllables *-markably* constitute the head.

The part before the onset is called the **prehead**. By definition, the prehead contains no accented syllables. In the example the prehead is *It was re-*.

If an IP contains no accented syllables before the nucleus, there is no head. If it contains no unaccented syllables before the first accent (onset or nucleus), there is no prehead.

The boundaries of prehead, head, nucleus and tail do not necessarily coincide with word boundaries, although they always coincide with syllable boundaries.

Although every IP contains a nucleus, not all IPs contain a prehead, a head or a tail.

For most utterances, the speaker can select from a wide range of possible intonation patterns. Depending on the circumstances and the meaning, the nucleus can be put in various places. For example, the statement *We're planning to fly to Italy* could be said as:

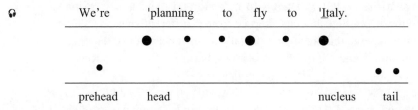

Here, the nucleus is *It-* and the tail is *-aly*. The onset is *plan-*, and the head is *planning to fly to*. The prehead is *We're*.

However, the same statement could also be said in any of the following ways, depending on the circumstances under which it is uttered. (The underlining shows the location of the nucleus. The mark ' shows the accented syllables.)

🎧   We're 'planning to '<u>fly</u> to Italy.
🎧   We're '<u>plan</u>ning to fly to Italy.
🎧   '<u>We</u>'re planning to fly to Italy.

The question of **tonicity** (or **nucleus placement**) is the topic of chapter 3.

Tone. Having decided the tonicity – that is, having selected a suitable location for the nucleus – what kind of pitch movement (what **tone**) is the speaker going to associate with it?

For example, a speaker wanting to say *You mustn't worry* can choose between several possible tones:
(fall)

(rise)

(fall–rise)

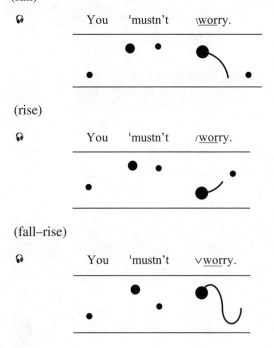

The basic choice between fall, rise and fall–rise is discussed in chapter 2. In general, a fall tends to indicate that the information conveyed is, or could be, complete, whereas a rise or fall–rise tends to indicate that there is something more to come (either from the same speaker, or from a different speaker). The default tone (= the tone used if there are no special circumstances) for statements, exclamations, commands and wh questions is a fall, but for yes–no questions it is a rise. A fall–rise often signals particular implications.

We also have to make decisions about which words (if any) in addition to the nucleus are to be accented. There may be different kinds of prenuclear pitch pattern. There are also tone choices involving more subtle distinctions than a simple fall vs. rise vs. fall–rise. For example, a fall can be a high fall, a low fall or a rise–fall. These further choices are discussed in chapter 5.

Although logically the speaker first has to decide the tonality, then the tonicity, and last of all the tone, it is convenient for our discussion to treat the three Ts in reverse order, namely: tone (chapter 2), then tonicity (chapter 3), then tonality (chapter 4). After that we deal with the less crucial choices in chapter 5, and bring everything together in chapter 6.

EXERCISES

E1.4.1 Say whether the following pairs differ in tonality, tonicity or tone.

1 (i)   So! | You want to kill me!
  (ii)   So you want to kill me!

2 (i)   I'm 'angry about his be'haviour.
  (ii)   I'm 'angry about his behaviour.

3 (i)   She \wants to be invited.
  (ii)   She /wants to be invited?

4 (i)   'Some of us | are 'very 'pleased.
  (ii)   'Some of 'us | are 'very pleased.

5 (i)   I \don't think | it's \fair.
  (ii)   I vdon't think | it's \fair.

E1.4.2 For each of the following, identify the nucleus and (if present) the onset, prehead, head and tail. Tone is not relevant.

'Never!
A'mazing!
'Thirty-'five.
I 'don't be'lieve it.
Is 'that what you think?

I 'just don't a'gree with you.
We've had a 'wonderful holiday.
There's a'nother train 'coming.
'When will you de'cide?
It's im'possible.

1.5   The functions of intonation

Native speakers of English exploit intonation patterns in many subtle ways that are not obvious at first sight. If you speak English as a second or foreign language, these uses of intonation may have no parallel in your first language. This can lead to a breakdown in communication when a native speaker is interacting with a non-native speaker. In a conversational situation, many a non-native speaker may fail to understand some or all of that part of the native speaker's message that is conveyed by intonation patterns. The native speaker, unaware both of his or her own use of intonation and of the non-native's failure to pick up on it, wrongly assumes that the message has been fully understood. Later, it becomes evident that the message has *not* been fully understood, and neither participant in the conversation knows why.

It may well be the case that English makes more elaborate use of intonation to signal meaning than do most other languages. This is a further reason why it should not be neglected by learners and teachers of English as a foreign language.

What, then, are the functions of English intonation? We can recognize several.

- The **attitudinal** function. The most obvious role of intonation is to express our attitudes and emotions – to show shock or surprise, pleasure or anger, interest or boredom, seriousness or sarcasm, and many others. We do this by **tone**.

- The **grammatical** function. Intonation helps identify grammatical structures in speech, rather as punctuation does in writing. We use intonation to mark the beginning and end of grammatical units such as clause and sentence (the **demarcative** function). We do this by **tonality**. We also use intonation to distinguish clause types, such as question vs. statement, and to disambiguate various grammatically ambiguous structures (the **syntactic** function). We do this mainly by **tone**.

- The **focusing** (also called **accentual** or **informational**) function. Intonation helps to show what information in an utterance is new and what is already known. We use it to bring some parts of the message into focus, and leave other parts out of focus; to emphasize or highlight some parts and not others. We do this by **tonicity** and by the placement of other accents. This is one of the most important functions of English intonation, and perhaps the function most readily taught in the EFL classroom. We combine accentuation with the choice of **tone** to present some longer stretches of the message as constituting the foreground of the picture we paint, while leaving other stretches as background. These are **pragmatic** functions.

- **The discourse** (or **cohesive**) function. Intonation signals how sequences of clauses and sentences go together in spoken discourse, to contrast or to cohere. It functions like the division of written text into sentences and paragraphs. It enables us to signal whether or not we have come to the end of the point we are making; whether we want to keep talking or are ready to give another speaker a turn.

- The **psychological** function. Intonation helps us organize speech into units that are easy to perceive, memorize and perform. We can all repeat an arbitrary string of three, four or five numbers, but not a string of ten – unless we split them into two units of five. This is why we need tonality.
- The **indexical** function. Just as with other pronunciation features, intonation may act as a marker of personal or social identity. What makes mothers sound like mothers, lovers sound like lovers, lawyers sound like lawyers, clergymen sound like clergymen, newsreaders sound like newsreaders, officials sound like officials? Partly, their characteristic intonation.

1.6   Intonation in EFL: transfer and interference

As in other areas of foreign or second language learning, learners of English will tend to start by assuming that English is like their own first language. They will **transfer** the intonation habits of the L1 to the L2. To some extent, this assumption may well be correct. All those elements of intonation that are truly universal must, by definition, apply to English just as they do to other languages.

Depending on the learner's L1, there may indeed be many other, non-universal, elements of intonation that are the same in English as in the L1, thus allowing their **positive transfer** to the learner's use of English (his or her so-called **interlanguage**). For example, German and Dutch have tonicity systems extremely similar to that of English, so that German and Dutch learners already know this part of English intonation. French, however, does not use tonicity in the same way, and French learners typically have difficulties with English tonicity because of their **negative transfer** of the French system to English. Unchecked, the assumption that English is like your L1 thus leads to **interference** from the L1 as inappropriate elements are transferred.

A more complex example of positive transfer of German tonicity into English is seen in the following example:

> *English*:   I've 'lost my 'bag.
> *German*:   Ich   habe   meine   'Tasche   verloren.
>   I   have   my   bag   lost.

In English, the ordinary intonation pattern for this sentence involves a nucleus on the word *bag*, which happens to be the last word. The ordinary intonation pattern of German equally involves a nucleus on *Tasche*, the German for 'bag', although because of the different word order in German it is not the last word. The German word order is different from the English. Despite this, in German as in English the principle applies that in such sentences the nucleus goes on the grammatical object (the last lexical noun phrase). Thus the superficial difference between the two languages (nucleus on the last word in English, but not in German) is less important than the deeper, more abstract rule which the two languages share (nucleus on the object noun).

As an example of negative transfer of an intonation pattern from an L1 into English, consider this example:

> A: What job would you like to have?
> B: I haven't thought about it.

Native speakers of English would normally place the nucleus for B's reply on *thought*:

> B: I haven't 'thought about it.

French people, whose language does not share the English rule directing accents away from function words, would be likely to say:

> B: I haven't thought about 'it. *or*
> B: I haven't thought a'bout it.

In the corresponding Japanese sentence the last word is a negative particle such as *nai*, which in Japanese carries the equivalent of the nucleus. So a Japanese speaker of English would tend to place the English nucleus on the word that incorporates the translation of *nai*, namely *haven't*:

> B: I 'haven't thought about it.

Germans, though, enjoy the benefit of positive transfer from their own pattern:

> Darüber   habe   ich   nicht   'nachgedacht.
> about-it   have   I   not   thought

– and place the nucleus on *thought* even though the word order is different.

English compound words are a source of difficulty for many learners. Even speakers of Germanic languages such as German and Danish, who have a compound stress rule in their L1 identical to that of English, encounter negative transfer in cases where English does not use an expected compound, or where the English compound is late-stressed:

> A: 'Was   wollen   Sie   'trinken?
>   what   will   you   drink
>
> B: 'Ich   nehme   'Weißwein.
>   I   take   white   wine

Compare English:

> A: 'What would you like to 'drink?
> B: 'I'll have some white 'wine.

Although German *Weißwein* has compound stress ('*Weißwein*), its English equivalent *white wine* has phrase stress (ˌ*white* '*wine*). The same difference is seen in '*Hauptstadt* as against ˌ*capital* '*city*.

Naturally, speakers of languages that make little or no use of tonicity are likely to make many inappropriate tonicity choices in English. Typically, they tend to accent the last word in an intonation phrase, even in cases where L1 speakers of English would not do so. On occasions this can make such a speaker sound bizarre or absurd to the listener, since it sends out the wrong signals about where the new information in the message ends, or about what is in focus and what is not.

English:	In '<u>most</u> cases | 'standards have greatly im'<u>proved</u>.
French:	Dans la plupart des '<u>cas</u> | . . .
French English:	In most '<u>cases</u> | . . .
English:	I can '<u>see</u> someone.
French:	Je vois quel'<u>qu'un</u>.
French English:	I can see some'<u>one</u>.

It is not known whether tonality, too, causes problems of negative transfer. Tone certainly does, since many languages have characteristic tone patterns or tone uses that sound strange or misleading in English, e.g. the rise used by many Norwegians and Danes on a simple statement, where most native English speakers would be likely to use a fall.

TOPICS FOR DISCUSSION OR ESSAY

1   Explain the terms *stress* and *tone*. What does it mean to say that some languages use them lexically?

       (For those whose L1 is not English) Is your first language a tone language? If so, demonstrate this by finding sets of words distinguished only by tone. If not, what use does your language make of pitch differences?

2   Is English a tone language? What use does English make of variation in the pitch of the voice?

3   What are 'the three Ts'? Explain the terms *tonicity, tone* and *tonality*.

4   What functions does intonation perform in English? Does it perform the same functions in other languages you are familiar with?

5   How might the intonation of a learner's L1 cause problems in learning and using English intonation?

2 Tone: going up and going down

FALL, RISE AND FALL–RISE

2.1 Falling and non-falling tones

The most basic distinction among English nuclear tones is that between falling and non-falling.

The various different kinds of falling tone (high fall, low fall, rise–fall) evidently have some degree of meaning in common. In this chapter we do not distinguish between them, but treat them all as just falls. There is also something in common in all the various kinds of non-falling tone (high rise, low rise, mid level, fall–rise), which we refer to as non-falls. However, here it is often necessary to distinguish between rises on the one hand and fall–rises on the other.

A popular idea among language students is that statements are said with a fall, questions with a rise. Although there is an element of truth in this generalization, it is very far from the complete truth. In English, at any rate, statements may have a fall – but they may also have a non-falling tone (a fall–rise or a rise). Questions may have a rise – but they may also have a fall. In general there is no simple predictable relationship between sentence type and tone choice. Nevertheless, it is useful to apply the notion of a **default** tone (= unmarked tone, neutral tone) for each sentence type.[1] As we shall see, the default tone is

- a fall for statements, exclamations, wh questions and commands;
- a rise for yes–no questions.

Another useful generalization is that the default for utterances involving two intonation phrases is to have

- a fall on the main part, and
- a non-fall on the subordinate or dependent part.

In sections 2.2–4 we study the anatomy of falls, rises and fall–rises, learning to recognize and reproduce these different tones. In sections 2.5–19 we consider their use in **independent tones**, as seen in short utterances that involve only a single intonation phrase. Then, in 2.20–5, we look at **dependent** tones and the tones of successive IPs in sequence. Finally, in 2.26–7, we discuss general tone meanings and tabulate all the tone meanings we have identified.

In considering tone meanings, we classify sentences according to their **discourse function**. We look in turn at statements, questions, exclamations, commands and interjections.

EXERCISES

E2.1.1 Listen and repeat. Listen to the word *now* spoken with various kinds of falling tone. For the moment, the important thing is just to perceive that in each the pitch of the voice falls: it starts higher, ends lower. Although they differ in various ways, each is a fall. Repeat them yourself, feeling the pitch of the voice fall. If you can whistle, whistle them too.

🎧   \now   \now   \now   \now   \now

E2.1.2 Listen and repeat. Listen to further monosyllabic words spoken with a falling tone. Some have no final consonant; some have a voiced final consonant; some have a voiceless final consonant. Does this have any effect on how the pitch movement sounds?

🎧   \three   \go   \four   \stay   \sure
          \bad   \nine   \good   \sing   \come
          \nice   \stop   \first   \right   \six

E2.1.3 In class, learners should practise these (and all pair-work exercises in this book) first speaking together in chorus, and then speaking individually.

o marks the 'context' turn in a conversation (to provide a context)
• marks the drill turn in the conversation (the point of the exercise)

🎧   o 'Whose is \this?   🎧 • \Mine.
                                    🎧 • \Yours.
                                       • \John's.
                                       • \Anne's.
                                       • \Lynn's.

🎧   o 'Where do you \come from?   🎧 • \Spain.
                                        🎧 • \France.
                                           • \Wales.
                                           • \Greece.
                                           • \Leeds.

E2.1.4 Listen and repeat. Listen to the word *now* spoken with various kinds of rising tone. Again, for the moment, the important thing is just to perceive that in each the pitch of the voice rises: it starts lower, ends higher. Although they differ in various ways, each is a rise. Repeat them yourself, feeling the pitch of the voice rise. If you can whistle, whistle them too.

🎧   /now   /now   /now   /now   /now

E2.1.5 Listen and repeat. Listen to further monosyllabic words spoken with a rise. Does the phonetic structure of the word have any effect on how the pitch movement sounds?

🎧   /three   /play   /sure   /go   /why

             /bad   /mine   /yours /good   /time

             /nice   /stop   /right   /thanks /test

E2.1.6 Pair-work practice.

🎧   o 'This money is \John's.   🎧• /John's?

                                         🎧• /Whose?

      o 'These are \Sophie's.   • /Sophie's?

                                           • /Whose?

🎧   o I'd 'like some \chicken, please. 🎧• /Chicken?

                                         🎧• /Grilled?

                                         • /Fried?

                                         • /Wings?

      o We're 'all \doomed.   • /Doomed?

                                         • /All of us?

E.2.1.7 Listen to the difference between a fall and a rise. Depending on the tone used for *who?* in this response, the meaning is quite different (see 2.16).

🎧   A: Bill could ask a friend.

          B1: \Who? (= Which friend could Bill ask?)

🎧   A: Bill could ask a friend.

          B2: /Who? (= Who did you say could ask a friend?)

Decide whether each test item is a fall, like B1, or a rise, like B2.

🎧   A: Bill could ask a friend.

          B: Who? (*ten items*)

2.2   Falls

      In a falling nuclear tone the pitch of the voice starts relatively high and then moves downwards. The starting point may be anywhere from mid to high. The endpoint is low. There may be some upward movement before the pitch moves downwards (discussed further in 5.5).

In the simplest cases the fall takes place on a single syllable. We see this in cases where the nuclear syllable is the *only* syllable in the IP, or where the nuclear syllable is the *last* syllable in the IP. The fall then happens on that syllable.

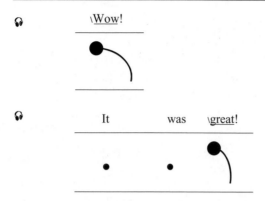

In identifying the nuclear tone we must disregard all the pitch levels and possible pitch movements that are found earlier in the intonation phrase, i.e. *before* the nucleus. (We shall analyse these **prenuclear patterns** in chapter 5.)

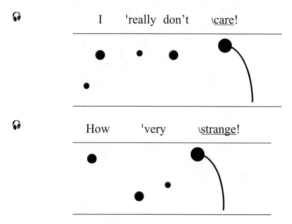

In both these examples the pitch movement on the nucleus is a fall. The preceding pitch patterns are irrelevant in determining the nuclear tone.

There is very often a **step up** in pitch as we reach the beginning of the nuclear fall. Do not let this mislead you into thinking that the tone is rising.

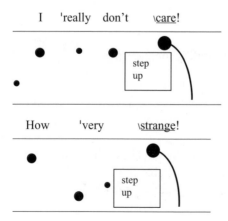

There may even be some upward movement at the beginning of the nuclear syllable. But as long as the pitch then comes down, it is a falling tone.

Often there are syllables *after* the nucleus, i.e. a **tail**. After a falling nucleus, the tail is always *low*. The fall (= the downward pitch movement) happens on or from the syllable that bears the nucleus (the lexically stressed syllable). The syllable(s) after the nucleus are low pitched.

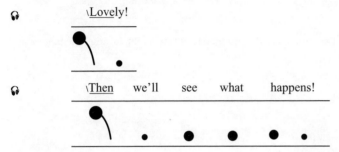

If the vowel in the nucleus syllable is short, or if this vowel is followed by a voiceless consonant, there may be insufficient time for the fall to be heard on the nuclear syllable itself. The effect is then one of a jump from a higher-pitched syllable (the nucleus) to one or more low-pitched syllables (the tail). The overall pitch pattern is still a fall.

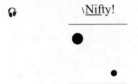

Again, in identifying a nuclear tone (in these cases as falling) we disregard any prenuclear pitch pattern:

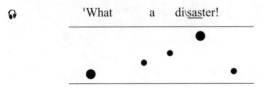

For a discussion of different varieties of falling tone, see 5.5.

EXERCISES

E2.2.1 Listen and repeat.

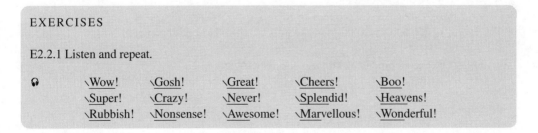

\Wow!	\Gosh!	\Great!	\Cheers!	\Boo!
\Super!	\Crazy!	\Never!	\Splendid!	\Heavens!
\Rubbish!	\Nonsense!	\Awesome!	\Marvellous!	\Wonderful!

E2.2.2 Pair-work practice.

○ I'll be 'there by \five.	• \Great!
○ It's 'nearly ˅eight.	• \Goodness! | I'm going to be \late.
○ 'Care for a /drink?	• \Thanks! | I'd \love one.
○ Can I 'tell /Lucy about it?	• \No! | She'll 'tell \everyone.
○ I 'painted it my\self.	• \There's a clever girl.

E2.2.3 Listen and repeat. Ignore the prenuclear material: concentrate on the falling tone that takes place on, or starts at, the nucleus.

Ri\diculous!
'How ri\diculous!
But that's ri\diculous!
How 'absolutely ri\diculous!
I think that's 'really quite ri\diculous!

In\credible!
'How in\credible!
That's in\credible!
How 'utterly in\credible!
They're going to find it 'utterly in\credible.

You're \right!
You're \right, you know.
You're 'absolutely \right!
I think you're 'absolutely \right!
You're going to be proved 'quite \right!

E2.2.4 Pair-work practice.

○ We've 'just got en\gaged.	• 'How \marvellous!
○ She's had a 'baby \boy.	• But that's \wonderful!
○ I got 'seventy per\cent.	• 'Well \done!
○ We won 'seven-\nil.	• 'What an a\chievement!
○ I 'missed the \train.	• 'How an\noying!
○ 'Now they want us to re-\register.	• 'What a pa\laver!
○ The 'sausages got \burnt.	• 'What a \pity!
○ 'Now he's crashed his \car.	• 'Oh \dear!
○ And 'then the \ceiling fell down.	• 'What a di\saster!
○ He 'couldn't make himself \heard.	• 'How pa\thetic!

For further practice on producing falls in exclamations, turn to 2.17.

2.3   Rises

In a rising nuclear tone the pitch of the voice starts relatively low and then moves upwards. The starting point may be anywhere from low to mid, and the endpoint anywhere from mid to high. (Some other possibilities are discussed in 5.5.)

If the nucleus is on the last or only syllable in the intonation phrase, then the rise takes place on that syllable:

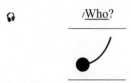

Again, in identifying the nuclear tone we must disregard any prenuclear pitch pattern.

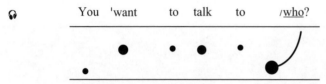

There is often a **step down** in pitch as we reach the beginning of the nuclear rise. Do not let this mislead you into thinking that the tone is falling.

If there is a tail (= syllables after the nucleus), the rising pitch movement does not happen wholly on the nuclear syllable, as in the case of a fall. Rather, the rise is spread over the nuclear syllable and all the following syllables – over the whole of the nucleus plus tail:

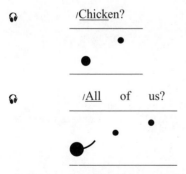

This means that the last syllable is actually the highest pitched, even though it is unaccented. Some people find this difficult to perceive, and instead tend to hear the nucleus later in the intonation phrase than it really is. In fact, if there is no prenuclear material the nucleus, perceptually the most salient syllable for native speakers, is actually the lowest-pitched syllable in the IP:

○ Her 'name's Mel\pomene.   • /What did you say her name was?!

/What   did   you   say   her   name   was?

EXERCISES

E2.3.1 Listen and repeat.

/What?   /Who?   /Where?   /When?   /Eh?
/Jim?   /Madge?   /Bill?   /Bob?   /Sue?
/Never?   /Always?   /Thousands?   /This one?   /Carrots?

E2.3.2 Pair-work practice.

○ You'll 'have to take the \tube.   • /What?
    • /Sorry?
    • /Pardon?
    • /What did you say?
    • /What was that?

○ I'll 'ask \James to help.   • /James?
○ She was 'reading the \Times.   • The /Times?
○ I'd 'like a \melon, please.   • A /melon?
○ It's 'time to re\lax.   • Re/lax?
○ I 'think it was \marvellous.   • /Marvellous?

○ We'll 'need an as\sistant.   • /Linda?
    • /Mary?
    • /Peter?
    • /Anna?
    • /Judith?

E2.3.3 Listen to the recording and identify the tones. The nucleus is already underlined for you, and the accent mark ' is used as a placeholder for the nuclear tone mark. (The onset accent, too, is shown, if there is one.)

A: 'Who's 'that over there?
B: It's 'Jim, | I 'think.
A: 'What's he 'like?
B: Oh he's 'one of our best 'students.
A: 'What's he 'studying?
B: 'Modern 'languages.

A: 'Which languages?
B: 'English, | 'French | and 'Spanish.
A: 'That | sounds 'interesting.

2.4   Fall–rises

In a fall–rise nuclear tone, the pitch of the voice starts relatively high and then moves first downwards and then upwards again. The starting point may be anywhere from mid to high, the midpoint is low, and the endpoint is usually mid. (Some other possibilities are discussed in 5.15.)

If the nucleus is on the last or only syllable in the intonation phrase, then the entire fall–rise movement takes place on that syllable:

🎧   vMine.

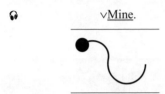

As usual, in identifying the nuclear tone we must disregard any prenuclear pitch pattern:

🎧   I   think   it's   vmine.

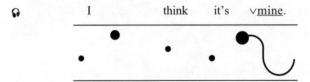

If there is a tail (= syllables after the nucleus), the falling–rising pitch movement is spread out over the nucleus and tail. The falling part takes place on the nuclear syllable, or between that syllable and the next. The rising part takes place towards the end of the tail and extends up to the last syllable of the IP:

🎧   o 'Are you ∕ready yet?   • vAlmost.
🎧   o 'This one's ＼mine.   • vMine, you mean.
🎧   o 'Was she ∕hurt?   • vFortunately, | she ＼wasn't.

🎧   .vAlmost.

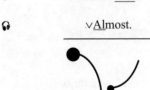

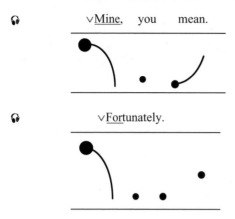

ⱱMine, you mean.

ⱱFortunately.

EXERCISES

E2.4.1 Listen and repeat.

ⱱNearly.	ⱱPartly.	I ⱱthink so.	He ⱱsays so.	I ⱱhope so.
ⱱTrue.	ⱱSoon.	ⱱNo.	Toⱱday.	Aⱱgain.
ⱱVirtually.	ⱱHappily.	Reⱱgrettably.	Reⱱportedly.	Alⱱlegedly.

E2.4.2 Pair-work practice.

o 'Are you ⁄sure, then? • I ⱱthink so.
o 'Did he ⁄finish it? • He ⱱsays so.
o 'Is it ⁄ready now? • ⱱPartly.
o Have they 'finished the ⁄housework? • ⱱMost of it.
o You 'promised it for \Thursday. • ⱱFriday.

o You 'said it was \black. • ⱱWhite.
o You were \there, | \weren't you? • ⱱYes.
o There are 'four \questions. • ⱱFive.
o 'This is \Jessica's book. • ⱱMine.
o He 'sings \tenor. • ⱱBass.

E2.4.3 Listen and repeat.

ⱱFortunately, | I was \wrong.
ⱱThen, | I saw a \dog.
Toⱱday | we're 'going to do \grammar.
Mrs ⱱAshton | will be 'taking the \children.
As for ⱱyou, | I'll 'deal with you \later.

E2.4.4 Listen to the recording and identify the tones. The nucleus is already underlined for you. The onset, too, is shown (if there is one).

A: I'm 'not really 'sure, | but I 'think I may have to 'cancel our meeting.
B: Oh I'm 'sorry about 'that.‖ 'What's the 'trouble?‖ Has 'something come 'up?
A: Well 'actually | it's my 'mother.‖ She 'needs to go into 'hospital | and she 'wants 'me | to 'take her there.

STATEMENTS

2.5   The definitive fall

Although simple independent statements can take any tone, they most often have a **fall**. A fall is the **default** (= neutral, unmarked) tone for a statement. We say statements with a fall unless there is a particular reason to use some other tone.

All the uses of the falling tone have some degree of meaning in common. As with other tone meanings, it is difficult to define this shared meaning precisely in words. But in general we can say that by using a fall we indicate that what we say is potentially **complete** and that we express it with **confidence**, **definitely** and **unreservedly**. The fall thus also tends to signal **finality**. We call this tone meaning the **definitive fall**.

'This is a ⟍pen.
We're ⟍ready.
My 'name is ⟍John.
I'm de'lighted to ⟍meet you.
It's 'ten fif⟍teen.

EXERCISES

E2.5.1 Listen and repeat. At this stage, do not worry about the prenuclear pitch pattern: concentrate on getting the fall on the nuclear syllable.

I 'think it's ⟍great.
We're 'all ⟍here.
They're 'waiting out⟍side.
It's 'half past e⟍leven.
I'll 'go and get some ⟍milk.

E2.5.2 Listen and repeat. Keep the tail low and level.

She 'lives in ⟍Kent.
She 'lives in ⟍Kenton.
She 'lives in ⟍Kensington.
She 'lives in ⟍Kettering, you know.
She 'lives in ⟍Kennington as far as I can tell.

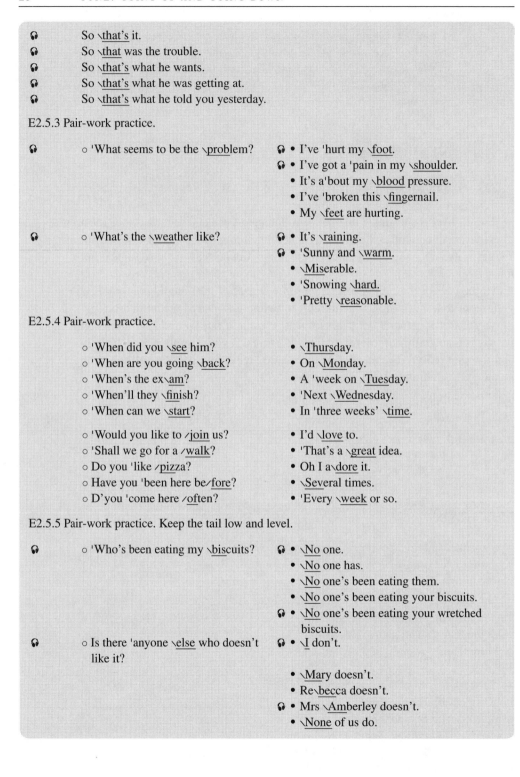

So ˎthat's it.
So ˎthat was the trouble.
So ˎthat's what he wants.
So ˎthat's what he was getting at.
So ˎthat's what he told you yesterday.

E2.5.3 Pair-work practice.

o 'What seems to be the ˎproblem?
• I've 'hurt my ˎfoot.
• I've got a 'pain in my ˎshoulder.
• It's aˈbout my ˎblood pressure.
• I've 'broken this ˎfingernail.
• My ˎfeet are hurting.

o 'What's the ˎweather like?
• It's ˎraining.
• 'Sunny and ˎwarm.
• ˎMiserable.
• 'Snowing ˎhard.
• 'Pretty ˎreasonable.

E2.5.4 Pair-work practice.

o 'When did you ˎsee him?
• ˎThursday.
o 'When are you going ˎback?
• On ˎMonday.
o 'When's the exˎam?
• A 'week on ˎTuesday.
o 'When'll they ˎfinish?
• 'Next ˎWednesday.
o 'When can we ˎstart?
• In 'three weeks' ˎtime.

o 'Would you like to ˊjoin us?
• I'd ˎlove to.
o 'Shall we go for a ˊwalk?
• 'That's a ˎgreat idea.
o Do you 'like ˊpizza?
• Oh I aˎdore it.
o Have you 'been here beˊfore?
• ˎSeveral times.
o D'you 'come here ˊoften?
• 'Every ˎweek or so.

E2.5.5 Pair-work practice. Keep the tail low and level.

o 'Who's been eating my ˎbiscuits?
• ˎNo one.
• ˎNo one has.
• ˎNo one's been eating them.
• ˎNo one's been eating your biscuits.
• ˎNo one's been eating your wretched biscuits.

o Is there 'anyone ˎelse who doesn't like it?
• ˎI don't.

• ˎMary doesn't.
• Reˎbecca doesn't.
• Mrs ˎAmberley doesn't.
• ˎNone of us do.

2.6   The implicational fall–rise

Sometimes statements are said with a tone other than a fall – namely, with a rise or fall–rise. One very typical meaning of a non-fall is **non-finality**. It shows that the speaker has not reached the end of what he or she wants to say:

ω	What did you do next?	• Well I 'opened the /door, | and . . .
		• Well I 'opened the vdoor, | and . . .

The rise or fall–rise thus indicates that the clause, phrase or word that bears it is part of a larger structure. We analyse this tone meaning in sections 2.20–5 (sequences of tones).

But what about non-fall tones on statements that are complete in themselves, i.e. **independent** non-falls? We analyse these tone meanings in the sections that follow now.

The most typical meaning of fall–rise tone is that the speaker *implies* something without necessarily putting it into words. We call this tone meaning the **implicational fall–rise**.

By making a statement with the fall–rise, the speaker typically states one thing but implies something further. Something is left unsaid – perhaps some kind of reservation or implication:

ω	Who's that?	• Well I 'know her vface.

The fall–rise implies something further: a **contrast** between what is expressed and what has not, or not yet, been expressed. In this case it might be:

- Well I 'know her vface, | but I 'can't remember her \name.

The speaker has the choice of making the contrast explicit, as in the second version, or leaving it implicit, as in the first. Whether explicit or implicit, the implication is still hinted at by the fall–rise intonation.

The unexpressed implication can usually be formulated in a clause beginning *but . . .* , which would make it explicit. The implicational fall–rise can be thought of as the tone that signals a *but . . .* to come.

More than one implication may be possible:

ω	Can we fix an appointment?	• I could 'see you on vWednesday.

Making it explicit we might have:

- I could 'see you on vWednesday, | but 'not on \Thursday. *or*
- I could 'see you on vWednesday, | but 'that might not suit \you.

Using a fall–rise but leaving the reservation unexpressed may lead the other speaker to pick up on the implication and ask for the reservation to be spelt out:

☞   A: 'What can we have for \tea?
            B: Well we've 'got some vstrawberries.
            A: So 'what's the \problem?
            B: We 'haven't got any \cream.

            A: 'What d'you think of \Hubert?
            B: He's 'very mevticulous.
            A: /But . . .?
            B: 'Utterly \boring.

The American gun lobby has a slogan:

        vGuns don't kill people, | \people kill people.

– where there is an explicit contrast between *guns* and *people* (as the subject of *kill*). The idea could be expressed more subtly (but still as tendentiously) by saying just:

        vGuns don't kill people.

– leaving it to the fall–rise to imply the corollary without expressing it.

    A speaker who uses a fall–rise has **reservations** about what is said. The speaker's statement may be true under some conditions, *but* not under others. Again, the reservation may or may not be made explicit. In the following examples it is given in parentheses: the words in parentheses might or might not be spoken aloud.

☞   Can we fix a date for the meeting?   • Well we could 'try vMonday (| though 'not if that's vdifficult for you).

       Have you ever visited France?   • I've 'been to vParis (| but 'not to many vother parts of the country).

       Is fruit expensive in this country?   • Well vapples are (| but I'm 'not sure about vother kinds of fruit).

       Is it an attractive building?   • Well vI think so (| but 'others may not a\gree).

The implicational fall–rise enables us to imply things without actually saying them. It makes it possible to be tactful and politely indirect; it also makes it possible to be hypocritical and devious.

       Are you free next week?   • Well on vMonday I am (| but 'later I may \not be).

       Do you smoke?   • I 'do ocvcasionally (| but 'not vregularly).

☞   What's she like as a colleague?   • Well she vworks very hard.

In the last example the unspoken implication might be *but she has no imagination* or *but she's not a good teacher* or *but she doesn't get on with her colleagues* or something else uncomplimentary.

There is an English expression (with, by the way, difficult-to-explain tonicity in the second intonation phrase):

It's 'not what she ∨said, | but the 'way that she \said it.

This suggests that the words if written might have been unexceptionable; but as spoken their intonation implied something different. They probably had a fall–rise.

EXERCISES

E2.6.1 Listen and repeat. Concentrate on getting the fall–rise nucleus.

- 🎧 I en'joy ∨dancing.
- 🎧 I've re'paired the ∨windows.
- 🎧 You could 'try the ∨salmon.
- 🎧 He was 'only ∨joking.
- 🎧 They're 'only staying for ten ∨minutes.

- 🎧 It 'wasn't really ∨bad.
- 🎧 I'm 'free to∨day.
- 🎧 She could 'read a ∨book.
- 🎧 I could 'let you have ∨two.
- 🎧 They could 'go on ∨foot.

E2.6.2 For each example in E2.6.1, supply a continuation with *but . . .* , making explicit a possible implication.

> *Model:* I en'joy ∨dancing, | but I 'don't like the \music.

E2.6.3 Practise these replies both with and without the parenthesized part.

🎧
- ○ 'Do you /smoke?
- ○ Can I 'take your /shredder?

- • I 'do ∨sometimes (| but 'not in the ∨house).
- • You can 'use it for ∨now (| but you must 'give it \back).

🎧
- ○ What a 'great i\dea!

- ○ What a 'nasty cold \day!

- ○ She 'didn't mean to /do it.

- • It 'does ∨sound great (| but I 'wonder if there's a \catch in it).
- • It's certainly ∨cold (| but I 'wouldn't say ∨nasty).
- • She 'may not have ∨meant to do it (| but she \did do it).

o Do you a⁄gree with them?	• vYes (| 'up to a vpoint).
o You 'won't vleave me, | \will you?	• vNo (| but you must 'stop behaving so neu\rotically).
o But you \promised me you'd play.	• vTrue (| but I 'didn't say vwhen).
o 'When will you be coming \back?	• vSoon (| but I 'can't say exvactly).
o Do you 'play ⁄squash?	• vSometimes (| but not voften).

E2.6.4 Practise these responses both as they are written and then with a *but . . .* continuation you must supply yourself.

o 'Can you play ⁄chess?	• I vused to be able to.
o I vthink they'd accept.	• vMelanie would.
o But you 'have to \work on Sundays.	• vUsually I do.
o 'Have you ⁄finished?	• vNearly.
o I've told you the e'xact \truth.	• I 'wish I could bevlieve that.

E2.6.5 Listen to the recording and identify the tones. The place of the nucleus is already shown for you.

ᴦ

A: 'Planning to go a'way this year?\|\|
B: We've 'just 'been away.\|\| We had a 'week in 'Cornwall.\|\|
A: And 'how 'was it?\|\|
B: Oh we had a 'marvellous time.\|\| The 'only 'problem \| was the 'weather.\|\| Un'fortunately \| it 'rained most of the time.\|\|
A: So 'what did you 'do during all this rain?
B: Well the 'great at'traction \| was the 'Eden Project.\|\| I found it 'utterly 'fascinating.

2.7   More about the implicational fall–rise

The fall–rise can also be used to signal that the speaker is **tentative** about what he or she says. This is a special case of the implicational fall–rise: the speaker makes a statement but at the same time implies something like *but I'm not sure* or *but I don't want to commit myself to this.*

Is this the way to Holborn?	• I vthink so (| but I'm 'not quite \sure).
What shall we have to drink?	• We 'could try a vriesling.

If we think someone has made a mistake, and we want to correct them, it is polite to do so in a tentative way. This explains the use of the fall–rise for **polite corrections**.

ᴦ

She's coming on Wednesday.	• On vThursday.
How many students? Twenty?	• vThirty.
I'll come with you.	• No you vwon't!

In contrast, to use a falling tone for a correction would be abrupt and perhaps rude:

🎧   She's coming on Wednesday.   • \No, | on \Thursday.

The fall–rise is often used when we want to make a **partial** statement; that is, to say that something applies partly, to some extent, but not completely:

                    So you both live in London?   • vI do (| but 'Mary lives in \York).
🎧   What was the food like?   • Well the vfish was good.

Many corrections are like this: partly we agree with the other speaker, partly we disagree. Partial corrections, too, take a fall–rise:

                    I hear you passed all your exams.   • vMost of them.
                                                          • Well not vall of them.
🎧   Green and blue are primary colours.   • Well vblue is (| but vgreen isn't).

Partial statements can involve subtle implications. There is an interesting example discussed by O'Connor & Arnold (1973: 68–9; I have modernized the language):

🎧   (i) What a lovely voice!   • \Yes, | she has a 'lovely vvoice (| but she
                                                            'can't vact).
🎧   (ii) I don't think much of her acting • Well she has a 'lovely vvoice (| 'even if she
                        ability.   can't \act).

In (i) the second speaker concedes that the performer in question sings well, but implies by the use of the fall–rise that he has reservations about other aspects of her abilities. So he agrees by the words he uses, but disagrees by his choice of tone. In (ii), on the other hand, he asks the first speaker to concede that the performer in question does at least have vocal ability. In each case we have a kind of partial correction: in (i) a partial agreement, in (ii) a partial disagreement.

The fall–rise is often used in **negative** statements:

                    She 'wasn't very vpleased.
                    I'm 'not suggesting these 'changes will be veasy.
🎧   I 'don't want to sound vrude (| but is 'that your /dog?)

                    She's refused to pay.   • Oh I 'don't think that's vtrue.
🎧   Why are you complaining?   • It's 'not just vme. (\Others are, | \too.)
                    Are you free over the weekend?   • 'Not on vSaturday (though I am on vSunday).

The implication is that the corresponding positive statement is not true. There is a contrast, implicit or explicit, between a negative (something that we present as not true) and a positive (something we present as true). The negative part is said with a fall–rise tone. The positive part may either be left implicit (unexpressed), or else be made explicit by being put into words. If it is made explicit, it may

come either before or after the negative part, and may have either a definitive fall
or an implicational (polite-correction) fall–rise:

He says they're moving to London.   • 'Not vLondon.
                                          • He 'didn't say vLondon.
                                          • He 'didn't say vLondon, | he said \Manchester.
                                          • He said \Manchester, | 'not vLondon.

She 'didn't say she vwould do it (, | she said she \wouldn't).
She said that she \wouldn't do it, | 'not that she vwould.

Let us return to one of our earlier examples of the implicational fall–rise. There
are two ways in which the implication might be made explicit:

Can we fix an appointment?   (i) • Well I could 'see you on vWednesday | but
                                              on 'Thursday I'm \busy.
                                        (ii)• Well I could 'see you on vWednesday | but
                                              'not on vThursday.

In (i) the implication is spelt out positively, with a definitive fall on *busy*, but in
(ii) it is expressed negatively, with a negative fall–rise on *Thursday*. Consider the
likely tone choices in the following answers. The positive answer would probably
have a fall, the negative one a fall–rise.

How did it go?   (*positive*)   • Oh it was 'very suc\cessful.
                     (*negative*)   • Well I 'wouldn't say it was sucvcessful.
Have you been to the   (*positive*)   • Yes I've had some 'great \times there.
Gigolo Club?

                     (*negative*)   • 'Not since it revopened.

The fall–rise tone has a special function in a negative sentence. Namely, it indicates
that the **scope** of negation includes the word bearing the nucleus, but not the main
verb (unless the main verb itself bears the nucleus). A falling tone, on the other
hand, does not restrict the scope of the negation in this way. In the following
examples labelled (i), the fall means the scope is not limited; in those labelled
(ii), the fall–rise means it is limited. The one labelled (iii), which has a rise, is
ambiguous.

(i)   I 'won't eat \anything. (= I'll eat nothing.)
(ii) I 'won't eat vanything. (= I'll eat only certain things.)
(iii) 'Will he eat /anything?

(i)   She 'didn't do it because she was vtired. (= She did it, but for some other
      reason.)
(ii) She 'didn't vdo it | because she was \tired. (= She didn't do it. Here's
      why.)

EXERCISES

E2.7.1 Listen and repeat these **tentative** statements. Think of a context where each might be used.

I ∨think so.
I'll ∨try.
She ∨might.
They ∨could.
∨Probably.

E2.7.2 Pair-work practice.

○ ˈWhen can we \meet?	• ∨Wednesday might do.
○ Is /Mary coming to the party?	• I ∨think she is.
○ Will you be coming to the /meeting?	• I ∨might be able to.
○ ˈI think it's too am\bitious.	• ˈThat's ∨one way of looking at it.
○ ˈHow are we going to \manage?	• ∨Victor might help out.
○ Your ∨price is rather high.	• I'm preˈpared to ne∨gotiate.
○ They're ˈasking us to sur\render.	• We ˈdon't have to ac∨cept.
○ So I ˈjust can't af\ford it.	• You could ˈalways make an ∨offer.
○ ˈHow can I get in \touch with him?	• You could ˈsend an ∨email.
○ ˈWhat can I \tell her?	• You could ˈtry the ∨truth.

E2.7.3 Pair-work practice: polite corrections.

○ You have to ˈchange at \Ilford.	• ∨Stratford. • At ∨Stratford. • ∨Stratford, you mean. • It's ˈactually ∨Stratford. • You change at ∨Stratford.
○ ˈNo one \ever phones her.	• ∨Sean does.
○ There's ˈno one \in today.	• ∨John's here.
○ She's ˈworking in \Oxford.	• ∨Cambridge.
○ I ˈdon't think prices are ∨falling.	• ∨Some are.
○ We're ˈgoing to \Denver.	• ∨Boulder.
○ The ˈwedding's in Ma\jorca.	• Ma∨deira.
○ The ˈmeeting's in \here, | /isn't it?	• In the ∨annexe, sir.
○ She ˈkeeps it in the \shed.	• In the ∨greenhouse.
○ So she's ˈcoming this \morning.	• I said this ∨evening.
○ What a ˈpretty blue \dress she had on!	• It was a ∨black dress.
○ That's ˈBeethoven's \ninth!	• It's his ∨fifth.
○ ˈCiaran was \early | to/day.	• He was ∨late.
○ There were \ten people there.	• ∨Nine.
○ She had an ˈawful pink \hat.	• ∨Mauve.
○ ˈThis is \Don's book.	• ∨Mine.

E2.7.4 Explain the difference of tone meaning between the following.

○ I'm 'told this was \Mike's idea.

(i) • No ∨mine.
(ii) • No \mine.

E2.7.5 Listen to the following, and decide on the basis of their intonation whether they are relatively polite or relatively brusque.

○ It goes in the ac\cusative. • No in the 'dative.
○ He's from \France. • From 'Germany.
○ She said her \foot was hurting. • Her 'arm.
○ It's a 'Jack \Russell. • A dal'matian.
○ We 'saw a \wolf. • A 'fox.

E2.7.6 Pair-work practice: partial statements.

○ Are they 'both going to be at the /party? • ∨Roy will be. | But 'Debbie can't \make it.
○ 'What about 'Philip and \Nolan? • I 'know ∨Philip can come.
○ And the /Smiths? • Well ∨she should be able to manage it.
○ 'Will there be /food? • For 'those who arrive before ∨ten.
○ Is your 'flat /big enough? • Well we've 'got the ∨space.‖ It's the \parking | ∨I'm worried about.

E2.7.7 Pair-work practice: partial corrections. Practise these with and without the part in parentheses.

○ 'Red and 'yellow are 'primary \colours. • ∨Red is. (| But ∨yellow isn't.)
○ 'Wasps and 'spiders are \insects. • ∨Wasps are. (| But ∨spiders aren't.)
○ So you're 'both going to \Athens. • Well ∨I am. (| But my ∨partner isn't.)
○ 'Raj and 'Ali are from \India. • ∨Raj is. (| But not ∨Ali.)
○ So you 'watched television all \morning. • 'Only till e∨leven. (| Not after ∨that.)
○ We had 'wonderful \meals. • Well ∨dinner was OK. (| But I thought 'lunch was disap\pointing.)
○ It's 'quite \easy | to get to /Manchester. • It's 'OK as far as ∨Wilmslow. (| But the \last part's slow.)
○ The ∨teachers are pretty good. • Well ∨some of them are. (| But others are \hopeless.)
○ 'Bread's \good for you! • ∨Wholemeal is. (‖ But 'cheap ∨white bread | is 'full of \additives.)
○ ∨Fruit's cheap today. • ∨Apples are. (| But 'pears are still ex\pensive.)

E2.7.8 After practising these, choose one and write a dialogue in which it is the punch line.

It's 'not ∨black, | it's \white.
It's 'not ∨hot, | it's \cold.

It's 'not really ˇyellow, | it's a 'sort of ˏorangy colour.
She's 'not ˇhappy, | she's 'desperately ˏmiserable.
I'm 'not just ˇpleased, | I'm 'absolutely deˏlighted.

You 'mustn't ˇmultiply, | you must diˏvide.
It's 'not 2ˇx, | it's '2ˏy.
She's 'not ˇfifty, | she's ˏsixty.
We're 'not going by ˇcar | but by ˏtrain.
It's 'not made of ˇwool | but ˏcotton.

E2.7.9 Pair-work practice: negative statements.

o Are you 'using your ⁄shredder?
o Is it 'open every ⁄day?
o 'How did Marilyn ˏtake it?
o He'll be 'here in ten ˏminutes.
o D'you 'think they'll ⁄win?

• 'Not at the ˇmoment.
• 'Not on ˇMondays.
• She 'wasn't very ˇpleased.
• I 'wouldn't ˇbet on it.
• It's 'not very ˇlikely.

o Is ⁄this the one we chose?
o So ˏKieran won it!
o You 'might win a ˏprize.
o But I 'thought you said he'd ˏdo it.
o 'Could I borrow your ⁄knife?

• I 'don't ˇthink so.
• I 'don't think he ˇdid.
• I 'don't think I ˇwill.
• That 'isn't what I ˇmeant.
• It 'isn't very ˇsharp.

E2.7.10 Practise these and construct further similar examples of your own.

I 'said I'd ˏborrow one, | 'not ˇbuy one.
I 'didn't say I'd ˇbuy one, | I 'said I'd ˏborrow one.

It was ˏJanet in the picture, | 'not ˇJackie.
It 'wasn't ˇJackie in the picture, | it was ˏJanet.

o They've 'moved to ˏSussex.

• Not ˇSussex, | ˏEssex.
• To ˏEssex, | not to ˇSussex.

E2.7.11 For each question, formulate a positive answer (with a fall) and a negative answer (with a fall–rise).

Model:
o 'Have you been to the Old ⁄Vic?

• ˏYes, | ˏseveral times.
• ˏNo, | 'not ˇrecently.

Have you seen their new play?
Would you care for a beer?
Do you travel much?
Do you like my new hairstyle?
Can I tempt you with a sandwich?

E2.7.12 Explain the difference in meaning in the following pairs.

1 (i)   I 'just don't want ˏanything.
  (ii)   I 'don't want just ˇanything.

2 (i)   I'm 'not going to come to the 'party because ＼Sophie invited me.
  (ii)   I'm 'not going to come to the 'party because ∨Sophie invited me.

2.8   Declarative questions

In English – unlike Spanish or Greek, for example – yes–no questions
usually have a special interrogative grammatical form, involving the inversion of
the subject and the verb. We discuss their intonation in 2.13. However, we do also
sometimes use **declarative questions**, which are grammatically like statements.
They can be identified as questions only by their intonation, or by the pragmatics of
the situation where they are used. They are usually said with a rise: a **yes–no rise**.

- You'll be 'coming to ／dinner? (= Are you coming to dinner?)
- He 'took his ／passport? (= Did he take his passport?)
  You 'think I'm ／crazy? (= Do you think I'm crazy?)
  I had an a'mazing ex＼perience.   • You ／did? (= I hear what you say.)

Sometimes they are said with a **fall–rise**:

- You 'didn't go and ∨tell him? (= Does that mean that you told him?)

and sometimes, confusingly, with a **fall**:

- So we'll be 'free by ＼six, then? (= Do you mean we'll be free by six?)
  You mean he 'didn't turn ＼up?

It can be difficult for the hearer to know whether a question or a statement is
intended, particularly when a falling tone is used:

- So there were ＼three of them.   • Are you ／asking me | or ＼telling me?

EXERCISES

E2.8.1 Pair-work practice.

- o You 'oughtn't to eat that ∨pie.
- o 'Someone's been in the ＼house.
- o It re'leases the body's ＼energy flows.
- o No ＼you take the car.
- o 'Let's get a ＼pizza.

- o They'll 'have to close ＼down.
- o The 'answer is ＼thirty.
- o You can 'take the ∨scissors.
- o I'll 'get it to you by ＼Friday.
- o He's 'lost his ＼job.

- • You mean it's ／poisonous?
- • We've had ／burglars?
- • You 'really be／lieve that?
- • It 'won't incon／venience you?
- • You've 'got enough ／money?

- • You 'really ／think so?
- • You're ／sure of that?
- • You 'won't be ／needing them?
- • You 'can't do it before ／then?
- • They've ／fired him?

2.9 Uptalk

Since about 1980 a new use of a rising tone on statements has started to be heard in English. It is used under circumstances in which a fall would have been used by an earlier generation (and a fall is still felt to be more appropriate by most native speakers of English).

◉   (i) \Hi. | 'I'm 'Cathy \Pomeroy. | I'm a 'customer \service agent.
◉   (ii) \Hi. | 'I'm 'Cathy /Pomeroy. | I'm a 'customer /service agent.

The traditional intonation pattern, with a definitive fall, is (i). The new pattern is (ii). It has been variously referred to as the **high rising terminal** (HRT), **upspeak** and **uptalk**. It is speculated that it originated in New Zealand, though other claimed sources are Australia, California and British regional accents.

To older people who do not use it the uptalk pattern sounds like a pardon-question rise (see 2.16). It is as if the uptalker is asking a question, checking whether something is the case or not, rather than giving information. In example (ii) it is as if the speaker were not sure of her identity, or felt she could not assert it. But the pragmatic context calls not for checking or querying, but for assertion of something the speaker certainly knows. Hence to non-uptalkers it feels like an inappropriate choice of tone.[2] Here are some examples overheard during 2004–5. In each case I myself would have used a fall where I heard a young speaker actually use a rise.

It'd be 'safer if you stayed with /friends for a couple of days.
I'll 'really really \really | be pissed /off | if I'm 'still here for vChristmas.
There was this /girl | who lived like 'three doors /down from me.
We're 'working vpeople, | but our 'pay doesn't re/flect that.
It vmight be | 'over there by the /fence.
◉ \Sorry. | I 'just wanted to use the /phone.

What do you feel about his criticism? • It can be 'quite /harsh sometimes.
Where are you working? • I'm in an 'office in Princess /Hall.
How do you find out about the arrangements? • 'Emails and /posters.

(*Students commenting on a speech pathology video:*)
He vseems | to have some /language impairment.
◉ He's vnot mentally ill, | but he's pre/tending to be.

The journalist Matt Seaton (2001) claims that his six-year-old Londoner daughter returned from an American summer camp and reported as follows: *Well, we went canoeing on the lake? Which was, like, really really fun? And then we had storytelling in the barn? And we all had to tell a story about, like, where we're from or our family or something?* The question marks, of course, indicate the to him unexpected rise tone.

What should the learner of EFL do about uptalk?

-     If you were born before about 1980, *do not use* uptalk.
-     If you were born later, you can imitate its use by native speakers: but do not overdo it. Uptalk is never essential. Bear in mind that using uptalk may annoy older people listening to you.

EXERCISES

E2.9.1 Answer these questions (a) with a fall and (b) with a rise.

> What's your name?
> Where do you come from?
> What's your favourite food?
> Would you prefer coffee or tea?
> Tell me, how old are you, Miss Thomas?

2.10   *Yes*, *no* and elliptical answers

The **answer** to a yes–no question is usually not a complete statement. Rather, it is just *yes* or *no* (or an equivalent). Quite often, we support the *yes* or *no* by an elliptical verb phrase. Or we may just use the elliptical verb phrase on its own:

Do you know Peter?
- \Yes.
- \Sure.
- Of \course.
- \Yes, | I \do.
- I \do.
- Of \course I do!
- Of \course I know Peter!

Have you ever been to Minsk?
- \No.
- \Never.
- Of \course not.
- \No, | I \haven't.
- I \haven't, | /actually.
- I don't think I \have.
- Of \course I haven't.
- No I \haven't been to Minsk.

The tone for these answers may be any of the tones that can be used in full statements. Typically, it will be a definitive fall; but other tones are possible:

Are you going to object?
- (\Yes,) | I \am.
- (/Yes,) | I /am. (. . . and I'll tell you \why.)
- (vYes,) | I vam. (. . . | though 'not imvmediately.)

Have you done your homework?	• (\No,) | I \haven't. • (/No,) | I /haven't. (. . . and I'm not \going to.) • (vNo,) | I vhaven't. (. . . but I vwill.)
Do you sell stamps?	• We /do. • \Yes, | we \do. • Well we vdo. (. . . | but we've 'sold \out.)

These grammatical patterns can be used not only to answer a direct question but
also to express our agreement with what the other person is saying, or alternatively
to contradict them. A straightforward agreement typically uses a fall:

So you've done your homework.	• \Yes. • I 'certainly \have. • \Yes, | I \have. • Of \course I have. • vYes. (. . . but not vall of it.)
Look, | it's snowing. It wasn't very good.	• 'So it \is, | \isn't it? • \No. (= You're right, it wasn't.) • It 'definitely \wasn't. • \No, | it \wasn't. • vNo. (. . . though it 'wasn't vhopeless.)

To **contradict** what the other person says, it is possible to use a definitive fall or
a tentative fall–rise; but the most usual tone is a rise:

You haven't brought the milk.	• I /have.
It was brilliant.	• It /wasn't.

If we put *(oh) yes* or *(oh) no* before the elliptical verb phrase in a contradiction,
English has fixed idiomatic tone patterns, and in particular disallows a sequence
of two falls. (You cannot contradict a negative statement by saying *yes* alone.)
This pattern is used only to contradict a statement, not to answer a question:

You haven't brought the milk!	• \Yes, | I /have. (= You're wrong.) • \Oh yes, | I /have. • Yes I vhave. *not* × • \Yes, | I \have.
It was brilliant.	• \No, | it /wasn't! (= You're wrong.) • \Oh no, | it /wasn't. • No it vwasn't. *not* × • \No, | it \wasn't.
Do you sell stamps?	*not* × • \Yes | we /do.

Contradictions can also be said with a definitive fall: the difference is that a (high)
fall implies warmth and solidarity with the other person – i.e. is supportive – while
the rise implies defensiveness and unfriendliness – that is, it is unsupportive:

You haven't paid for the coffee.   • I \have! (= It's OK, nothing's wrong.)
You haven't paid for the coffee.   • I /have. (= Don't accuse me wrongly.)

EXERCISES

E2.10.1 Pair-work practice.

    ○ Are you 'coming /with us?   • \Yes, | I \am.
    ○ Have you 'got your /passport?   • \Yes, | I \have.
    ○ Did you 'lock the /door?   • Of \course I did.
    ○ Will you be 'back before /seven?   • \Yes, | of \course I will.
    ○ 'Can you speak /French?   • \Yes, | I \can speak French.

    ○ Have you 'ever been to /Mali?   • \No, | I \haven't.
    ○ 'Will you be /joining us?   • \No, | I \won't.
    ○ 'Has she brought the /ham?   • \No, | she \hasn't.
    ○ 'Did they ask for an ex/tension?   • \No, | they \didn't.
    ○ 'Is he /satisfied?   • \No, | he \isn't satisfied.

E2.10.2 Pair-work practice: contradicting.

    ○ You've 'finished all the \milk!   • \No, | I /haven't.
    ○ They 'all \failed the exam.   • \No, | they /didn't.
    ○ 'Chloë's coming \with us.   • \No, | she /isn't.
    ○ He 'usually finishes by \ten.   • \No, | he /doesn't.
    ○ I can 'fit it in after \tea.   • \Oh no, | you /can't. (| We're going \out.)

    ○ You \can't eat | all that /chocolate!   • \Yes, | I /can.
    ○ You 'haven't finished your \homework.   • \Yes, | I /have.
    ○ There's 'never been a war in vCanada.   • \Yes, | there /has.
    ○ This 'isn't the tallest building in the   • \Oh yes, | it /is.
       vworld, though.
    ○ She 'didn't bring the vmoney.   • \Oh yes, | she /did.

E2.10.3 Supply a suitable context in which each of the following might be said:

1   \Yes, | they \do.
2   \Yes, | they /do.
3   \No, | they \don't.
4   \No, | they /don't.
5   \Oh yes, | I /am.
6   \Oh no, | I'm /not.

E2.10.4 Give an answer, with appropriate intonation, contradicting each of these assertions:

    'Sophie's got a new \hairdo.
    You 'haven't done any \cooking.
    They've 'all for\gotten.

'Darren's been at the \wine again.
I'm just a com'plete \failure.

E2.10.5 Pair-work practice.

    o 'Is it going to /rain?   • \Yes, | I think it \is.
    o 'Are we going to /finish on time?   • \Yes, | I think we \are.
    o I've made a 'dreadful mi\stake!   • \Yes, | I think you \have.
    o They 'haven't bought any \fruit!   • \No, | I 'don't think they \have.
    o Did we /score?   • \No, | I 'don't think we \did.

    o Is 'that Mrs /Bailey?   • \Yes, | I vthink so.
                               • \Yes, | I vthink it is.
                               • vNo, | I 'don't vthink so.
                               • \No, | I 'don't vthink it is.
                               • I'm 'not really \sure.

E2.10.6 Consider each of the responses given below. Is the intonation pattern plausible? Explain.

    A: 'Is this the /book you wanted?   B: vYes.
                                          B: \Yes.
                                          B: /Yes.
                                          B: \Yes, | it /is.
                                          B: \Yes, | it \is.

    A: 'Are you /ready?   B: \Yes, | I \am.
                                          B: vYes.
                                          B: \Yes | I /am.
                                          B: /Yes, | I /am.
                                          B: \Yes, | I vam.

2.11   Independent rises

    As well as for declarative questions and in uptalk, rises are used for short responses **encouraging** further conversation. They signal no more than that the social interaction is running smoothly.

    'Have a cup of \tea.   • That's 'very /kind of you.

Learners of English should be careful, however, not to use this tone for non-routine answers:

    'Where are you \from, then?   • ?Norway.

With a rise on *Norway*, this could sound rude (suggesting, perhaps, that this is routine information that the person asking the question ought to know already). For a straightforward statement in answer to the question, use a fall.

Rises are also used for various interjections (see 2.19) and for dependent parts of a larger structure (see 2.20–4). But they are fairly unusual with statements that are truly independent.

> I 'just asked for some extra \time. | It's a 'perfectly reasonable re/quest.

The rise here perhaps signals that the second sentence is not actually independent, but an afterthought to, or qualification of, the first.

Further discussion of rises in statements must wait until the analysis of prenuclear patterns, in chapter 5.

EXERCISES

E2.11.1 Pair-work practice.

ᘐ   o 'Any problems with the /builders?   ᘐ• I 'don't /think so.
                                                 ᘐ• 'Not /really.
                                                 ᘐ• No 'everything's O/K.
                                                    • It's 'all going /smoothly.
                                                    • They're 'just getting on with the /job.

QUESTIONS

2.12   Wh questions

Wh questions (= question-word questions, special questions) are those that are formed with a question word such as *who, what, which, when, where, why, how*. They ask for a more specific answer than just 'yes' or 'no'.

> 'Where's my \knife?
> 'Why are you com\plaining?
> 'How did it get \broken?

The default tone for wh questions is a **fall**. As with statements, this tone meaning is the **definitive fall**:

ᘐ   'When did you ar\rive?
ᘐ   'Who's \that?
ᘐ   'Which is the \shift key?
            'Where's the \grater?
            'How do you spell \friend?

So 'who did you ˎsee?
'What does inˎtestate mean?
'What ˎbooks have you read recently?

Nevertheless, a wh question can also be said with a non-fall: a rise or, less commonly, a fall–rise. This has the effect of making it *more gentle*, kindly, encouraging, sympathetic or deferential, as opposed to the businesslike fall. We call this tone meaning the **encouraging rise**.

🎧   'When did you arˏrive?
🎧   'What's the ˏtime?
          'How long will you be staying in ˏLondon, sir?
          'How many people in your ᵛparty, madam?

Contrast the two tone meanings, definitive fall and encouraging rise:

(i)   'Why are you ˎangry? (*unmarked*)
(ii)   'Why are you ˏangry? (*interested, sympathetic*)

🎧   (i) 'What's your ˎname?   (*unmarked, businesslike*)
🎧   (ii) 'What's your ˏname? (*encouraging, kindly*)

A separate type of wh question is the echo question, discussed in 2.16 below.
    A short wh question that the speaker immediately answers himself (one type of rhetorical question) usually has an interested rise:

          I'm 'coming ˎback.‖ ˏWhy? | Be'cause I ˎlove you.
          We can 'conquer ˎpoverty.‖ ˏHow? | By 'educating the ˎworkforce.
🎧   You 'can't ˎgo.‖ 'Why ˏnot? | Be'cause I ˎsay so.

EXERCISES

2.12.1 Pair-work practice: monosyllabic.

o I've 'just seen ˎMiriam.   • ˎWhere?
o I'm 'going to reˎsign.   • ˎWhy?
o We'll 'find someone ˎelse.   • ˎWho?
o I'll 'play them a reˎcording.   • ˎHow?
o 'Come and see me toˎmorrow.   • ˎWhen?
o 'Borrow someone's ˎdictionary.   • ˎWhose?
o She 'flew with one of the low-ˎcost airlines. • ˎWhich?
o I'm 'going for a ˎdrive.   • ˎWhere?
o She 'says she'll comˎplain.   • ˎWhy?
o I'll 'send him an ˎemail.   • ˎWhen?

2.12.2 Pair-work practice: with tail.

- ○ I've got a'nother \question.
- ○ I was 'told you'd re\signed.
- ○ I \know he'll be there.
- ○ We 'mustn't \use them.
- ○ They 'may not let us \in.

- • \Now what?
- • \Who told you?
- • \How d'you know, though?
- • \Why mustn't we use them?
- • \Then what'll we do?

2.12.3 Pair-work practice: with prenuclear accent (head).

- ○ We're 'going on a \trip.

- • 'Where \to?
- • 'Who \with?
- • 'What \for?
- • 'How \soon?
- • 'Which \one?

2.12.4 Listen and repeat.

I'm 'not \standing for it. | 'Why \should I?
I 'can't believe he \did that. | 'How \could he?
So you've \found the papers! | 'Where \were they?
So I've \missed your birthday. | 'When \was it?
I'll 'pick you up tomorrow \morning. | 'What \time?

E2.12.5 Pair-work practice: longer wh questions.

- ○ So 'that's my \plan.
- ○ He's gonna have to \pay for it.
- ○ There's been some 'sharp \practice.
- ○ We're running a 'one-day \seminar.
- ○ I've 'bought a new \table.

- • And 'when are you going to com\plete it?
- • 'Why do you want to \punish him?
- • 'How d'you make \that out?
- • 'What are you going to \charge?
- • 'Where are you going to \put it?

E2.12.6 Dialogue practice.

A: /What was that you said?
A: Oh, we went to \Spain.
A: 'Just outside \Malaga.
A: A \week.‖ 'Six \nights, | to be ex/act.

A: \Oh, | the /usual things.‖ 'What do \you do on holiday?

B: 'Where did you go for your \holiday?
B: 'Which \part?
B: 'How long did you \stay?
B: 'Are you pleased you /went?‖'What did you do while you were \there?
B: 'Why do you \ask?

E2.12.7 Pair-work practice: encouraging rise.

- ○ I 'don't think I'll \go.
- ○ Oh, this 'wretched com\puter!
- ○ I saw \Zoë | at the /party.
- ○ I 'used to live in \Belper.
- ○ I'm a'fraid they've gone \out.

- • 'Why /not?
- • 'What's /wrong with it?
- • 'Who was she /there with?
- • And 'where d'you live /now?
- • 'How soon will they be /back?

E2.12.8 Practise these responses first in a straightforward businesslike way (with a fall) and then in a softened, friendly way (with a rise).

- o I'm 'leaving to\morrow.
- o So I've 'been here a few \weeks now.
- o I was 'wondering if I could have some more \leaflets.
- o They've 'gone for a \walk.
- o We're 'having a \marvellous time.

- • 'What time's your 'flight?
- • 'Where are you 'living?
- • 'How many would you 'like?
- • 'How soon will they be 'back, d'you think?
- • 'Who's in 'charge of the group?

E2.12.9 Explain the difference in tone meaning in these pairs. Which would be likely to be used by an immigration officer speaking to an arriving passenger at an airport? Who might use the other one?

1 (i)   'How long will you be \staying?
  (ii)   'How long will you be /staying?

2 (i)   'Where will you be \living?
  (ii)   'Where will you be /living?

2.13   Yes–no questions

Yes–no questions (= general questions, polar questions) ask whether something is the case or not. Such questions are capable of meaningfully being answered 'yes' or 'no' (though there may be other possible answers such as 'perhaps' or 'I'm not sure'). The default tone for a yes–no question is a **rise**. We call it the **yes–no rise**.

🎧   'Are you /ready?
🎧   Is 'that the /time?
           'Will you be at the /meeting?
           Have you 'been here /long?
           'Has he a/greed to it?

           I'm 'just going to the \supermarket.   • Can 'I come /too?

Yes–no questions can be positive or negative. Whatever their polarity, they usually have a yes–no rise:

           'Won't you be at the /meeting?
           'Haven't you /finished yet?
           'Don't you like your /soup?
           'Haven't we met be/fore?

Some utterances with the grammatical form of yes–no interrogatives are not questions so much as requests. They, too, usually have a yes–no rise:

> 'Would you pass me the ⁄water?
> 'Will you send him a ⁄letter?
> 'Could I have some ⁄paper?
> 'Couldn't I take the ⁄car?

It is also possible for a yes–no question to be said with a **fall**. This makes the question more insistent. It is more businesslike, more serious, perhaps more threatening. We call this tone meaning for yes–no questions the **insistent fall**.

> A: I'll 'ask you once ＼more: | 'Did you take the ＼money?
> B: ＼No, | I ＼didn't.
> A: 'Can you ＼prove that?

The insistent yes–no fall is often used in guessing games.

> A: 'Guess where I ＼come from.
> B: From ⁄France?
> A: ∨No.
> B. From ＼Italy, then?
> A: ＼No.
> B: D'you come from ＼Spain?

The insistent yes–no fall is also regularly used when a speaker repeats a question because the other person didn't hear it properly:

> A: 'Have you come ⁄far?
> B: ⁄Sorry?
> A: I ∨said, | 'have you come ＼far.

In colloquial speech the initial auxiliary verb and pronoun are often omitted:

> 'Got the ⁄keys? (= 'Have you got the ⁄keys?)
> [Do you] 'see what I ⁄mean?
> [Have you] 'all ⁄got that? (= Do you all understand?)
> [Are you] 'short of ⁄cash?
> [Would you] 'like a ⁄drink?
> [Is it] 'still ⁄snowing?

EXERCISES

E2.13.1 Listen and repeat.

> Have you 'finished your ⁄essay?
> 'Did you remember to ⁄tell her?
> 'Can you speak ⁄French?
> Are you 'going to com⁄plain?
> Is the 'water ⁄hot enough?

'Did he a⁄pologize?
Was she 'pleased to ⁄see you?
'Were the ⁄children there?
'Have you vacuumed the ⁄carpets?
Will your ⁄mother be coming?

E2.13.2 Listen and repeat.

'Haven't they done e⁄nough?
'Didn't you bring an um⁄brella?
'Couldn't you send a ⁄text message?
'Isn't she ⁄ready yet?
'Aren't you going to intro⁄duce us?

'Won't it be a bit ⁄cold?
'Wasn't she here ⁄last week?
'Hasn't he ⁄finished yet?
'Don't you feel a 'bit over⁄dressed?
'Couldn't we ask for some ⁄more?

E2.13.3 Dialogue practice.

A: Hul⁄lo.   B: Is 'that James ⁄Smith's house?
A: ⁄Yes.   B: 'Could I speak to ⁄Mrs Smith, please?
A: I'm a'fraid she's not ⟍here.   B: 'Has she been gone ⁄long?
A: ⟍Oh, | for about an ⟍hour.   B: 'Could I leave a ⁄message?
A: Of ⟍course.   B: Could she 'phone my ⁄office?

E2.13.4. Pair-work practice: what are the words omitted at the beginning of the responses?

o What 'lovely ⟍cherries!   • ⁄Want some?
o It's going to ⟍snow.   • ⁄Think so?
o I'm 'wondering about ⟍Clare.   • ⁄Seen her lately?
o The 'chocolates were de⟍licious. • ⁄Eaten them all?
o ⟍David's back home.   • ⁄Seen anything of him?

E2.13.5 Pair-work practice: long tail.

o I 'wonder why she was up⟍set.   • 'Was it the unex⁄pectedness of it all, do you
                                          suppose?
o 'What did you think of my ⟍song?   • Do you ⁄always sing as flat as that?
o If 'only I had a bit more ⟍capital!   • 'Won't ⁄anyone lend you the money?
o It's 'really up to ⟍you, Michael.   • Would you 'very much ⁄mind if I refused?
o We'll 'need a ⟍sound system.   • 'Could we ⁄hire one, do you think?

E2.13.6 Pair-work practice: yes–no questions with a falling tone.

o He 'says he's \innocent.	• But 'can he \prove it?
o 'Let's drop in on the \Robinsons.	• 'Have we got \time, though?
o It would be 'nice to have a new \kitchen.	• But 'can we af\ford one?
o 'Gavin ex\plained it all to me.	• Yes but 'did you under\stand the explanation?
o I 'can't get my \email to work.	• 'Have you tried re\booting?

E2.13.7 Pair-work: ask the questions with a rise. The other speaker didn't catch what you said. Repeat them with a fall.

Model: A: 'Would you like some /tea?
B: /Sorry, | /what was that?
A: 'Would you like some \tea?

'Did you bring some 'money?
'Will you be staying 'long?
'Shall we buy some 'fruit?
'Could I borrow your 'stapler?
'Were they sur'prised at what she did?

2.14   Tag questions

Tag questions (question tags) are short yes–no questions tagged onto the end of a statement or command. We shall consider their intonation at this point, even though they of course involve dependent rather than independent intonation phrases.

Most tag questions can be said either with a fall or with a rise, and there is an important difference of tone meaning between these two possibilities.

If a tag question is genuinely asking for information, the tone will be a **yes–no rise**. This allows the speaker to check whether the other person agrees with what he or she has just said. It is open to the other person to agree or disagree:

The 'answer is \twenty, | /isn't it? (= Am I right?)
We could 'start with the \kitchen, | /couldn't we? (= That's just my suggestion.)
They 'haven't for\gotten, | /have they? (= Can that be the reason they're not here?)

'What does \chaise mean?	• \Chair,	/doesn't it?
'Where are they going to\morrow?	• \Leicester,	/aren't they?

The other possibility is an **insistent fall**. With a falling tag the speaker insists, assumes or expects that the other person will agree. Rather than genuinely asking for information, the speaker appeals for agreement:

🎧   The 'view is mag\nificent, | \isn't it? (= I'm sure you agree.)
🎧   We've 'been here be\fore, | \haven't we? (= We both know we have.)
              'Seven 'fives are 'thirty-\five, | \aren't they? (=You know they are.)
              Well it's 'not very ᵥgood, | \is it? (= You'll agree it's not very good.)

In some cases the falling-tone tag has the force of an exclamation. Exclamations always have a fall (see 2.17):
    Notice the difference of tone meaning in the following examples:

🎧   (i) It's \snowing, | \isn't it? (= You can see it is.)
🎧   (ii) It's \snowing, | /isn't it? (= I can't see, I'm not sure.)

🎧   (i) It's 'not ᵥright, | \is it? (= I'm \sure it's not.)
🎧   (ii) It's 'not ᵥright, | /is it? (= I'm not sure, I'd like your views.)

The effect of a tag with an insistent fall can even be to *force* the other person to agree. It becomes a way of exercising control:

🎧   ᵥMummy, | 'can I have some /cake?   • We'll have to \see, | \won't we?
🎧   'Why did I only get a \C?   • Because you made a 'lot of mi\stakes, | \didn't you?

Most tags, as in the examples given so far, reverse the polarity of the clause to which they are attached: that is, if the main clause is positive, the tag is negative; whereas if the main clause is negative, the tag is positive (see 4.10). Another kind of tag is the **constant-polarity** tag. Here the main clause is positive and the tag is also positive. Constant-polarity tags, if they have their own tone, always have a **rise**:

              It's \snowing, | /is it? (\Oh, | I \see.)
              So you 'think you'll \win, | /do you? (ᵥI don't think you will.)
🎧   What a 'lovely \dress!   • You \like it, | /do you?

As mentioned in 4.10, tags are not necessarily made into a separate IP and therefore do not necessarily have their own tone. As a result, it can be difficult for the analyst to determine the correct analysis. In the case of a falling pattern followed by a rising pattern, it is not always clear whether we have a fall tone followed by a rise tone, or a single fall–rise tone. There is a subtle difference between these two:

🎧   (i) So you've 'qualified as a ᵥlawyer, have you?
🎧   (ii) So you've 'qualified as a \lawyer, | /have you?

Version (i) is a declarative question with a high fall–rise (see 5.6). Version (ii) is a statement followed by a question. The difference in meaning between them corresponds to the difference between the corresponding tagless clauses:

(i)   So you've 'qualified as a ∨lawyer? (= Have . . . I got that right?)
(ii)   So you've 'qualified as a ∖lawyer! (= I . . . note this new information.)

Tags attached to clause types other than statements are more restricted in their possibilities.

When attached to an **exclamation**, a tag virtually always has an insistent fall:

🎧   'What a sur∖prise, | ∖wasn't it?

When attached to a **command**, a tag often comes in the tail rather than having its own intonation phrase (see 4.10):

🎧   'Come over ∕here a minute, will you?
🎧   'Open the ∖window, would you please?

If the tag after a command does have its own IP, the tone is usually an encouraging rise, giving a softening effect:

          'Come over ∖here a minute, | ∕will you?
          'Open the ∖window, | ∕would you, please? (= 'Would you open the
          ∕window?)[3]

After a command, a tag with a fall sounds very insistent. Not all speakers find this construction intonationally well-formed:

          'Answer the ∖phone, | ∖will you? (= 'Will you answer the ∖phone.‖ O'bey
          me im∖mediately.)

Tag questions are sometimes included as parentheses within a statement. Usually they have an insistent fall, though a yes–no rise is also possible:

🎧   It's ∖strange, | ∖isn't it, | how she never wants to do her share of the ∕work.
          We 'find it ∖difficult, | ∖don't we, | to 'live a virtuous ∖life. (= I'm sure you
          agree.)
          We 'find it ∖difficult, | ∕don't we, | to 'live a virtuous ∖life. (= Or am I wrong?)

EXERCISES

E2.14.1 Performance practice: rising tag, genuine question, yes–no rise.

          'This one is ∖Wayne's, | ∕isn't it?
          We're sup'posed to give it back to∖day, | ∕aren't we?
          You're re∖lated to her, | ∕aren't you?
          We 'promised to let them have it by ∖Monday, | ∕didn't we?
          I could ex'press it as a ∖decimal, | ∕couldn't I?

E2.14.2 Pair-work practice: fall plus rising tag.

          o 'Whose is ∖this one?   • ∖Jessica's, | ∕isn't it?
          o 'How many do they ∖want?   • ∖Seven, | ∕don't they?

○ 'When did we last ˎmeet? • In ˎApril, | ˏwasn't it?
○ The 'meeting's in 'Gˎ3. • That 'won't be ˎbig enough, | ˏwill it?
○ He's at St ˎJoseph's. • He teaches ˎphysics, | ˏdoesn't he?

○ 'Who d'you think'll ˎhelp? • ˎLenroy will, | ˏwon't he?
○ I've 'had a letter from ˎSophie. • She's in ˎPoland, | ˏisn't she?
○ Yes, I've ˎfinished the course. • Your e'xams were in ˎJune, | ˏweren't they?
○ 'Marvellous ˅play. • One of ˎPinter's, | ˏwasn't it?
○ So 'now we've ˎmoved. • You've gone to ˎStreatham, | ˏhaven't you?

E2.14.3 Pair-work practice: fall–rise plus rising tag, polite correction plus check.

○ He's ˎCzech. • ˅Polish, | ˏisn't he?
○ It's a sort of ˎgreen. • ˅Blue, | ˏisn't it?
○ 'Three nines are twenty-ˎeight. • Twenty-˅seven, | ˏaren't they?
○ They're from Uˎganda. • Rwˏanda, | ˏaren't they?
○ They're in ˎZurich. • ˅Bern, | don't you ˏmean?

E2.14.4 Performance practice: falling tag, appealing for agreement, insistent fall.

It's a 'beautiful ˎday, | ˎisn't it?
'Two and two makes ˎfour, | ˎdoesn't it?
The 'first three ˅notes | are 'do, re, ˎmi, | ˎaren't they?
The 'Vatican's in ˎRome, | ˎisn't it?
ˎAh, | you're ˎMargaret, | ˎaren't you?

We could 'order a ˎpizza, | ˎcouldn't we?
Looks 'pretty ˎmiserable, | ˎdoesn't it?
'Better than the ˅first one, | ˎwasn't he?
De'licious ˅cake, | ˎisn't it?
'Pretty deco˅rations, | ˎaren't they?

E2.14.5 Pair-work practice: fall plus falling tag, agreeing and appealing for agreement.

○ So we've had to ˎcancel it. • ˎPity, | ˎisn't it?
○ What a 'terrible ˎaccident! • ˎShocking, | ˎwasn't it?
○ It 'looks like ˎrain. • It ˎdoes, | ˎdoesn't it?
○ We've 'spent more than we ˎmeant to. • ˎYes, | we ˎhave, | ˎhaven't we?
○ 'Apples are quite exˎpensive here. • They ˎare, | ˎaren't they?

○ We 'don't need ˅both of them. • ˎNo, | we ˎdon't, | ˎdo we?
○ She 'hasn't been here be˅fore. • No she ˎhasn't, | ˎhas she?
○ They 'haven't sung ˅this one before. • They ˎhaven't, | ˎhave they?
○ We 'can't start a˅gain. • No we ˎcan't, | ˎcan we?
○ You 'haven't got a ˎticket! • No I ˎhaven't, | ˎhave I?

E2.14.6 Explain the difference in tone meaning in the following pairs. Practise saying them in appropriate contexts.

1 (i)   'That's cor\rect, | \isn't it?
  (ii)   'That's cor\rect, | /isn't it?

2 (i)   You're from \Italy, | \aren't you?
  (ii)   You're from \Italy, | /aren't you?

3 (i)   We 'didn't ∨win, | \did we?
  (ii)   We 'didn't ∨win, | /did we?

E2.14.7 Performance practice: constant-polarity tag, rising.

You're 'ready to \go, | /are you?
So 'this is \Humphrey, | /is it?
So we're 'facing a bit of a \problem, | /are we?
You pre'fer the \other one, | /do you?
She'll be 'here to\morrow, | /will she?

o They 'want a \rise.   • Oh they \do, | /do they?
o He's 'going to \challenge you. • He \is, | /is he?
o What a 'lovely \dress!   • You \like it, | /do you?
o Yes I've \told | /Heather.   • Oh you've \seen her, | /have you?
o 'How about asking \Neil?   • You 'think he'd a\gree, | /do you?

There are further examples of tag questions in 3.16 and 4.10.

2.15   Independent elliptical questions

One way of reacting to a statement made by another speaker is to use a short yes–no question, consisting just of an elliptical (= shortened) verb phrase. This resembles a tag question; but unlike a tag question it involves a change of speaker. The default tone for an independent elliptical question is a yes–no rise:

    I'm 'thinking of taking a \break.   • /Are you?
    He's 'just seen \Peter.   • /Has he?

This is a kind of minimal response to keep the conversation going. It may indicate anything from boredom to surprise, depending on the pitch range used. It means much the same as:

    He's 'just seen \Peter.   • /Really?

Independent elliptical questions of this type have the same polarity (positive or negative) as the clause just uttered by the other speaker:

    It 'wasn't very ∨good.   • /Wasn't it?
    They 'didn't have any \bread. • /Didn't they?

⚇   A: She 'won't be at all ˅pleased.
            B: ╱Won't she?
            A: ╲No, | she ╲won't.

Independent elliptical questions can also be said with an insistent fall. The tone
meaning is one of slight surprise or scepticism, but accepting that the other speaker
has expressed an opinion. This tone can sound hostile:

⚇   I 'really ╲like it here.   • ╲Do you? (I was a'fraid you ╲wouldn't.)
            Well, it's ╲over | ╱now.   • But ╲is it? (Per'haps it ˅isn't over, | after
                                                    ╲all.)
            There's 'nothing wrong with ˅greed. • ╲Isn't there? (I don't a╲gree with you.)

Much less common is a reverse-polarity negative elliptical yes–no question as a
reaction to a positive statement by the other speaker. This is a kind of exclamatory
fall (2.17):

            We 'really ╲thrashed them | ˅this time.   • ╲Didn't we just!
⚇   Her daughter's 'awfully ˅clever.   • ╲Yes, | ╲isn't she!

E2.15.1 Pair-work practice: elliptical question with rising tone, minimal response.

            ○ I've got 'something to ╲tell you.   • ╱Have you?
            ○ He's 'just turned ╲thirty.   • ╱Has he?
            ○ The 'Johnsons weren't in╲vited.   • ╱Weren't they?
            ○ I 'thought she was ╲fascinating.   • ╱Did you?
            ○ He 'comes from Bul╲garia.   • ╱Does he?

E2.15.2 Pair-work practice: elliptical question with falling tone, mild surprise, acceptance.

            ○ She's 'thirty-╲five.   • ╲Is she? (| I 'didn't ╲know.)
            ○ I 'love ˅Marmite.   • ╲Do you?
            ○ He's 'not going to ˅like it.   • ╲Isn't he? (| 'Too ╲bad.)
            ○ I'm 'off to New ╲York tomorrow.   • ╲Are you?
            ○ They 'won't be here before ˅ten.   • ╲Won't they?

E2.15.3 Explain the difference in tone meaning.

            ○ I a╲dore | ╱Mahler.   (i) • ╱Do you?
                                           (ii) • ╲Do you?
            ○ You're 'too ╲late.   (i) • ╱Am I?
                                           (ii) • ╲Am I?

E2.15.4 Reverse-polarity elliptical questions, exclamatory.

- ○ I thought 'Judi 'Dench was \great.
- ○ They've done 'terribly ⌄well.
- ○ The 'meal was a\trocious.
- ○ The 'flowers look \super.
- ○ We can be 'really \proud of ourselves.

- • \Yes, | \wasn't she!
- • Yes \haven't they!
- • \Yes, | \wasn't it!
- • \Don't they just!
- • \Yes, | \can't we just!

There are further examples of these patterns in 3.16.

2.16 Checking

If while you are speaking you want to check whether you have said the right thing, or whether your hearer has understood what you said, you can use an interjection such as *OK?* or *right?*. These interjections are a kind of yes–no question, and are accordingly usually said with a yes–no rise:

I'll 'get in touch with \Martin, | /right?
You can 'have it to\morrow, | 'all /right?
I'll 'pay you \back, | 'O/K? (*compare:* I'll pay you\back.‖ Is 'that O/K?)

In some varieties of English various other such interjections are used – though not in mainstream British standard English:

I'll 'do it to\morrow, | /yeah?
You 'think you're \clever, | /huh?
'Why did you \do it, | /eh?

To ask another speaker to repeat something because you did not hear it properly, you can say *What?* or *Sorry?* or *Pardon?*, with a rise. We call this tone meaning a **pardon-question rise**.

- 'Could you turn the /music down?
- 'Would you pass me the /salt?
- I 'want to \tell you something.
- We could 'ask ⌄Millington.

- • /What?
- • /Pardon?
- • You /what? (= | I can't \hear you.)
- • /Eh? | /What did you say?

With a pardon question you can query either the entire previous utterance, as in the examples just given, or just one element in it. In either case, the tone is the pardon-question rise:

- I 'chose \Thora.
- 'This is \Mel.
- Are we 'going to /win?

- • /Who?
- • /Nell?
- • Are we 'going to /win? | Of \course we are!

A typical conversational interchange might go as follows. Speaker A makes a statement, perhaps with an implicational fall–rise. Speaker B didn't quite catch it, and utters an interjection with a pardon-question rise. Speaker A repeats what he said, this time with a definitive fall:

> A: The ∨cruise documents have come.
> B: ∕Huh?
> A: (I ∨said, |) the ∖cruise documents have come.

The following conversational interchange is similar. But here speaker A asks a yes–no question. B asks a pardon question. When A repeats his yes–no question, again he switches to an insistent fall tone:

> A: Has 'Mrs ∕Partington been in?
> B: ∕Sorry?
> A: Has 'Mrs ∖Partington been in?

To check whether you have understood the other speaker correctly, you can suggest an interpretation, to see if it is correct. This too requires a rise: it is a kind of yes–no question, and takes a yes–no rise.

> We'll 'need some ∖vegetables.   • ∕Carrots? (= D'you mean ∕carrots?)
> It'll cost 'quite a ∨lot.   • A ∕thousand?
> I was 'talking to my ∖friend the other day.   • ∕Mary? (= By 'friend', do you mean Mary?)

An **echo question** uses some or all of the same words as used by the previous speaker, but with a pardon-question rise. This may be a simple request for repetition or clarification, or it may also express surprise and amazement at what the other speaker has said:

> You'll 'have to do it a∖gain.   • I'll 'have to do it a∕gain?
>   • Do it a∕gain?
>   • A∕gain?
> They've 'finished the ∖job.   • 'Finished the ∕job?
> Have you 'got your ∕pen?   • My ∕pen?
> 'Where's the ∖bathroom?   • The ∕bathroom?

There may be broad focus, querying the whole of the previous speaker's utterance, or narrow focus on some particular element. In the latter case the nucleus may be placed on a different item than the one on which the previous speaker placed it, often with ellipsis of some of the words:

> You'll 'have to do it a∖gain.   • ∕I'll have to?
> They've 'finished the ∖job.   • ∕Finished it?
> She's 'seeing him to∖morrow.   • ∕Seeing him?

It is also possible to query two or more words individually, placing a pardon-question rise nucleus on each:

> I was 'talking to James ∖Smith.   • ∕James | ∕Smith?
> You'll 'need a digital ∖camera.   • A ∕digital | ∕camera?

A special type of echo question is a **second-order question**, which echoes the other speaker's question to query it, perhaps with narrowed focus:

Have you 'got your /pen?	• Have /I got my pen?
'Where did it \happen?	• /Where? | Or \when?

A different kind of pardon question is a **please-repeat wh question**, which involves changing the focused element into a question word. The tone is always a rise. In the simplest form of please-repeat wh question there is no fronting of the question word:

⊙ She 'took a \tonga.	⊙ • She 'took a /what?
	• She did /what?
	• She /what?

Alternatively the wh word may be fronted. If so, it still bears the nucleus and has a rising tone:

She 'took a \tonga.	• /What did she take?
	• /What did you say she took?

Any element of the first speaker's utterance may be queried in this way. The nucleus always goes on the question word:

'Martin's lost his \cat.	• /Who's lost his cat?
	• 'Martin's done /what?
	• 'Martin's done /what to his cat?
	• 'Martin's lost his /what?

Broad-focus (see 3.9) pardon questions request a repetition of everything the other speaker has just said. Like repetition wh questions, they have a pardon-question rise on the question word.

She 'took a \tonga.	• /What was that again?
	• /What did you say?
	• /What?
	• /Sorry?

On the other hand, if the speaker asks not for a repetition but for a clarification, we have an ordinary wh question (see 5.9), which will most likely be said with a definitive fall:

She 'took a \tonga.	• 'What's a \tonga?

The difference between the definitive fall on a wh question and the pardon-question rise using the same syntax is seen in this pair of examples:

(i) 'Sophie's brought her \friend along.	• \Who? (= \which friend?)
(ii) 'Sophie's brought her \friend along.	• /Who? (= /who has?)

The appropriate answer to *who?* in (i) is the friend's name. The appropriate answer to *who?* in (ii) is *Sophie*.[4]

EXERCISES

E2.16.1 Attach one of the following, with a rising tone: *OK?, right?, all right?, yeah?, huh?.*
Think of an appropriate context where each sentence might be said.

> *Model:*   I'll 'bring it on \Friday.
>   → I'll 'bring it on \Friday, | 'O /K?

So you're \pleased with the presents.
We can 'start next \month.
You can 'pick her up at \Gatwick.
They'll be 'waiting out\side.
So 'Vernon could collect the \flowers.

We 'need some \bin liners.
'Don't forget the \scouring pads.
'Ask them about the \tiles.
So we'll 'just have to ac\cept it.
I'll 'try and do it by next \week.

E2.16.2 Pair-work practice.

o 'May I have a /word?   • /Pardon?
o I'm 'trying to make a \call.   • /What?
o I 'want to reach \Madelaine.   • /Sorry?
o I 'wonder if I might \trouble you. • I /beg your pardon?
o 'Could you get me some /milk?   • You /what?

o 'Let's switch 'over to the BB\C.   • /What was that again?
o They're 'playing \basketball.   • Come a/gain?
o 'Put in a \page break.   • /Sorry?
o The \trains are delayed.   • /What?
o It 'needs re-a\nalysis.   • /Pardon?

E2.16.3 Pair work. One person says something, with a non-fall tone. The other says *sorry?* or an equivalent phrase, with a rise. The first person then repeats their words, but using a fall.

> *Model:*   A: I'm 'not going to take out a ˅bank loan.
>   B: /Sorry?
>   A: I'm 'not going to take out a \bank loan.

I 'don't like her ⌄cats.
'Have you tried ⁄yoghurt?
It 'won't take ⌄long.
'Are you planning to re⁄tire soon?
'Could I have a look at your ⁄newspaper?

E2.16.4 Pair-work practice: pardon questions and echo questions.

○ He's 'been on a ⌵haj.
- A ⁄haj?
- A ⁄what?
- He's ⁄what?
- He's 'done ⁄what?
- A ⁄badge?

○ I'm 'going to visit ⌵Chloë.
- ⁄Who?
- ⁄Who are you going to visit?
- You're 'going to do ⁄what?
- You're 'going to do ⁄what to her?
- ⁄We are?

○ I've 'broken my ⌵humerus.
- Your ⁄what?
- Your ⁄humourless?!?
- You've 'done ⁄what to it?
- You've 'broken your ⁄what?
- ⁄You have? (| Of ⌵all people!)

E2.16.5 Pair-work practice: second-order questions.

○ 'Have you done the ⁄ironing?
○ 'Can we af⁄ford it?
○ 'What ⌵is it?
○ 'How much will it ⌵cost?
○ 'Where do you ⌵live?

- 'Have I done the ⁄ironing? | ⌵Yes!
- 'Can we af⁄ford it? | Of ⌵course.
- 'What ⁄is it? | A ⌵leek!
- 'How much will it ⁄cost? | A ⌵lot.
- 'Where do ⁄I live? | In ⌵Sydenham.

E2.16.6 Dialogue practice. You could extend this dialogue by adding further conversational exchanges in the same vein.

A: 'How much would a new ⌵carpet cost?
B: A new ⁄carport?
A: ⌵No, | a ⌵carpet.
B: ⌵Oh, | a ⌵carpet.‖ 'Quite a ⌵lot, | I should ⁄think.
A: Well I've 'just been looking at this ⌵catalogue.
B: You've been 'doing ⁄what?
A: 'Looking at a ⌵catalogue.
B: ⁄And?
A: Well there's a 'very reasonable ⌵offer here.
B: An ⁄author?‖ 'What d'you ⌵mean?
A: ⌵No, | an ⌵offer.‖ I 'don't think you're ⌵listening to me.

E2.16.7 Pair-work practice: please-repeat wh questions.

o I'm 'going on a \cruise.
- You're /what?
- On a /what?
- /What are you going on?
- You're doing /what?
- You're going on a /what?

o 'Seymour's won a \prize.
- /Who's won a prize?
- He's won a /what?
- /What has he won?
- /What has he done?
- /Who has?

E2.16.8 Pair-work practice: mixed rises and falls.

o We'll be 'battling with paedi\atrics.
- /What'll we be battling with?
- 'What's paedi\atrics?
- 'Who's \we?
- /What'll we be doing?
- 'What do you \mean, with paediatrics?

o They're 'trying to sell us in\surance.
- They're 'trying to sell us /what?
- /What are they trying to do?
- \Who is?
- 'What \sort of insurance?
- They're 'trying to do /what?

E2.16.9 Explain the difference by answering the questions.

o 'Jake's been \seeing someone.
(i) • /Who?
(ii) • \Who?

o There's 'something I must \do.
(i) • /What?
(ii) • \What?

o She's 'taking \ramipril.
(i) • /What's that?
(ii) • 'What's \that?

o 'This is some ver\miculite.
(i) • /What is it?
(ii) • 'What \is it?

OTHER SENTENCE TYPES

2.17   Exclamations

Exclamations (= expressions of surprise, anger or excitement) virtually always have a **fall**. We call this tone meaning the **exclamatory fall**. It can be seen as a sub-type of the definitive fall.

Some exclamations have a special grammatical form. In English these begin with *what* or *how*, and in writing usually have an exclamation mark:

> 'What a \pity!
> What a 'good i\dea!
> 'How \odd!
> What 'pretty \eyes she has.
> How 'very \nice of him!

Other exclamations may be interjections, statements, or yes–no interrogatives. But they are all said with an exclamatory fall:

> \Wow!
> \Dreadful!
> I 'don't be\lieve it!
> 'Welcome to \Brighton!
> You were \marvellous, darling!
> 'Isn't she \pretty!
> 'Wasn't it \awful!

> 'Will you be going to Oak /Hill?   • 'Will I \heck!
> He's 'feeling a bit an\noyed.   • \Is he just!

Exclamations are thus the simplest kind of utterance for the student of EFL. The rule is: if it's an exclamation, say it with a fall. Exclamatory falls are excellent drill material for anyone who wants to practise producing falling tones. (It is not true that every sentence written with an exclamation mark necessarily takes a fall. In particular, commands (see 2.18) may be written with an exclamation mark and pronounced with a fall–rise.)

EXERCISES

E2.17.1 Performance practice: exclamations.

> 'What a sur\prise!
> 'What a disap\pointment!
> 'What a \waste!
> 'What a to-\do!
> What a 'silly \joke.
>
> 'How \wonderful!
> 'How in\credible!
> 'How \awful!
> 'How an\noying.
> How 'very disap\pointing!
>
> What a 'funny way to \do it!
> What a ri'diculous thing to \ask!

What a re'markable person he \was.
What a 'glorious day it has \been!
What 'great \times we used to have!

What an 'interesting \lecture that was.
What 'beautiful \lips you have.
What a 'marvellous \holiday we had.
What 'great \legs she has!
What a 'silly little \man he is.

E2.17.2 Pair-work practice: exclamatory yes–no questions.

o I 'can't find them \anywhere.
o So she 'never \finished it.
o 'These are my two \sons.
o I 'did enjoy the ex\vcursions.
o We 'really 'thrashed U\vnited.

• 'Isn't that \strange!
• 'Wasn't it a \pity!
• 'Haven't they \grown!
• \Yes, | 'weren't they \fun!
• \Didn't we just!

E2.17.3 Pair-work practice.

o I've 'just been pro\moted.

• \Wow!
• \Great!
• 'Good for \you!
• What 'wonderful \news!
• I 'don't be\lieve it!

2.18   Commands

The default tone for commands is the definitive **fall**:

'Stop that \noise!
'Stand \up when you answer.
'Tell me the \truth.

In short commands (as with statements) a **rise** is often used to **encourage** the other speaker to continue:

I've got 'something to \tell you.   • 'Go /on.

For **warnings** we often use an implicational fall–rise:

'Watch vout!
'Wait for vme!
'Do be vcareful.

The implication here is something like this:

'Do as I vsay, | or 'something \bad will happen.

If said with a fall tone, these would indeed be not so much warnings as straight-forward commands:

> 'Wait for \me!
> 'Do be \careful.

Like negative statements, **negative** commands often have a fall–rise without nec-essarily implying a warning:

> 'Don't start until you're vready.
> 'Don't forget the vsalt.

Commands said with the interested rise (with a high prenuclear pattern; see 5.8) sound **soothing** and kindly. We use this tone when speaking to children, for example. To adults, it can sound patronizing.

> 'Come to /Daddy.
> 'Don't /worry.
> Now 'take your /time.

The differences in these tone meanings can be seen when we compare them on the same sentence:

(i)   Now 'move a\long, please. (*firm, authoritative*)
(ii)   Now 'move avlong, please. (*urgent, warning*)
(iii)   Now 'move a/long, please. (*routine, friendly*)

EXERCISES

E2.18.1 Pair-work practice: commands with a fall.

o 'Thanks very \much.
o My \phone's broken.
o I 'can't understand vthis.
o My \tea's too hot.
o She 'still hasn't been in vtouch.
o I 'can't find anywhere to veat.
o I 'keep getting it \wrong.
o I'm 'not feeling \well.
o 'What about this \money?
o The \lid doesn't fit.

• 'Don't \mention it.
• 'Use \mine.
• 'Let \me have a look at it.
• 'Put some more \milk in it.
• 'Send her another \email, then.
• 'Go to a \pub.
• 'Try a\gain.
• 'Go and lie \down.
• 'Put it in the \safe.
• 'Turn it the 'other way \round.

o 'Watch me jump \down.
o 'What's the \matter?
o 'May I borrow your /pen?
o 'Shall we have a game of /ping-pong?
o D'you 'think these /trousers'll fit me?

• \Don't! | You'll \hurt yourself.
• \Look! | It's \snowing!
• \Yes. | \Do.
• \Yes. | \Let's.
• \Try them.

E2.18.2 Pair-work practice.

   ○ I 'hope I'm not div͟sturbing you.

                                                              • 'Come \i͟n!
                                                              • 'Sit \do͟wn!
                                                              • 'Pull up a \cha͟ir!
                                                              • 'Make yourself at \ho͟me!
                                                              • Go 'right a\he͟ad.

   ○ 'What should I do \ne͟xt?

                                                              • 'See if she's \re͟ady.
                                                              • 'Enter the \da͟ta.
                                                              • 'Add the \se͟asoning.
                                                              • 'Formulate a hy\po͟thesis.
                                                              • 'Take a \bre͟ak.

E2.18.3 Performance practice: warnings.

   'Keep away from the v͟wires!
   'Stand v͟back!
   Watch 'out for the v͟boom!
   'Mind my v͟fingers!
   'Watch what you're doing with that v͟knife!

   v͟Run!
   v͟Quick!
   v͟Try!
   v͟Now!
   v͟Jump!

E2.18.4 Pair-work practice.

   ○ 'Can I use the /ca͟r?
   ○ I 'think he'll probably av͟gree.
   ○ I'm /so͟rry.
   ○ /Wh͟at did you say?
   ○ v͟Actually, | the \re͟d one might be better.

               • Well 'take v͟care.
               • 'Make sure he v͟does.
               • Well 'say it as if you v͟meant it.
               • 'Do try and v͟listen!
               • Well 'make up your v͟mind.

E2.18.5 Explain the difference in these pairs:

1 (i)   'Keep away from the v͟edge.
   (ii)   'Keep away from the \e͟dge.

2 (i)   'Keep your v͟voice down.
   (ii)   'Keep your \vo͟ice down.

3 (i)   Be v͟careful.
   (ii)   Be \ca͟reful.

4 (i)   v͟Jump!
   (ii)   \Ju͟mp!

5 (i)   Make 'sure they're v͟big enough.
   (ii)   Make 'sure they're \bi͟g enough.

E2.18.6 Performance and pair-work practice: negative commands.

'Don't touch that ⌄knob!
'Don't try and ⌄influence me.
'Don't think I'm going to come ⌄back to you.
'Don't forget your ⌄passport.
'Don't offer him ⌄money.

o So we'll 'see you on \Friday.
o I'm 'going a\head with it.
o I 'think it's going to \rain.
o ⌄I could carry the leaflets.
o So it's 'all \settled then.

• 'Don't forget to re⌄mind me.
• Well 'don't say I didn't ⌄warn you.
• Oh 'don't say ⌄that.
• 'Don't ⌄strain yourself.
• 'Don't be too ⌄sure.

o My \leg's hurting.
o I'll 'make a start on the \dishes.
o I'll 'bring my \case down.
o 'All a/board, then.
o I'll 'just call the \waiter.

• Oh 'don't ⌄you start!
• No 'don't ⌄you do them – | \I will.
• 'Don't ⌄you lift it. | Get \Jim to.
• 'Don't ⌄you drive. | You've been \drinking.
• 'Don't ⌄you pay. | Let \me.

E2.18.7 Performance practice: soothing, possibly patronizing.

'Don't /worry.
'Cheer /up.
'Never /mind.
'Sit /down.
'Go to /sleep.

E2.18.8 Pair-work practice.

o I 'just can't \manage it.
o I 'do find this ⌄difficult.
o I'm a'fraid I'm in your \way.
o 'Am I dis/turbing you?
o 'Am I in the /way?

• Well 'keep /trying.
• 'Don't /worry. | It's 'nearly /over.
• 'Don't /move. | There's 'lots of /room.
• No 'come /in.
• No 'go a/head.

2.19 Interjections and greetings

The categories of interjection and exclamation partly overlap. So, not surprisingly, the default tone for interjections is an exclamatory (or definitive) fall:

\Thank you.
'Oh \good!
\Sure.

However, many short interjections can be said with an encouraging rise, inviting the other person to speak or to continue speaking:

(*answering the phone*)	• Hul/lo.
(*bank clerk to the next customer*)	• Good /morning. (-How can I \help you?)
I've 'bought a new \hat, darling.	• /Uh-huh. (\Tell me about it.)
Oh ∨Mary.	• /Yes?

The interjection *oops*, *whoops* (uttered when you have just made a mistake or dropped something) seems always to have a rise (including under 'rise' its variant, the mid level; see 5.7).

In other cases a rise on an interjection signals no more than a routine acknowledgement:

Here's your \change, love.	• /Thank you.
You'll 'need this \form.	• /Right.

The difference in meaning between a definitive fall and an encouraging rise can be seen in the following pair of examples:

☊ (i)	'Unscrew the \cylinder head.	• \Right. (I \will.)
☊ (ii)	'Unscrew the \cylinder head.	• /Right. (And 'what \next?)

The fall on *right* in (i) implies the potential completion of the conversational interchange, whereas the rise in (ii) can be taken by the first speaker as an invitation to issue a further instruction. It means something like 'please continue speaking'.

Not all encouraging rises on interjections mean 'please continue speaking'. In the following examples the meaning is more 'please continue with your course of action':

It's my e\xam | to/morrow.	• 'Good /luck!
Would you 'like me to do it /now?	• 'Yes /please.

In calling someone by name, we normally use a rise or fall–rise if trying to get their attention. A fall, on the other hand, is a straightforward greeting (or, of course, an exclamation):

Pro'fessor /Jones: | I 'wonder if I could have a \word.
Pro'fessor ∨Jones: | I 'wonder if I could have a \word.
Pro'fessor \Jones! | How 'nice to \see you!
/Peter? (Is 'that /you?|| It's \me!)
\Peter! ('Fancy seeing \you!)

For most **greetings**, both falls and rises are perfectly possible and acceptable. A definitive fall is more formal, an encouraging rise more personal:

(i)	Hel\lo!
(ii)	Hel/lo.

(i)   Good \morning!
(ii)   Good /morning.

Variant (i), with a fall, means just 'I am greeting you', whereas variant (ii), with a rise, expresses an added interest in the person addressed, 'as I greet you, I am acknowledging you'.

A vocative after *hello* or *hi* usually has its own, rising, tone (see 4.4). In this case *hello* may be stress-shifted (see 5.10) so that the accent falls on the first syllable:

\Hi, | /Kevin.
Hel\lo, | /Margaret.   *or*   \Hello, | /Margaret.
Hul\lo, | /Tim.   *or*   \Hullo, | /Tim.

One or two greetings are tonally restricted. Whereas *hello* may have any tone, *hi* (if said with an ordinary tone, not a stylized one; see 5.15) can only have a fall. The same is true of *hey*. Likewise *cheers*, in its British sense of 'thank you', always has a fall:

\Hi!
\Hi, Julia.
\Hi, | /Ashley.
\Hey, | \you! || I want to \talk to you.
\Cheers, mate.

Said with a fall, *thank you* has the straightforward meaning 'I am thanking you'; with a rise, it suggests 'as I thank you, I am acknowledging you'. This is, however, a routine kind of acknowledgement. To express genuine gratitude, it is necessary to use a fall, variant (i):

(i)   \Thank you. (*straightforward*)
(ii)   /Thank you. (*routine acknowledgement*)

For saying **farewell**, *goodbye* and its equivalents often have a rise. Since *goodbye* signals the completion of a conversational exchange, you might expect it normally to be said with a definitive fall; but in practice a rise is much more frequent. Why? Because it is an encouraging rise, expressing good will and an acknowledgement of the other person. The same applies when a television presenter signs off.

🎧   I'm \off | /now. || 'Good/bye.
         'Good /night. || 'See you to/morrow.
         'So /long then.
         'That's it from /me.

But to get rid of an unwelcome guest you would say:

         'Good\bye.

Strangely, the informal *see you* tends to have a fall–rise rather than a rise:

         ∨See you.

EXERCISES

E2.19.1 Performance practice: interjections with a fall.

\Oh!
\Great!
\Wow!
\Gosh!
'Yip\pee!

\Gosh it's cold today!
\Wow! | Look at \that!
\Super! | I'm really \pleased with it.
My \goodness!
\Blimey! | Get a load of \that!

E2.19.2 Pair-work practice.

o 'Joseph said you'd re\fused. • \Nonsense!
o 'Did you finish the re/port? • \Heavens yes! | \Ages ago.
o 'Can I tell /Tina about it? • \Goodness no!
o I'll be 'there by \six. • \Great. | See you \then.
o I 'painted it my\self, Dad. • \There's a clever boy!

E2.19.3 Pair-work practice: interjections with a rise, encouraging, or routine.

o Is it 'really /yours? • Of /course.
o Shall we 'meet at /ten? • O/K.
o Good \morning, sir! • Good /morning.
o I've 'taken some more \paper. • /Uh-huh.
o 'Here's your \change. • /Thanks.

o 'Take these \cases up. • 'Very /good, sir.
o 'Would you bring me some /water? • 'Very /good, madam.
o 'Let me do it \my way. • 'No /problem.
o We 'finished on \time. • 'Well /done.
o 'Here's my \coursework. • /Thank you.

A: 'Grasp the patient's \hand. B: /Right.
A: 'Find a suitable /vein. B: 'O/kay.
A: Say ''just a small /prick'. B: /Uh-huh.
A: In'sert the /needle. B: /Right.
A: In/ject, | and with\draw the needle. B: 'O\kay!

E2.19.4 Get someone to tell you something. Each time they pause, say /*uh-huh* to show that you are listening.

Model: o I've just been into \town. • /Uh-huh.

E2.19.5 Explain the difference in meaning.

1 (i)   ○ You'll 'need a \screwdriver.   • \Right.
  (ii)   ○ You'll 'need a \screwdriver.   • /Right.

2 (i)   ○ I came 'top of the \class.   • 'Well \done.
  (ii)   ○ I came 'top of the \class.   • 'Well /done.

3 (i)   ○ 'Here are your \tickets.   • \Thank you.
  (ii)   ○ 'Here are your \tickets.   • /Thank you.

E2.19.6 Performance practice: greetings with a rise, showing interest in the addressee.

> Good /morning.
> Good /evening.
> Hel/lo.
> Good 'after/noon.
> Good 'after/noon, Archibald.

E2.19.7 Practise saying *thank you* (i) in a routine sort of way (rise), and (ii) when you are expressing real gratitude (fall). Which is appropriate in response to each of these?

> 'Here's your \change.
> I've 'brought you a little \present.
> We were 'wondering if you could come to \dinner tomorrow.
> So I can re\duce the price | by 'twenty per\cent.
> (*pointing*) 'This /way.

> 'Try some of these \peanuts.
> Would you 'care for a /drink?
> (someone makes room for you in a crowded tram)
> Your \bill, sir.
> 'Room service will be along \later.

E2.19.8 Practise saying goodbye, with a rise or fall–rise. What would it mean if you were to use a fall instead?

> 'So /long.
> 'Cheeri/o!
> 'Good/bye then.
> 'Good/bye! | 'Come again /soon.
> ⱽSee you then.

E2.19.9 Performance practice: greetings with a fall, more formal.

> Good \morning!
> Good \evening!
> \Hi!
> Hel\lo, Jeremy.
> \Morning, Mrs Allardyce.

> Hel\lo! | 'Anyone /there?
> Good \morning. | I'd 'like to speak to the \manager.
> Good 'after\noon. | I 'wonder if I could see Mr \Carter, please.

\Hi. | 'My name's 'Ricky \Pearce. | I 'telephoned \earlier.
Hel\lo. | I'm en'quiring about my ac\count.

SEQUENCES OF TONES

2.20   Leading and trailing tones

Many phrases or clauses do not stand alone, but are attached to some
other element. They are not complete in themselves, but are dependent on some
other (independent) structure. Usually they precede this other, main, element; but
sometimes they follow it.

If a dependent element precedes the main element, we say it is **leading**. If it
follows the main element, we say it is **trailing**. In either case, the unmarked tone
for a dependent element is a **non-fall** (= a fall–rise or a rise).

With a **leading** dependent element, this non-fall is most usually a **fall–rise**.
We call this tone meaning the **dependent fall–rise**. It indicates that there is more
material still to come, and is thus an indication of non-finality:

> 'After ∨lunch | we could 'call on \Mary.
> 'British ∨Airways | 'flies there on \Tuesdays.
> 'First we find the ∨socket, | 'then we insert the \pin.

Alternatively, a leading dependent element may have a rise (including the possibility of a mid-level tone). We call this tone meaning the **dependent rise**.

> 'After /lunch | we could 'call on \Mary.

With a **trailing** dependent element, the most usual tone is a rise. The tone
meaning of this **trailing dependent rise** is merely to indicate that it belongs with
what went before:

> I'm 'rather an\noyed, | /frankly.
> We're 'going to \Spain | in /August.
> They're ar'riving to\morrow, | as far as I /know.

The following pairs each contain the same material, but in different orders. In
the variants numbered (i), the dependent element has a leading fall–rise. In the
variants numbered (ii), it has a trailing rise. The independent element in each case
has a definitive fall:

(i)   If you're ∨ready, | we could be\gin.
(ii)   We could be\gin | if you're /ready.

🎧   (i) If 'I were ᵛyou, | I'd re\ject it.
🎧   (ii) I'd re\ject it | if I were /you.

(i)   They're 'not from ᵛSpain, | they're from \Portugal.
(ii)   They're from \Portugal, | they're 'not from /Spain.

It is possible for a dependent fall–rise to be, at the same time, an implicational fall–rise, as in the following example, where *you* is in contrast with *me*.

I 'don't know about ᵛyou, | but 'I'm \starving.

So the typical patterns are:

• **fall–rise plus fall**, for the order dependent–independent, and
• **fall plus rise**, for the order independent–dependent.

Alternatively, but less commonly, as we have seen, a leading dependent tone can be a rise, while a trailing dependent tone can be a fall–rise.

ᵛPersonally, | I 'thought it was \terrible. (*leading fall-rise*) *or*
/Personally, | I 'thought it was \terrible. (*leading rise*)

I 'thought it was \terrible, | /personally. (*trailing rise*) *or*
I 'thought it was \terrible, | ᵛpersonally. (*trailing fall-rise*)

Students of EFL may need to spend time practising the leading fall–rise. It is a tone very characteristic of mainstream English (RP and GA), yet rare or absent in most other languages.

EXERCISES

E2.20.1. Performance practice: leading fall–rise.

'When I come ᵛback | we can have a 'bite to \eat.
If I'm ᵛright, | he'll 'pass with \ease.
The 'thing ᵛis, | we 'can't risk an\tagonizing her.
'As you ᵛknow, | we'll be 'staying at the \Sheraton.
'As you can iᵛmagine, | there's 'plenty of \work to do.

🎧   On the ᵛtable | you'll 'find a \jug.
🎧   If 'I were ᵛyou, | I'd 'wait and see what \happens.
If it's 'OK by ᵛyou, | I'd 'rather have a \pizza.
'Come to ᵛthink of it, | I 'ought to get my \own room tidied up.
'Under the ᵛcircumstances, | we'd 'better ac\cept.

E2.20.2 Pair-work practice.

o 'How d'you get to \work?   • ᵛUsually | I 'take the \train.
o D'you en/joy your job?   • ᵛFrankly, | I \loathe it.

○ Are they /really going to settle?
○ 'What's the 'Lake District \like?
○ D'you 'like my new /hat?

• Ap∨parently | they \are.
• If the ∨weather's good, | it's \marvellous.
• If you 'don't mind my ∨saying so, | it's \terrible.

E2.20.3 Performance practice: trailing rise.

I'm 'getting a bit fed \up, | /frankly.
The 'service is sus\pended | on /Sundays.
I'm 'off to Ma\jorca, | as a matter of /fact.
I'll do it to\morrow, | if I can fit it /in.
We could 'do it to\gether, | if that's OK with /you.

You'll find a \jug | on the /table.
I'd 'wait and see what \happens, | if I were /you.
'I'll have a \pizza, | if it's OK by /you.
I 'ought to get my \own room tidied up, | come to /think of it.
We'd 'better ac\cept, | under the /circumstances.

E2.20.4 Pair-work practice.

○ 'What can I \do for you, sir?
○ And for /you, madam?
○ 'Which \train'll she be on?
○ 'How are you getting \on, Martha?
○ D'you 'see much of /Paul these days?

○ 'How's it \looking?

• I'd like this \tie, | /please.
• Some \paper, | if you'd be so /kind.
• The e'leven oh \seven, | I i/magine.
• It's my 'final e\xam | to/morrow.
• Yes I \do, | /actually.

• 'Pretty \bad, | I'm a/fraid.
• 'Quite \good, | I'm glad to /say.
• 'Cata\strophic, | /frankly.
• 'Not \bad, | /actually.
• 'Reasonably o\kay, | I /think.

E2.20.5 Explain the difference in meaning:

1 (i)   I'll have a \word with them | when they come /back.
  (ii) I'll have a ∨word with them | when they come \back.
2 (i)   I'll \do it | if it's what you /want.
  (ii) I'll ∨do it | if it's what you \want.

E2.20.6 Performance practice: structuring a talk.

∨First, | I'll give a 'short intro\duction.‖ ∨Next, | I'll 'outline the \problem.‖ After ∨that, | I'll ex'plain how I tried to \solve it.‖ In the ∨fourth section, | I'll 'analyse my \findings.‖ And at the ∨end | I'll 'summarize what I've \done.

E2.20.7 Performance practice.

He 'lives in \Luton, | 'not /Harpenden.
The 'meeting's in \Hamburg, | 'not /Munich.

> They're 'getting married at a \registry office, | 'not in /church.
> He 'goes to a \gym, | 'not a /squash club.
> She 'asked for \pasta, | 'not /pizza.

2.21   Topic and comment

If an utterance starts with a fall–rise there is a high probability that this is a non-final fall–rise, and that by it the speaker is signalling that he has not yet completed what he is saying:

> I've 'washed my vface, | and 'now I'll clean my \teeth.

If you say *face* with a non-falling tone (a rise or a fall–rise), then the listener expects that there is something more to come: the information is incomplete. Hearing the subsequent fall on *teeth*, the listener concludes that now the information is complete.

The implicational meaning of the fall–rise tone (see 2.6) can be understood in this light. It can be seen as a special case of the dependent fall–rise, the difference being that the speaker may choose to leave the further material unexpressed. The independent element is implicit rather than explicit.

An alternative tone pattern for the example just considered has a fall not only on *teeth* but also on *face*. Using this pattern, the speaker presents the information as two separate and potentially complete items:

> I've 'washed my \face,|| and 'now I'll clean my \teeth.

Hearing *face* with a falling tone, the hearer might suppose at this point that there is no more to come. He'd be wrong.

It is tempting to sum up the meaning of falls, on the one hand, as 'complete' or 'final'; and of non-falls, on the other hand, as 'incomplete' or 'non-final'. However, this is not necessarily so.

A fall does not necessarily mean that we have come to the end of our 'turn' in the conversation, and will now await input from the person we are talking to.

More accurately, perhaps, we might say that the basic meaning of a falling tone is something like 'major information' or 'primary information'. Correspondingly, the shared general meaning of non-falling tones is something like 'incomplete information', 'minor information', 'secondary information'. We use falls and non-falls together to indicate the structuring of our message, showing what is primary (by a fall) and what is secondary (by a non-falling tone).

We can often divide an assertion into two parts: a **topic** (a subject or theme) and a **comment** (the thing we say about the subject or topic, a 'rheme'). The topic is typically said with a non-falling tone (a dependent fall–rise or rise), the comment with a falling tone (a definitive fall):

My vbrother (*topic*) | will be 'very \angry (*comment*).
In the /morning (*topic*) | we'll 'do some \sight-seeing (*comment*).

The relationship between non-falling topic and falling comment is preserved if we change the sentence structure so as to reverse the order of the two parts:

He'll be 'very \angry, | will my vbrother.
We'll 'do some \sight-seeing | in the /morning.

What is the difference in tone meaning between the two dependent tones? One difference is that the fall–rise not only announces the topic but also draws attention to it, while the rise merely announces it. Consider the following example:

(i)   Your 'passport will be ready to\morrow.
(ii)   Your /passport | will be 'ready to\morrow.
(iii)   Your vpassport | will be 'ready to\morrow.

Version (i) is straightforward, and is typical of a rapid, routine style of speech. Version (ii) makes *your passport* into a separate intonation phrase, and is thus typical of a slower, more deliberate form of delivery. Version (iii) is like (ii), except that it adds emphasis to the topic (*your passport*) as against the comment (*will be ready tomorrow*). Version (iii) could also signal a contrast between the topic, *your passport*, and some other possible topic, e.g. *your ticket*.

It is also possible to announce a new topic with a fall. Newsreaders often do this at the start of a new item of news:

Po'lice in North \Yorkshire | say they are 'seeking a /man | in con'nection with . . .

EXERCISES

E2.21.1 Performance practice: first item presented as incomplete.

'Physics is vone thing, | and 'chemistry's a\nother.
She 'doesn't eat vmeat, | and she 'doesn't drink \alcohol.
I 'got vup | and 'had my \breakfast.
I've got a 'brother named vBrad, | and a 'sister named Lou\ise.
We're getting a 'new vcarport | and a 'new \driveway.

E2.21.2 Performance practice: first item presented as potentially complete.

'Physics is \one thing, | and 'chemistry's a\nother.
She 'doesn't eat \meat, | and she 'doesn't drink \alcohol.
I 'got \up, | and 'had my \breakfast.
I've got a 'brother named \Brad, | and a 'sister named Lou\ise.
We're getting a 'new \carport, | and a 'new \driveway.

E2.21.3 Performance practice: topic followed by comment.

My ᵛfather | was a \bricklayer.
My ᵛmother | 'worked in a \factory.
My ᵛbrother | is an ac\countant.
My ᵛsister | is a \nurse.
And my ᵛuncle | is a \teacher.

The ᵛdoctor | thinks I've got 'raised \blood pressure.
This ᵛbeer | 'tastes \awful.
What I'm ᵛsaying | is that you 'shouldn't de\spair.
What ᵛyou need | is some 'fresh \air.
What he 'fails to underᵛstand | is that I'm 'just not \interested.

E2.21.4 Pair-work practice.

○ 'Why do people go \running?
○ Well 'whose fault \was it, then?
○ 'Who's doing the \interviews?
○ 'What do you think of Tracey \Emin's stuff?
○ 'Derek's made another com\plaint.

• Well ᵛI run | because I en\joy it.
• ᵛMum says | it was \yours.
• ᵛMolly told me | it was \you.
• ᵛThat sort of art | 'leaves me \cold.
• ᵛSome people | are \always complaining.

E2.21.5 Match the response to the context.

Model:	context (a)	Who's having the sticky-toffee pudding?
	context (b)	Which dessert did you order?
	response (i)	ᵛI'm	having the 'sticky-toffee \pudding.
	response (ii)	\I'm	having the sticky-toffee /pudding.

Answer: context (a), response (ii); context (b), response (i)

1	context (a)	What will you do after we finish?
	context (b)	When do you eat?
	response (i)	I 'usually cook a \meal	in the /evening.
	response (ii)	I 'usually cook a ᵛmeal	in the \evening.
2	context (a)	Is this the way to the station?
	context (b)	Is the library down here?
	response (i)	No ᵛthat's	the way to the \library.
	response (ii)	No \that's	the way to the /library.
3	context (a)	Which newspaper do you read?
	context (b)	Which of you reads the *Guardian*?
	response (i)	Oh \I	read the /*Guardian*.
	response (ii)	Oh ᵛI	read the *Guardian*.
4	context (a)	Who's going to drive?
	context (b)	Would you rather drive or navigate?

| | *response (i)* | Oh v<u>I'll</u> | \<u>drive</u>. |
| | *response (ii)* | Oh \<u>I'll</u> | /<u>drive</u>. |

5	*context (a)*	So is Susan some sort of assistant, then?
	context (b)	So is the delegation being led by Bob?
	response (i)	No v<u>Susan's</u>	in \<u>charge</u>.
	response (ii)	No \<u>Susan's</u>	in /<u>charge</u>.

E2.21.6 Think of a context in which each of the following might be said. (For a model, see E.2.21.5.)

| 1 (i) | No v<u>Linda's</u> | my \<u>wife</u>. |
| (ii) | No \<u>Linda's</u> | my /<u>wife</u>. |

| 2 (i) | Well v<u>I</u> think | he's a 'great \<u>guy</u>. |
| (ii) | Well \<u>I</u> think | he's a great /<u>guy</u>. |

| 3 (i) | No v<u>Peter's</u> | the \<u>tall</u> one. |
| (ii) | No \<u>Peter's</u> | the /<u>tall</u> one. |

| 4 (i) | Oh my v<u>brother</u> | lives in \<u>Birmingham</u>. |
| (ii) | Oh my \<u>brother</u> | lives in /<u>Birmingham</u>. |

| 5 (i) | Well, v<u>Chloë's</u> | doing 'pharma\<u>cology</u>. |
| (ii) | Well, \<u>Chloë's</u> | doing pharma/<u>cology</u>. |

2.22   Open and closed lists

As we have seen, a leading non-fall at the beginning of an utterance leaves us waiting for the fall that will complete the pattern. It thus indicates that the sentence is **incomplete**. It signals **non-finality**. Putting it another way, a non-fall leaves matters **open**.

A fall, on the other hand, indicates that the sentence is potentially complete. It tends to signal finality. It suggests that matters are **closed**.[5]

We see the distinction between the **closed fall** (= definitive fall) and the **open non-fall** (= non-final fall–rise or rise) most clearly in the intonation of **lists**:

(i) You can have /<u>coffee</u> | or \<u>tea</u>.
(ii) You can have /<u>coffee</u> | or /<u>tea</u>.

The fall on *tea* in (i) signals that there are no more options: you must choose either coffee or tea. The rise on *tea* in (ii) signals that there may be other possibilities too, as yet unmentioned, e.g. *or you could have an \orange juice*.

(iii)   /<u>Chicken</u> | or \<u>beef</u>?
(iv)   /<u>Chicken</u> | or /<u>beef</u>?

In (iii) the addressee (the passenger on an airline, perhaps) is being invited to choose between the two possibilities, chicken and beef. In (iv) she is being invited to choose one of those two, or – if she prefers – some other option.

(v)   ⁄One, | ⁄two, | ⁄three, | ⁄four, | \five.
(vi)   We've been to ⁄Manchester, | ⁄Edinburgh | and \London.

Example (v) demonstrates how you might count a small child's fingers for her. The rises in the first four intonation phrases leave the list open. The fall on the fifth closes it. In (vi) the non-falls (which might be rises or fall–rises) on *Manchester* and *Edinburgh* indicate that there is more to come. The fall on *London* indicates that we have come to the end.

Although the intonation patterns in these examples are valid, they are not the only way of treating lists. First, we do not have to give each item its own IP: openness of a list can be signalled simply by not yet having reached the nucleus, i.e. by giving the non-final items head accents rather than nuclear accents:

(i′)   You can have 'coffee or \tea.
(ii′)   You can have 'coffee or ⁄tea.
(iii′)   'Chicken or \beef?
(iv′)   'Chicken or ⁄beef?
(v′)   'One, 'two, 'three, 'four, \five.
(vi′)   We've been to 'Manchester, 'Edinburgh and \London.

Secondly, the list as a whole may require a non-falling tone, in which case it may be impossible for the hearer to know whether the speaker intended the list to be left open or not:

> Well you can have 'coffee or ᵥtea, | and then we've some 'rather special \sandwiches to offer you.

Here the dependent fall–rise on *tea* (signalling that the utterance, rather than the list, is not yet complete) leaves us uncertain whether there are other possibilities.

Alternative questions are sets of two or more yes–no questions linked by *or*. They are treated as lists. A closed list ends in a definitive fall, and in principle an open list (if nuclear) ends in a dependent rise. However, the speaker has some discretion to ignore this rule.

> Is 'Mary ⁄ready, | or does she 'need some more \time?
> Would you 'like your coffee ⁄now, | or at the \end of the meal?
> Is that a ⁄gun in your pocket? | Or are you 'just pleased to \see me?
> Is it a ⁄bird? | Is it a ⁄plane? (‖ \No, | it's \Superman!)
> Am I asking ⁄fifty dollars? | Or ⁄forty dollars?‖ \No, | it's 'yours for \twenty!

EXERCISES

E2.22.1 Pair-work practice: closed lists.

- o   'Count from 'six to \ten.
- o   'What are the 'last three letters of the \alphabet?

- • ⁄Six, | ⁄seven, | ⁄eight, | ⁄nine, | \ten.
- • ⁄X, | ⁄Y, | and \Z.

o 'How many people are \waiting?
o 'What's the \choice?
o 'When could I \see you?

• \Two: | /Ethan | and \Andy.
• Just /chicken | or \fish.
• Well, /Monday | or per'haps \Tuesday.

E2.22.2 Pair-work practice: open lists.

o 'Go on /counting.
o 'Say the 'alphabet \backwards.
o 'Count 'backwards from a \hundred, | 'taking away \seven | 'each \time.
o 'What have you got a\vailable?

o 'Who was at the \party?

• E/leven, | /twelve, | /thirteen, | /fourteen . . .
• /Z, | /Y, | /X, | /W . . .
• 'Ninety-/three, | 'eighty-/six, | 'seventy-/nine . . .
• There's /chicken, | or /fish, | or /ham . . . (| 'All \sorts of things.)
• /Derek, | and /Steve, | 'Jim and /Linda, | /Verity . . . (| \Lots of people.)

E2.22.3 Practise enumerating the people in the room, the different sports you play, the members of your family, the days of the week, the months of the year, the places you like to visit, the subjects you are studying, etc. Use rise or fall tones appropriately.

E2.22.4 Performance practice: alternative questions, closed list.

Would you prefer /coffee | or \tea?
Are you 'coming /with us, | or are you 'staying at \home?
Did you 'write your /essay, | or did you 'just mess a\round?
'Shall we sing a /hymn, | or 'would you prefer a \psalm at this point?
Is he a /tenor | or a \bass?

Have you got 'change for a /fifty, | or shall I \owe it to you?
'Would you like to go /out to eat, | or 'shall we just open a \tin?
'Did she say she was coming /back, | or 'is she going straight \home?
Can I /go now, | or have I 'got to wait till the \end?
Are you /sure it's all right, | or are you 'just \hoping it is?

E2.22.5 Pair-work practice.

o 'This box \is heavy!

o This 'drawing is \excellent.

o Is 'something /up?

o He was 'very vrude, | \wasn't he?

o \That | was a bit unex/pected.

• D'you 'want a /hand, | or can you 'manage on your \own?
• D'you 'really /mean that, | or are you 'just being po\lite?
• Was that a 'knock at the /door, | or am I i\magining things?
• Is he /always like that, | or had 'something up\set him?
• \Yes: | am I going /crazy, | or did he 'just agree he'd \pay for it?

2.23   Adverbials

Adverbs and adverbial phrases that qualify a whole clause or sentence (rather than qualifying just one word) often have their own intonation phrase. If placed at the beginning, they usually have a leading non-final fall–rise (or rise). If placed at the end, they tend to have a trailing rise.

🎧   Un⌄fortunately | I've 'lost your ⌍letter. *or*
🎧   Un⌿fortunately | I've 'lost your ⌍letter.
🎧   I've 'lost your ⌍letter, | un⌿fortunately.

Most adverbials, like *unfortunately* in this example, limit the sense of the main clause in some way. So we call this pattern with an adverbial a **limiting non-fall**. Here are some more examples:

> (*leading*)
> ⌄Frankly, | I'm 'rather an⌍noyed.
> ⌄Next week | I'm 'going to ⌍Frankfurt.
> If ⌄I were you, | I'd 'buy a Mer⌍cedes.
>
> (*trailing*)
> I 'thought it was ⌍dreadful, | ⌿frankly.
> I 'can't ⌍stand her, | to be ⌿honest with you.

However some adverbials are said with a falling tone. Their meaning is not to limit the sense of the main clause, but rather to reinforce it. We call this tone meaning with an adverbial a **reinforcing fall**.

> D'you 'think I ought to ⌿say something?   • Of ⌍course, | you must pro⌍test.
>   • You must pro⌍test, | of ⌍course.
>
> I've 'never heard anything so ri⌍diculous | in 'all my born ⌍days.
🎧 >   I 'promise to ⌍love you | for ⌍ever.

It would be bizarre to say:

> ✕ I 'promise to ⌍love you | for ⌿ever.

– because *for ever* is not a limitation but its opposite, a reinforcement.

Some adverbials can be used either way: with a reinforcing fall or with a limiting (dependent) non-fall:

> (*reinforcing*)   ⌍Clearly, | we're 'going to be disap⌍pointed.
> (*limiting*)   ⌄Clearly, | we're 'going to be disap⌍pointed.
>
> (*reinforcing*)   On the ⌍contrary, | I'm de⌍lighted.
> (*limiting*)   On the ⌄contrary, | I'm de⌍lighted.

The same distinction applies in various kinds of adverbial clause and the like:

(*reinforcing*)	I'll 'ring you in an ＼hour, | when I'm ＼ready.
(*limiting*)	I'll 'ring you in an ＼hour, | if I'm ∕ready.
(*reinforcing*)	He'll be 'back to＼morrow, | I'm ＼sure.
(*limiting*)	He'll be 'back to＼morrow, | I ∕think.

There are some adverbials that regularly take a falling tone when initial, even though they are not obviously reinforcing. They can be seen as tonally idiomatic. Examples include *at least* and *at any rate* and also *by the way* and *incidentally*, used to introduce a side-issue.

> We 'finish work to ＼morrow –‖ at ＼least, \| ∨most of us do.
> 'Inci＼dentally, \| 'when are we going to get ＼paid?
> By the ＼way, \| I was de'lighted with the ∨dress.

If they follow the main clause, these adverbials usually form part of the tail, i.e. do not have their own IP:

> 'When are we going to get ＼paid, incidentally?
> I was de'lighted with the ∨dress, by the way.

EXERCISES

E2.23.1 Pair-work practice: leading adverbials, limiting.

○ 'What d'you do on ＼Sundays?	• Well ∨usually | I 'go to see my ＼mother.
○ D'you 'like ∕whisky?	• ∨Personally, | I 'never ＼touch the stuff.
○ 'Can you come to the ∕party?	• Un∨fortunately, | I'm ＼busy that night.
○ 'What did you think of ＼Craig's behaviour?	• ∨Frankly, | I was dis＼gusted.
○ 'What can I do about the ＼dog?	• Well if ∨I were you | I'd 'ask your ＼neighbour to look after him.
○ 'Done much ∕travelling?	• Well ∨last year, | I 'went to ＼China.
	• 'Next ∨month | I'm 'going on a ＼cruise.
	• 'When I was ∨younger | I went 'backpacking around the ＼world.
	• 'Two ∨years ago | I 'visited Bot＼swana.
	• In ∨January | I went to ＼Norway.

E2.23.2 Practise expressing your opinions, starting off as follows.

> ∨Personally, \| . . .
> ∨Actually, \| . . .
> As 'far as ∨I'm concerned, \| . . .
> 'On the ∨whole, \| . . .
> In ∨my view, \| . . .
>
> To be ∨candid, \| . . .
> If you 'ask ∨me, \| . . .

What ∨<u>I</u> would say | is . . .
As 'far as I can ∨<u>see</u>, | . . .
Well ∨<u>I</u> think | . . .

E2.23.3 Pair-work practice: trailing adverbials, limiting.

○ 'Don't you /<u>like</u> it?   • I \<u>don't</u>, | /<u>frankly</u>.
○ 'What's his \<u>cooking</u> like?   • Quite \<u>good</u>, | /<u>really</u>.
○ 'Whose \<u>turn</u> is it?   • \<u>Mine</u>, | /<u>actually</u>.
○ You're 'off \<u>soon</u>, | /<u>aren't</u> you?   • To\<u>morrow</u>, | as a matter of /<u>fact</u>.
○ 'Shall we tell /<u>Rita</u>?   • She al'ready \<u>knows</u>, | ap/<u>parently</u>.

E2.23.4 Pair-work practice: leading adverbials, reinforcing.

○ Do they /<u>know</u>?   • \<u>Surely</u>, | they \<u>must</u> know.
○ 'Katie was rather an\<u>noyed</u>.   • \<u>Naturally</u>, | she \<u>would</u> be.
○ So you 'didn't like the \<u>steak</u>.   • On the \<u>contrary</u>, | I \<u>loved</u> it.
○ 'What's it going to \<u>cost</u>?   • \<u>Obviously</u>, | quite a \<u>lot</u>.
○ Were you sur/<u>prised</u>?   • Of \<u>course</u>, | we \<u>all</u> were.

E.2.23.5 Practise these leading fall-tone adverbials, then make sentences of your own beginning in the same way.

'By the \<u>way</u>, | I 'didn't catch your \<u>name</u>.
'By the \<u>way</u>, | 'did you bring your /<u>swim</u>suit with you?
'Inci\<u>dentally</u>, | 'this is where we're going to hold the \<u>party</u>.
'Inci\<u>dentally</u>, | 'who's the tall \<u>blonde</u> woman?
'After \<u>all</u>, | it 'isn't very im∨<u>portant</u>.

E2.23.6 Performance practice: trailing adverbials, reinforcing.

I'll 'pay you ∨<u>back</u>, | \<u>naturally</u>.
You can 'always ask for a ∨<u>refund</u>, | \<u>obviously</u>.
We can 'change it ∨<u>later</u>, | of \<u>course</u>.
He'd be 'willing to do the ∨<u>mowing</u>, | \<u>surely</u>.
I'll 'come next \<u>week</u>, | as I \<u>promised</u>.

E2.23.7 Performance practice. Decide on a suitable tone for the adverbial.

?<u>Personally</u>, | I was 'rather disap\<u>pointed</u>.
By the ?<u>way</u>, | I was 'rather disap\<u>pointed</u>.
?<u>Obviously</u>, | I was 'rather disap\<u>pointed</u>.
?<u>Naturally</u>, | I was 'rather disap\<u>pointed</u>.
Of ?<u>course</u>, | I was 'rather disap\<u>pointed</u>.

I was 'rather disap∨<u>pointed</u>, | ?<u>actually</u>.
I was 'rather disap∨<u>pointed</u>, | as a matter of ?<u>fact</u>.
I was 'rather disap∨<u>pointed</u>, | ?<u>naturally</u>.
I was 'rather disap∨<u>pointed</u>, | to be ?<u>candid</u>.
I was 'rather disap∨<u>pointed</u>, | ?<u>personally</u>.

2.24   Fall plus rise

We have seen the use of a fall-plus-rise pattern for independent clause plus dependent clause (2.20), and for topic plus comment (2.21) or main clause plus adverbial (2.23). This pattern is also a very characteristic way for a speaker to emphasize something early in the utterance while still keeping a nuclear accent in its expected place on the last lexical item that adds new information. Thus alongside the patterns:

> I 'hope you'll be able to \come.
> 'Please shut the \window.

we can alternatively say:

> I \hope | you'll be able to /come.
> \Please | shut the /window.

In this way we can place emphasis on *hope* and *please* respectively, while respecting the fact that they are not the last lexical item in the sentence.

The fall-plus-rise pattern is particularly common where the first nucleus goes on a word referring to a mental state, or on an intensifying word:

> I'm \glad | you found it /interesting.
> I \do wish | you wouldn't com/plain so much.
> You've been ex\tremely | /patient with us.
> I'm a\ware | of your o/pinion, | /thank you. (= Keep quiet!)

It is also found in cases where the second nucleus falls on information that is new though fairly predictable:

> 'How can we \get there?   • \Maureen's | got a /car.
>   • \Walking's | the /easiest way.
>   • The \tube | would be /quickest.

The part with the fall contains the most important idea, while the part with the rise contains an idea of secondary importance. It differs from the usual topic–comment pattern of non-fall plus fall in that greater emphasis falls on the first part. Compare alternative formulations:

> 'How can we \get there?   • If you 'want a ⌄car, | \Maureen's got one.
>   • The ⌄easiest way | would be to \walk.
>   • The ⌄quickest route | would be the \tube.

There is also a spoken construction involving the displacement of the subject to the end of a statement. Here, too, we usually find a fall-plus-rise tone pattern. The main fall tone stays in its normal place on what would have been the last lexical item (etc.). The displaced subject, in a separate IP, has a dependent rise (or less commonly fall–rise):

'Brenda's \brilliant.	→	She's \brilliant, | /Brenda.
This 'weather's disap\pointing	→	'Disap\pointing, | this /weather.
'That one'll let you \down again.	→	He'll 'let you \down again, | will /that one.
vThat's | \lovely.	→	\Lovely, | vthat.

This construction is not usual in written English. In regionally flavoured British English the syntax may be subtly different, with copying of the verb. But the tone pattern is the same.

> She's \brilliant, \| /Brenda. (*standard*)
> She's \brilliant, \| is /Brenda. (*regional*)
> She's \brilliant, \| /Brenda is. (*regional*)

The presence of the intonation boundary functions as an indication of this grammatical construction, as shown in a minimal pair (example from Cruttenden, 1997: 70):

(i)   'Very \fattening, \| /biscuits, \| \aren't they? (= Biscuits are fattening.)
(ii)   'Very \fattening biscuits, \| \aren't they? (= These are fattening biscuits.)

The final rise also distinguishes the displaced subject from a vocative.

(i)   She's \brilliant, \| /Brenda. (= Brenda is brilliant.)
(ii)   She's \brilliant, Brenda. (talking to Brenda; someone else is brilliant)

Commands said with a fall-plus-rise pattern are pleading requests, rather than orders that are expected to be obeyed:

> \Do \| keep it /short. (*pleading*)
> 'Do keep it \short. (*authoritative*)

How do we distinguish this two-nucleus fall-plus-rise pattern from the single-nucleus fall–rise tone? After all, both involve a pitch pattern of a falling movement followed by a rising movement. Sometimes, in fact, they may sound almost identical, or indeed completely identical (example from O'Connor & Arnold, 1973: 83):

(i)   I vlike chocolate.
(ii)   I \like \| /chocolate.

The important point is that these two patterns have different tone meanings: they convey different speaker attitudes. Version (i) is an implicational fall–rise. It implies some kind of reservation (*but . . .*). It might be found in a context such as

🎧   (i) I've 'got some \chocolate here.   • Oh \dear.‖ I vlike chocolate, \| but I'm on a \diet.

Version (ii), on the other hand, implies no such reservations. It is a straightforward proclaiming definitive fall for the major focus, followed by a dependent rise for the minor focus:

🎧   (ii) I've 'got some ˅chocolate here.   • Oh ˅good.‖ I ˅like | ⁄chocolate.‖ 'Pass it ˅over.

Another example, also adapted from O'Connor & Arnold (1973: 84), is this:

🎧   (i) I be'lieve you're from ˅Sheffield.   • ˅No – | my ˅mother's from Sheffield;‖ 'I'm
                                                      from ˅Leeds.
🎧   (ii) I'm 'going to ˅Sheffield.   • ⁄Really?‖ My ˅mother's | from ⁄Sheffield.

Again, we see the implicational fall–rise in (i) but the definitive fall-plus-dependent rise in (ii).

   Support for this distinction also comes from changing the wording while keeping the tone meanings the same. Versions (i) keep a fall–rise if we do this:

        'What about ˅chocolate?   • Well I ˅like it, | but I'm on a ˅diet.
        I be'lieve you're from ˅Sheffield. • ˅No –‖ that's 'true of my ˅mother, | but ˅I'm
                                              | from ˅Leeds.

The phrase *I like it* must occupy a single intonation phrase, because there is clearly no reason to highlight the pronoun *it* (as would necessarily be the case if we had here a fall plus a rise). Versions (ii), on the other hand, keep a fall under rewording.

        I've 'got some ˅chocolate here.   • Oh ˅good.‖ I ˅love it.
        I'm 'going to ˅Sheffield.   • ⁄Really?‖ 'That's where my ˅mother's from.

There are also intonational grounds for distinguishing between the fall–rise tone and a fall tone followed by a rise. As discussed in 5.2, the unmarked head tone before a fall–rise nucleus is falling, but before a fall nucleus it is a high level. This test, too, supports our analysis.

(i)   I've 'got some ˅chocolate here.   • Oh ˅dear.‖ I`do ˅like chocolate, | but I'm on a
                                                  ˅diet.
(ii)   I've 'got some ˅chocolate here.   • Oh ˅good.‖ I'really ˅like | ⁄chocolate.‖ 'Pass
                                                  it ˅over.

However . . . given that there may sometimes be no perceptible phonetic difference between a fall–rise and a fall followed by a rise, examiners should not penalize confusion of the two.

EXERCISES

E2.24.1 Performance practice: first nucleus on a verbal expression referring to a mental state.

        I'm ˅sorry | you didn't ⁄like it.
        I'm ˅glad | you liked the ⁄flowers.
        I ˅love | the way he ⁄looks at me.
        He's ˅furious | about this new ⁄tax.
        I ˅wish | you wouldn't ⁄do that.

I'm \sure | I've seen him be/fore.
I'm \grateful | for your kind /words.
You 'ought to be a\shamed | to live in a house like /that.
He was 'rather sur\prised | you didn't ac/cept.
I was a\mazed | how ma/ture she seemed.

E2.24.2 Performance practice: first nucleus on a modal.

I \do wish | you wouldn't com/plain.
I \am surprised | he came /last.
I \do think | you ought to try /harder.
I \do | a/pologize.
We \were sorry | you couldn't /come.

You \must try | to be more /careful.
It \shouldn't | take /long.
I \don't think | he'll /mind.
I \can't | be everywhere at /once.
I \won't | ask you a/gain.

E2.24.3 Performance practice: first nucleus on an intensifier.

I'm \so | /sorry.
It's \awfully | /cold in here.
I'm \frightfully | /sorry about it all.
It was in\credibly | /careless of him.
I know ex\actly | how you /feel.

E2.24.4 Performance practice commands with *do*, *don't*, *please*.

\Do | try to be on /time.
\Please | be /punctual.
\Don't| try and avoid the /issue.
\Do | for/give me.
\Please | have a little /patience.

Now \do | be /reasonable.
\Please | hurry /up.
\Don't | take it to /heart.
Now \don't | take it out on /Roger.
\Do | get on and /finish.

E2.24.5 Pair-work practice.

o 'Who's \there?   • It's \only | /me.
o So 'Jim had to \wait a few minutes.   • Yes and he was \so | an/noyed.
o You can 'drop in \any time.   • That's \awfully | /kind of you.
o You 'don't /mind, do you?   • No I \quite | under/stand.
o I 'really \must go | /now.   • Oh \please | stay a little /longer.

o That 'cake was su\perb.   • Yes I a\dore | /fruit cake.

o 'Have a \nibble.
o It's a \marvellous present.
o 'How is she doing at \school?
o 'What sort of \wine shall we have?

- \Thanks. | I'm \fond | of /peanuts.
- I'm \glad | you /like it.
- \English | is her /best subject.
- A \riesling | would be /nice.

E2.24.6 Performance practice: displaced subject.

She's a 'good \cook, | /Jenny.
He's a \wonderful man, | /Stefan.
They're 'so \careless, | young people /nowadays.
It's 'rather \worrying, | this /last result.
He was a 'bit \pushy, | your friend /Peter.

E2.24.7 Supply a suitable intonation pattern.

It's quite a useful dictionary, the Chamberlain.
He's a good watchdog, my Rover.
They look nice, these pictures.
They'll still be here when you get back, those dirty dishes.
He'll be a few minutes late, (will) Mr Smith.

E2.24.8 Pair-work practice: commands: pleading, encouraging.

o It's 'all going \wrong.
o I 'don't \like it.
o I'm a'fraid I've \broken it.
o 'Let's \go.
o The \phone's ringing.

- \Cheer | /up.
- \Eat it | /up, | \there's | a good /boy.
- \Never | /mind.
- \Wait | a /minute!
- \Don't | just /sit there.|| \Answer it!

2.25   Tone concord

If two successive intonation phrases are grammatically parallel, this may be signalled intonationally by their having the same tone.

This is particularly evident in cases of non-defining apposition (see 4.8). Here there is regularly **tone concord** between the two intonation phrases. That is to say, the tone used for the first is repeated (copied) in the second. In the following, the tone on *colleague* is repeated on *Charles*:

(i)   'This is my \colleague, | \Charles.
(ii)   Now 'this is my vcolleague, | vCharles, | and 'he will be taking \over.
(iii) Then I've got my /colleague, | /Charles, | and 'also my friend \Rachel.

Tone concord is a tendency rather than an iron rule. It is also perfectly possible to say:

(iv)   'This is my vcolleague, | \Charles.

– or indeed to place both elements within a single IP (see 4.8), though this tends to imply defining rather than non-defining apposition:

(v)   'This is my colleague \Charles. (= Of my colleagues, this is Charles.)

The use of tone concord is particularly likely where the utterance as a whole is not yet finished, as in (ii) and (iii).

Tone concord can signal parallelism not only between nouns or noun phrases but also between other parallel structures: between other parts of speech and indeed between complete clauses or sentences.

> I re\ject it, | I de\spise it, | I won't ac\cept it.
> 'Jennifer's \better, | she's \well again.
> You say that 'nothing is worse than /war?‖ Well, dis\honour is worse than war, | \slavery is worse than war!

A tone can be reused where information is presented as two IPs rather than one, and where we string together near-synonyms for emphasis:

> We've 'built a \barbecue | on the \patio.
> \Don't be | ri\diculous.
> I \love you, | I a\dore you, | I 'can't live with\out you.

When *too* is used at the end of a sentence or clause to mean 'in addition' (see 3.19), and given a separate intonation phrase, it usually exhibits tone concord. The same is true of its synonyms *as well* and *also*, and of its negative synonym *either*.

> vAndy isn't the only one interested; | \Neil's interested, | \too.
> If vMartha wants to come, | as vwell, | we'll need a 'bigger \car.
> She 'didn't vask for it, | and she 'didn't \get it, | \either.

> \Peter wants some, | \too. (*definitive; concord, definitive*) *or*
> vPeter wants some, | \too. (*implicational, definitive*) *or*
> vPeter wants some, | vtoo. (*implicational; concord, implicational*)

EXERCISES

E2.25.1 Practise these examples of noun phrases in apposition, with tone concord. Then construct further examples of your own.

> 'This is \Melanie, | my 'co-\worker. (*AmE*: . . . my \co-worker.)
> 'This is E\lizabeth, | my \boss.
> Is 'that /Tyson, | /Jim's dog?
> I can't 'stand vTina, | your vroommate.
> 'Can I leave you to feed /Fritz, | the /cat?

E2.25.2 Explain why the following is ambiguous. Could altering the intonation remove the ambiguities?

> The vnext ones to arrive | were /Robby, | his /boyfriend, | and \Richard, | his \boss.‖
> So now we've got /Esther, | her /mother, | her vfriends, | the vGordons, | and \Sam.

E2.25.3 Performance practice: verbs, adjectives, etc.

That's \great, | \marvellous.
She was \pining for him, | 'wasting a\way.
I'll 'come along \later, | about 'six p.\m.
It was a 'sort of \red colour, | \scarlet.
It was 'pretty \useless, | \hopeless in fact.

E2.25.4 Performance practice: supplementary information.

I've 'left it out\side, | by the \door.
He's from \England, | from a 'little place near \Cheltenham.
We could 'play a \card game, | \whist for example.
Have you 'got some I/D? | Your /passport? | A /credit card?
I've got a vletter here, | from my vdoctor.

E2.25.5 Performance practice: final *too* and synonyms.

vI'll be there, | and I'll 'bring my \friend, | \too.
Did /Pauline go shopping with you, | /too?
It's an 'excellent vcar, | and 'not ex\pensive, | \either.
Are you 'going to bring /Victor with you, | as /well?
I've 'been to Javpan, | and I've 'been to Ko\rea, | \too.

- o 'Can you speak /French?
- o 'Did you see \Paul?
- o 'Did you do the /physics homework?
- o So you were 'all on your /own?
- o 'Where could I go \next?

- • \Yes, | and I can speak \German, | \too.
- • \Yes, | and \Lloyd, | \too.
- • vNo, | and I 'didn't do the \chemistry, | \either.
- • No, vWayne was there, | as vwell.
- • Well there's 'always vDevon, | and you could go to \Cornwall, | \too.

TONE MEANINGS

2.26   Generalized meanings of different tones

How can we generalize about the various tone meanings we have recorded so far? Two authors, Brazil (1985, 1994) and Gussenhoven (1984, 2004), have each made proposals in this area. This section is about their ideas.

One useful generalization about the function of a fall tone is to say that it **proclaims** something, while the function of a fall–rise is that it **refers** to something. These terms and this approach were devised by the late David Brazil, who indeed calls the fall the **proclaiming** tone and the fall–rise the **referring** tone (example from Brazil, 1997: 68).

(i)   'Mary vBrown's | a \teacher.
(ii)   'Mary \Brown's | a vteacher.

Pattern (i) is appropriate in a discourse in which we have already mentioned Mary Brown, perhaps along with various other people. Its meaning could be paraphrased as 'as for Mary Brown, she's a teacher'. Thus we **refer** to a topic already mentioned (*Mary Brown*), by using a fall–rise, and **proclaim** a new fact about this topic (that *she's a teacher*), by using a fall.

Pattern (ii), on the other hand, is appropriate in a discourse in which we are already discussing teachers. Its meaning could be paraphrased as 'talking of teachers, Mary Brown's one'. Thus we refer to the topic (*teachers*) by using a fall–rise, and proclaim the new fact about it (that *Mary Brown's one*) by using a fall. In this pattern (ii), the proclaiming (comment) precedes the referring (topic, theme), which is not the usual order of things: but it is a consequence of the rigidity of English word order (subject, *be*, complement), and clearly signalled by the choice of tones.

Referring in this way to a topic previously mentioned involves refocusing on it (see 3.32). If the topic of the discourse was already very explicit, we might alternatively choose not to refocus on it, and perhaps indeed not even to accent it. So instead of (i) it would also be possible to say:

(i′)   'Mary Brown's a \teacher.

and instead of (ii):

(ii′)   'Mary \Brown's a teacher.

or indeed, to use the fall-plus-rise pattern discussed in 2.24:

(iii′)   'Mary \Brown's | a /teacher.

To revert to our basic example:

(i)   'Mary vBrown's | a \teacher.
(ii)   'Mary \Brown's | a vteacher.

– we can use a diagram to represent the knowledge of two participants in any conversational exchange – the world view of the speaker and hearer respectively. These two world views are different, but they overlap (the common ground being represented in the diagram as the shaded area):

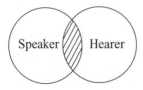

What the referring fall–rise does is to focus on some item that is already in the common ground. The proclaiming fall tone that accompanies it (whether it precedes or follows) then asserts (proclaims) something about this item, so that it too then becomes part of the common ground.

A speaker, by using the referring fall–rise, thus also makes an assumption about the hearer, namely that the topic referred to is indeed already part of the common ground between speaker and hearer.

The common ground shared between speaker and hearer is dynamic: it will tend to increase as the conversation progresses. It is referred to by Gussenhoven (1984, 2004) as the **background**. What the choice of tone does, according to Gussenhoven, is to indicate the relationship of the information contained in the intonation phrase to the conversational background.

The information in the current IP is, in Gussenhoven's terminology, the **variable** (abbreviated as V). There are three basic **manipulations** of the variable with respect to the background, each signalled by the choice of tone:

- **V-addition**, signalled by a **fall**, whereby the speaker declares that the variable is now to be treated as part of the background;
- **V-selection**, signalled by a **fall–rise**, whereby the speaker reminds the hearer that the variable is already part of the background;
- **V-relevance testing**, signalled by a **rise**, whereby the speaker leaves it to the hearer to decide whether the variable is relevant to the background.

Consider these examples:

(i)   When I've 'finished these ᵥletters | I'll 'make those ＼phone calls.

The first IP has a fall–rise (in our terms, a leading dependent fall–rise). For Gussenhoven, this is therefore an instance of V-selection. As the speaker says *When I've finished these letters*, by choosing a fall–rise tone he is seen as expressing a meaning such as 'you know I've got to finish these letters, don't you, because you know I have to send them off today'. When he says *I'll make those phone calls*, by choosing a fall tone he is expressing the meaning 'here is something new that you should take notice of'.

(ii)   I'll 'make those ᵥphone calls | when I've 'finished these ＼letters.

In (ii) the thing that the speaker assumes to be already agreed or presumed is his making the phone calls. What he wants the other person to take notice of is that this will take place after his writing the letters.

(iii)   Are you 'going to fetch the ⁄kids?

In (iii), with its rise tone, signalling relevance testing, the speaker communicates something such as 'as for your fetching the kids, is this something we should agree on as being part of the background of our conversational interaction from now on?'.

EXERCISES

E2.26.1 Pair-work practice.

    ○ I 'don't \like | /Benjy's.

- We'll 'leave you be\hind | if you don't want to /come.
- If you 'don't want to ∨come | we'll 'leave you be\hind.

    ○ It's 'rather ∨difficult.

- If you 'can't stand the ∨heat, | 'keep out of the \kitchen.
- 'Keep out of the \kitchen | if you can't stand the /heat.

    ○ I 'wonder if we ought to 'change the \boiler.

- If it's 'not ∨broke, | 'don't \fix it.

- 'Don't \fix it | if it's not ∨broke.

    ○ 'How are we \doing?

- If we 'go on like ∨this, | we'll be \fine.
- We'll be \fine | if we go on like /this.

    ○ 'Off we \go then!

- If we 'break ∨down | we'll be in real \trouble.
- We'll be in 'real \trouble | if we break /down.

E2.26.2 Pair-work practice.

    ○ 'William works in the uni\versity.
    ○ 'What's a \zeta function?
    ○ 'Could you take us into /town?
    ○ 'Do we need some more /Persil?
    ○ ∨Robert's | 'training as a so\licitor.

- Oh my \brother's | a /don.
- I've 'never been very \good | at ∨maths.
- I just \love | /driving.
- I've \done | the /washing.
- Oh \Paul's | a /lawyer, | \too.

E2.26.3 Think of a scenario in which each of the following might be uttered. (For a full answer, delay this exercise until you have studied chapters 3 and 4.)

(i)   My ∨parents | have been to \China.
(ii)   My \parents | have been to ∨China.
(iii)   My \parents | have been to /China.
(iv)   My \parents have been to China.
(v)   My 'parents have been to \China.

E2.26.4 Compare and contrast the analysis of general tone meaning proposed by Brazil and that proposed by Gussenhoven.

E2.26.5 'There is no such thing as "a questioning intonation": an utterance can only be heard as a question if it is produced in circumstances where a question would be appropriate' (Brazil, Coulthard & Johns, 1980: 143). Discuss.

2.27   Checklist of tone meanings

The table lists all the tone meanings discussed in this chapter (except 2.26).

Fall	**definitive** (includes exclamatory)	statement	2.5
		exclamation	2.17
		wh question	2.12
		answer	2.10
		command	2.18
		interjection	2.19
	insistent	yes–no question	2.13
		(includes tag question	2.14
		and elliptical question)	2.15
	reinforcing	adverbial	2.23
Non-fall (= fall–rise or rise)	**dependent** (includes open)	clause or smaller element	2.20–2
	limiting	adverbial	2.23
fall–rise	**implicational** (includes contrastive, reservation, tentative, polite correction, partial statement, negative, warning)	statement	2.6–7
		command	2.18
Rise	**encouraging** (includes soothing)	statement	2.11
		wh question	2.12
		command	2.18
	non-supportive (includes truculent, perfunctory)	statement	2.9
	yes–no (includes pardon question, uptalk)	yes–no question tag question	2.13
		indep. ellip. question decl.	2.14
		question	2.15
		statement	2.8
		pardon question	2.16
		interjection	2.10
			2.19

Notes

1. It is perhaps impossible to demonstrate conclusively that there is such a thing as a default tone for any sentence type, and some would deny that the concept of default, neutral or unmarked tone has any validity. It is not necessarily the case that the default tones, as described here, are statistically the most frequent. Nevertheless, it is at the

very least pedagogically useful to assume that there are default tones, and to regard any deviation from them as necessarily due to a reason that can in principle be made explicit.

2. Uptalk has evoked widespread comment both from the general public and from scholarly commentators. See for example McLemore (1991), Britain (1992), Bradford (1997), and for newspaper reports Seaton (2001), Diresta (2001).

3. These are not single fall–rise tones. They correspond in meaning to (i), not to (ii).

    (i)   Come over \here.| Open the \window.

    (ii)   Come over vhere. | Open the vwindow.

4. Similarly in Spanish: in response to *Se puso un camisón* 'she wore a nightgown', the fall *Cómo* asks 'how (did she do it)', but the rise ∕*Cómo* is a pardon question.

5. The terms 'open' and 'closed' as generalized tone meanings for non-falls and falls respectively are from Cruttenden (1997: 163).

3 Tonicity: where does the nucleus go?

BASIC PRINCIPLES

3.1 On a stressed syllable

Within each intonation phrase, we select one word as particularly important for the meaning. This is where we place the **nucleus** (or **nuclear accent**), the syllable that bears the nuclear **tone** (a fall, rise, or fall–rise, as discussed in chapter 2).

Phonetically, we **accent** a **syllable** by giving it a prominent change in pitch, or movement in pitch, or the start of a pitch movement. An accented syllable is always also rhythmically stressed, i.e. it has a rhythmic beat.

Pragmatically, we **accent** a **word** by accenting its stressed syllable (or at least one of them if it has more than one). This indicates the importance or relevance of the word for what we are saying.

In an IP there may be other accents in addition to the nuclear accent. If so, the nucleus is the **last** accent in the IP. Any other accents come earlier in the IP and are 'prenuclear'. The first is known as the **onset**. Prenuclear patterns are discussed in chapter 5.

The most important decision the speaker makes in selecting an intonation pattern is to decide where the nucleus goes: which is the last word to be accented. In doing this the speaker chooses the **tonicity** of the intonation phrase.

But how do we decide where the nucleus should go?

First, we know that the nucleus must go on a **stressed** syllable. By 'stressed syllable' we mean the syllable that has **lexical** stress. Lexical stress is part of the basic pattern of a word's pronunciation, as shown in dictionaries.

To make a word the nucleus of an IP, we put a nuclear tone on (or starting on) its lexically stressed syllable. To produce an English intonation pattern correctly it is essential, therefore, to know which syllable in each word bears the stress.

To accent the word *never* we accent the first syllable. For the word *annoyed* we accent the last syllable. For *tomorrow* it is the second syllable. To accent the word *fine*, we accent its only syllable.

In this book we show the location of an accent by placing the mark ' before the relevant syllable (or some more specific mark such as ◡). In addition, we show the nucleus by under<u>lin</u>ing the nuclear syllable. (Because we are using conventional orthography, for this underlining we follow the conventional rules for orthographic syllabification. In case of doubt, consult a dictionary.)

In the examples we show not only the nuclear accent but also other accents (particularly the onset), as appropriate. We do not show non-accent rhythmic stresses at all, since they have no effect on intonation. We concentrate on the most important accent, the nuclear accent.

Here are some examples involving one-word IPs:

Have you been to Canada?	• 'Never.
How did he look?	• An'noyed.
When's the test?	• To'morrow.
How are you feeling?	• 'Fine.
What was the trip like?	• Inde'scribable.

These IPs could be said with any tone – fall, rise, or fall–rise. The location of the nucleus (the tonicity) is a separate choice from the choice of nuclear tone:

To\morrow.   To/morrow.   To∨morrow.

In each case the syllable *-mor-* is the nucleus and bears a nuclear tone. Where the choice of tone is irrelevant, it is equally valid to write just *To'morrow*.

EXERCISES

E3.1.1 Place the nucleus on the lexically stressed syllable of the one-word response. You can do this both as a written exercise (answer by underlining the nucleus and placing ' before it) and as a spoken exercise (answer by using a nuclear tone on the nucleus).

| *Model:* | |
| o Have you been to Canada? | • 'Never. |

o What were they playing?	• Football.
o What won't he eat?	• Vegetables.
o What did he paint on his car?	• Stripes.
o What's she wearing?	• Clothes.
o When's the lecture?	• Tomorrow.

o What shape is the park?	• Square.
	• Oblong.
	• Triangular.
	• Circular.
	• L-shaped.

o How did she look?	• Annoyed.
	• Happy.
	• Ecstatic.
	• Disgruntled.
	• Okay.

E3.1.2 Use each of the following words first as a verb, then as a noun. (Check the lexical stress in a dictionary if necessary.) Create a sentence in which the word is the last word, and bears the nucleus. Be careful: there may be traps.

> ⍾ *Model:* digest
> (i) 'Some foods are difficult to di'<u>gest</u>.
> (ii) I 'read it in the Reader's 'Di<u>gest</u>.

rebel	insert
refuse	object
reject	control
promise	insult
permit	conduct

E3.1.3. Place the nucleus on the appropriate syllable of the last word in each of the following responses.

○ Where do you come from?
- Just outside Moscow.
- An island in the Pacific.
- A village in Germany.
- A suburb of Toronto.
- The south of Japan.

○ What'll you have to drink?
- A cup of coffee.
- Some Coca-Cola.
- A pint of bitter.
- Just a glass of water.
- Some lemonade.

3.2 On or near the last word

The nucleus is usually located on or near the last word of the intonation phrase. By definition, the nuclear accent is the last accent in the IP. So clearly the general tendency is for the nucleus to be **towards the end** of the IP. Provided that the last word in an IP is important for the meaning, it will be accented and thus bear the nucleus:

> I 'want to buy a '<u>lem</u>on.
> The 'bridge is about to col'<u>lapse</u>.
> She's 'just started a new re'<u>la</u>tionship.
> 'Could you tell me the '<u>time</u>?

It is only if the words towards the end of the IP are for some reason not accented that the nucleus will go on an earlier word.[1]

Initials, names of letters and numerals are treated like separate words. In a string of several letters or numerals, the nucleus generally goes on the last one:

In the e'<u>xam</u> | she got a '<u>C</u>.
My 'room number is 50'<u>6</u>.   (= five oh '<u>six</u>)
'Switch over to IT'<u>V</u>.   (= eye tee '<u>vee</u>)

EXERCISES

E3.2.1 Place the nucleus on the last word.

Model: 'Bring me the '<u>fold</u>er.

Pay attention.	A bar of chocolate.
Keep them talking.	Salt and vinegar.
I'm trying to sleep.	Put the cutlery in the drawer.
They wanted to help.	Go and try again.
It's stopped raining.	She was awfully tired.
Find the asterisks.	A nest of vipers.
A bunch of grapes.	I like your style.
A kilo of pears.	A jug of water.
One and a half.	Two and a quarter.
A can of soup.	As high as a kite.

E3.2.2 Pair-work practice, concentrating on nucleus placement. If no nuclear tone is specified, use any appropriate tone.

o And for '<u>you</u>?

- A 'half of '<u>lag</u>er.
- A 'pint of '<u>bit</u>ter.
- A 'gin and '<u>ton</u>ic.
- A 'piece of '<u>pie</u>.
- A 'slice of '<u>cake</u>.

- Some 'nuts and '<u>raisins</u>.
- A 'pound of '<u>cheese</u>.
- Some 'knives and '<u>forks</u>.
- A 'cup of '<u>coffee</u>.
- A'nother slice of '<u>pizza</u>.

o 'What do I do '<u>next</u>?
o 'Want to come '<u>climbing</u>?
o I'm 'rather '<u>worried</u>.
o 'How was the '<u>circus</u>?
o 'What's wrong with '<u>Martha</u>?

- You 'need to ap'<u>ply</u>.
- It's 'frightfully '<u>dangerous</u>.
- You must 'stay '<u>calm</u>.
- It was 'pretty a'<u>maz</u>ing.
- She's 'suffering from '<u>asthma</u>.

o 'Why are they \<u>worried</u>?
o This is the 'only so\<u>lution</u>.
o 'What shall I \<u>do</u>?
o 'Thanks for your ∨<u>help</u>.
o 'Shall we say ten o'/<u>clock</u>?

- They're ex'posed to pol\<u>lution</u>.
- I 'don't a\<u>gree</u>.
- 'Keep taking the \<u>tablets</u>.
- 'Have a nice \<u>day</u>!
- No I've 'got to go to the \<u>dentist</u>.

E3.2.3 Place the nucleus on the last initial, letter, or numeral.

> *Model:* the 'BB'<u>C</u>

> x + y = z
> Her number is 8346.
> 55 BC
> C2C
> as easy as ABC

E3.2.4 Pair-work practice.

- o 'What would you \<u>like</u>?
- o 'What's \<u>that</u>?
- o 'Who does she \<u>work</u> for?
- o 'What kind of a \<u>sandwich</u> is that?
- o 'Which /<u>union</u> do you belong to?

- o 'What's your \<u>number</u>?

- A'nother C\<u>D</u>.
- My 'new DV\<u>D</u>.
- 'B and \<u>Q</u>.
- A 'BL\<u>T</u>.
- The 'RM\<u>T</u>.

- '27\<u>9</u>.
- '308\<u>3</u>.
- '58\<u>8</u>.
- '65\<u>2</u>.
- '14\<u>4</u>.

3.3 Content words and function words

Words can be divided into two broad categories, **content words** and **function words**.

Content words are nouns, adjectives, most verbs and most adverbs: words that have meanings that can be defined in a dictionary and probably have straightforward translation equivalents in other languages. For example: *table*, *head*, *remember*, *yellow*, *suddenly*.

Function words, on the other hand, are pronouns, prepositions, articles, auxiliary verbs, modal verbs: words whose meaning may need to be explained in a grammar rather than a dictionary, and which may not have exact equivalents in other languages. For example: *me*, *at*, *the*, *are*, *would*.

Generally speaking, we accent content words but not function words. Hence the nucleus (which is one kind of accent) is typically placed on the **last content word** in the IP:

> I 'can't '<u>hear</u> you.
> I'm 'very an'<u>noyed</u> with her.
> 'Ask her what that '<u>noise</u> is.

In particular, the nucleus does not usually go on a personal pronoun, a preposition, an auxiliary verb or a modal verb. These words bear the nucleus only if special circumstances apply. If an IP ends with a personal pronoun or a preposition, the nucleus normally goes earlier.

---

personal pronouns: *I, me, you, he, him, she, her, it, we, us, they, them, one*
prepositions, such as *at, by, from, of, to, with, about*, etc.
auxiliary verbs: *be, have, do* and their forms *am, was, did*, etc.
modal verbs: *can, could, may, might, shall, should, will, would, must*

The way to select a suitable place for the nucleus, therefore, is to start from the end of the IP and work back. In the following examples we disregard the final pronoun:

> She's 'done it.
> I'll 'tell them.
> Can you 'see her?

In the next examples we disregard the final preposition:

> 'What are you 'looking at?
> 'Who was she 'talking to?
> She's the 'only person he con'fides in.
> I 'wonder where the words were 'taken from.

Some IPs end in a combination of preposition(s) and pronoun(s). They must both be disregarded:

> I'll be 'thinking of you.
> He 'keeps 'worrying about it.
> I've 'just received a 'letter from her.
> 'Tell me about it.
> 'Bring it to her.

In the next examples we disregard final auxiliary or modal verbs:

> 'Chloë earns 'twice as much as 'Robert does.
> 'Bill was talking at the 'same time as 'Jim was.
> He did 'better than I 'thought he would.
> ('First 'Peter took a drink, |) and 'then 'Mary did.

So – to decide where it is appropriate for the nucleus to go, start at the *end* of the IP. Work back towards the beginning, ignoring any function word. Unless special circumstances apply, the nucleus should probably go on the first content word you encounter as you move backwards.

   Here is an example. Suppose that you want to find a suitable location for the nucleus in the following sentence:

> I think you ought to tell me about it.

Start at the end and work backwards. Which word should bear the nucleus?

it? – No, it's a pronoun.
about? – No, it's a preposition.
me? – No, it's a pronoun.
tell? – Yes! This is the last content word. The nucleus goes here:

> I think you ought to 'tell me about it.

EXERCISES

E3.3.1 Place the nucleus on the last content word.

> *Model:* Can you 'see it?

I'll tell them.	I can't hear you.
Have you forgotten me?	I think I can see him.
I can't stand it!	What can I write with?
What are you looking at?	Who was she talking to?
Who did you go with?	Where does she come from?

E3.3.2 Pair-work practice.

○ 'Where are the \papers?	• I'll 'go and \get them.
○ 'Where's \Miriam?	• Dun\no. | I 'can't ∨see her.
○ 'Shall we ask /Roger?	• \No, | I 'can't \stand him.
○ I'm 'over \here!	• I 'can't ∨see you.
○ I'm 'going to re\port you.	• I 'didn't \do it!
○ 'What's the \matter?	• You must 'stop an\noying her.
○ 'Why are you com\plaining?	• They 'keep up\setting me.
○ 'What about her \parents?	• I'm de'termined to \ask them.
○ 'Why was he sur\prised?	• He 'thought he'd ex\plained it.
○ So 'what's \wrong?	• You 'didn't \tell me!

E3.3.3 Place the nucleus on the last content word.

> ☊   *Model:* I received a 'letter from him.

I'll be waiting for you.
There's a parcel for her.
Take your umbrella with you.
There's a fly in it!
We could try to reason with them.

She brought her baby with her.
I've bought a coffee table for you.
Here's some information about them.
I forgot to bring my books with me.
My tie's got a stain on it.

E3.3.4

> 🎧   *Model:* 'Why not go for a \walk? | 'That's what ∨Mary does!

> Bake cakes? | That's what Diane does.
> I earned quite a lot more than Rick did.
> Drop out of college? | That's what Wayne did!
> Do you like eating the same things as I do?
> Why not run a restaurant? | That's what Sarah's doing.

E3.3.5 Performance practice.

> She wrote 'more than I \thought she would.
> 'George ∨Tomlinson | scored 'more than I ex\pected he would.
> You've done 'better than I \thought you would.
> Pe∨nelope | had to wait 'longer than she \wanted to.
> It's 'bigger than I i\magined it would be.

E3.3.6 Pair-work practice.

🎧   o Did /James answer the phone?   • No \Nicky did.
🎧   o Will Na/tasha read the lesson?   • No \Jake will.
         o Did 'Joss deliver the /presents?   • No Sa\mantha did.
         o Is 'William the /treasurer?   • No Ma\ria is.
         o Did /Natalie make the cake?   • No \John did.

         o Will Re'becca be meeting us at the   • No but ∨Harry will.
            /airport?
         o Has 'Natalie done the /ironing?   • No but ∨Josh has.
         o Can 'Gary come to the /party?   • No but ∨Sammy can.
         o Could 'Amy borrow your /car?   • No but her ∨mother can.
         o Are 'beetles /insects?   • Yes ∨beetles are, | but ∨spiders aren't.

3.4   Compounds

When identifying the 'last content word' we have to bear in mind the existence of compounds. Most **compounds** in English are **single-stressed**, that is, the main lexical stress goes on the first element. (Alternative terms for 'single-stressed' are 'front-stressed' and 'early-stressed'.)

'bedtime, 'grassland, 'wheelbarrow, 'newsgroup, 'keyboard, 'highlight

If a compound is to bear the nucleus, then – just as with simple words – the accent is located on the lexically stressed syllable:

It's 'well past your 'bed<u>ti</u>me.
'Put the grass in the 'w<u>hee</u>lbarrow.
'Don't look at the 'k<u>ey</u>board!
'Where's your 'gr<u>and</u>mother?
'Here's another 'h<u>igh</u>light.

Many English compounds are written as two separate words, even though the main stress is still on the first element of the compound. These are called **open** compounds (or two-word compounds).

'library book, 'credit card, 'bus ticket, 'running shoe, 'slag heap, 'high school

It does not matter whether a single-stressed compound is written as one word, or hyphenated, or as two words.[2] As far as intonation is concerned, it makes no difference: all single-stressed compounds behave as if they were single words. If we place the nucleus on one, it goes on the stressed syllable of the first element:

Is 'that my 'l<u>i</u>brary book?
I've 'lost my 'cr<u>e</u>dit cards.
They were 'playing 'v<u>i</u>deo games.
I 'need some new 'r<u>u</u>nning shoes.
Are you 'still at 'h<u>igh</u> school?
At 'ten we have a 'ph<u>ys</u>ics class.

Compounds can be **nested**: that is, one of the elements of the compound may itself consist of more than one element. If the outer compound is single-stressed, the nucleus will still go on the first element:

'credit card bill = bill for using a credit card, ['['credit card] bill]

To refine our tonicity rule so as to allow for compounds, we need to change 'on the last content word' to an expression covering both simple words and compound words. Accordingly, from here on we shall refer to **lexical items** rather than to content words. A 'lexical item' is either a single word or a compound. Unless there is some reason for it to go elsewhere, the nucleus goes on the **last lexical item** in the IP.

This is the default tonicity rule: unless contrast is involved (see 3.10–13), we place the nucleus on the last lexical item in each IP. To do this we place the nuclear accent on the lexically stressed syllable of that item. This is 'neutral' or 'unmarked' tonicity.

Open compounds can be misleading for the student of EFL because superficially a compound may look like a phrase consisting of adjective plus noun. Compare *running shoes* and *running water*. The first is an open compound, single-stressed; *running* is a gerund (a verbal noun). The second is a phrase in which each word has its own lexical stress; *running* is a participle (a verbal adjective):

(i)   I 'need some new 'r<u>u</u>nning shoes.
(ii)   They made the 'outhouse into a 'b<u>ath</u>room | and installed 'running 'w<u>a</u>ter.

The last lexical item in (i) is *running shoes*, a single-stressed compound. The last lexical item in (ii) is *water*.

Unlike compounds, **phrases** consist of two or more lexical items. They have one lexical stress for each. The nucleus normally goes on the last of them:

It was a 'bitter disap\point·ment. (*bitter disappointment* is a phrase)

Phrases such as *bitter disappointment* are 'double-stressed', as opposed to the single lexical stress of compounds.

EXERCISES

E3.4.1 One-word compounds. Locate the lexical stress on each of the following words. Then make a sentence with the nucleus on this word and say the sentence aloud.

> *Model:* 'wheelchair
>   She was sitting in a 'wheelchair.

washbasin	greengrocer	grandfather
toothpick	newspaper	grasshopper
baby-sitter	capitalism	queue-jumping
sweat-inducing	brother-in-law	webmaster
daylight	dreadlocks	opinion-makers

E3.4.2 Place the nucleus on the last lexical item (which may be a compound), making sure to select the correct syllable.

> *Model:* They're 'acting as 'peacekeepers.

They've built a sandcastle.	Sit on the windowsill.
Buy her a T-shirt.	Blessed are the peacemakers.
Ask my grandmother.	Ten centimetres.
Another newspaper.	It was truly heart-rending.
She's a keen concert-goer.	Hire a cement mixer.

E3.4.3 Pair-work practice.

- o 'Who's \that? — • He's my \brother-in-law.
- o /What did you call him? — • A 'real \swashbuckler.
- o 'What's the \trouble? — • She's 'such a \stargazer.
- o 'What's he \doing there? — • He's the \doorkeeper.
- o 'What's /that thing? — • An 'old \typewriter.

- o 'What does she \do? — • She's a \pastrycook.
  - • She's a \schoolteacher.
  - • She's a \copywriter.
  - • She's a \dressmaker.
  - • She's a \metalworker.

       o 'What's his ＼job?   • He's a ＼scriptwriter.
                                 • He's a ＼gravedigger.
                                 • He's a ＼bricklayer.
                                 • He's a ＼bookmaker.
                                 • He's a ＼shopkeeper.

E3.4.4 Locate the lexical stress on each of the following **open** compounds. Then make a sentence with the nucleus on this item and say the sentence aloud.

> *Model:* departure lounge
>
>   They're in the de＼parture lounge.

railway station	teddy bear
tea trolley	rent rebate
progress report	oil painting
kiwi fruit	Fraud Squad
campaign manager	entrance fee

E3.4.5 Locate the nucleus on the last lexical item in the following sentences.

> *Model:* 'Ask about their 'business plan.

Bring me the alarm clock.	Find me some drawing pins.
He's an estate agent.	Clean the windscreen wipers.
Look at the fire engines!	Take her to the health centre.
I'm looking for a hardware store.	Ask him for his telephone number.
Could I have your credit card?	Store it in the bicycle rack.

E3.4.6 Performance practice: nucleus on open compound.

       I've 'lost my ＼credit cards!
       Is 'that my ／library book?
       They were 'playing com＼puter games.
       We've 'bought some new ＼dining chairs.
       We have 'only one ∨physics class.

       She 'can't find her ＼wedding ring.
       Do you 'like my ／mouse mat?
       You must 'reinstall the ∨printer driver.
       They 'live in a ＼tower block.
       I'm 'looking for my ＼lecture notes.

       The 'cheese is past its ＼sell-by date!
       We were 'looking at a ＼cruise ship.
       They 'went on a ＼field trip.
       She 'sat down at the ＼dinner table.
       Shall I 'buy a new ／coffee pot?

E3.4.7 Pair-work practice.

- o 'What does he \do?
  - He's a \football player.
  - He's a \heating engineer.
  - He's a psy\chology lecturer.
  - He's an \airline pilot.
  - He's a \car mechanic.

- o 'What's her \job?
  - She's a \bus driver.
  - She's a \language teacher.
  - She's a \software consultant.
  - She's a \shop assistant.
  - She's a 'speech and \language therapist.

- o 'What's \that?
  - It's a \fruit machine.
- o 'Where will it be \listed?
  - 'Try the \subject catalogue.
- o 'What are her \symptoms?
  - 'High \blood pressure.
- o 'What should she \do?
  - 'Watch her \salt intake.
- o 'How can I \write it?
  - 'Use a \word processor.

E3.4.8 Pair-work practice: supply your own appropriate intonation pattern.

- o What's the trouble?
  - You need new brake pads.
- o Where's Selfridge's?
  - In Oxford Street.
- o What happened to him?
  - A massive heart attack.
- o How can I identify it?
  - Look for the registration number.
- o What's in the box?
  - Ballot papers.

- o What are they hoping for?
  - An improved pay offer.
- o What have you bought?
  - A new vacuum cleaner.
- o What did you trade in?
  - My old washing machine.
- o What are you waiting for?
  - The next Wimbledon train.
- o Where was it issued?
  - The local passport office.

- o I'd like to borrow some books.
  - You'll need a library card.

  - Apply at the issue desk.
  - Ask for an application form.
  - Talk to the issue clerk.
  - Come back during opening hours.

E3.4.9 Some of the following are single-stressed open compounds, others are double-stressed phrases. Sort them out. If the nucleus goes on this item, which syllable bears the nuclear accent?

> *Models:*
> sentence construction – *compound* –'sentence construction
> brilliant idea – *phrase* – 'brilliant i'dea

house design	interesting lecture
further advance	second chance
site map	watering can
troubled waters	shallow water
drinking water	tap water

E3.4.10 Pair-work practice.

    ○ 'What's the \problem?

- I 'think it's the \power supply.
- It 'could be the con\trol unit.
- Per'haps it's the hard \disk.
- 'Might be some rusty \contacts.
- 'Let's look at the \operating system.

E3.4.11 Decide whether each of these is a compound or a phrase.

    An eating apple
    An exciting event
    A charming house
    A wishing well
    A tuning fork

E3.4.12 Locate the nucleus.

    I want to buy a fishing rod.
    I could see a galloping horse.
    Where's the writing paper?
    It was no better than a gambling den.
    What an interesting idea!

E3.4.13 Pair-work practice. Make sure you understand the reason for the place of the nucleus.

    ○ 'What do you still \need?

- A \carving knife.
- Some 'sparkling \water.
- A \serving spoon.
- Some \cooking oil.
- A \frying pan.

  ○ 'Where shall we have our \tea?   • In the \sitting room.
  ○ 'Where's \Jim gone?   • He's 'off on a \training run.
  ○ 'What's the \problem?   • I 'haven't got an \ironing board.
  ○ 'How were they \executed?   • By a \firing squad.
  ○ 'What's \Kevin doing?   • He's 'ironing \shirts.

3.5   Double-stressed compounds

    Confusingly, some English compounds are **double-stressed** (also called 'late-stressed' or 'end-stressed'). Their main lexical stress is on their second element. They are usually shown in dictionaries with a secondary stress mark followed by a primary stress mark:

,Christmas 'Eve, ,Town 'Hall, ,gold 'ring, ,ham 'sandwich.

However, the lexical stress pattern of a double-stressed compound is just like that of a phrase. Both the lexically stressed syllables are **accentable**.

If a double-stressed compound bears the nuclear tone, the nucleus goes on the second element. But the first element may also be accented, e.g. as the onset:

It was 'Christmas 'Eve.
There are some 'ham 'sandwiches.

In order to locate the nucleus correctly it is important to identify which compounds are, exceptionally, double-stressed. Here are some guidelines. The following types of compound tend to be double-stressed:

- proper names of people

  ,James Mc'Gregor, De,nise 'Harris

- proper names of roads and public places

  Vic,toria 'Road, ,Oxford 'Avenue (except those ending in *street*: 'Oxford Street)

- names of institutions such as hotels and schools

  ,Jury's 'Inn, the ,Marlborough Ho'tel, ,Goldsmith's 'College, ,Bailey's 'Restaurant, the ,Festival 'Hall (*but* 'high school, 'secondary school, 'Pizza Hut)

- compounds in which the first element names the place or time

  ,Town 'Hall, ,kitchen 'window, ,summer va'cation, ,evening 'meal (*but* 'Boxing Day, 'Christmas ,present, 'Christmas card, 'birthday card; *compare* ,Christmas 'Eve, ,Christmas 'Day, ,Christmas 'pudding)

- compounds in which the first element names the material or ingredient

  ,leather 'jacket, ,cheese 'sandwich, ,pork 'chop (except those ending in *juice* or *cake*: 'orange juice, 'carrot cake)

As can be seen, there are many irregularities and exceptions. In case of doubt, use your dictionary (or ask a native speaker) to check stress patterns.[3]

Although lexical stresses *before* the main stress in a lexical item are **accentable**, this is not true of lexical stresses *after* the main stress (shown as , above). The accentuation of words and phrases is discussed further in 5.9–10.

EXERCISES

E3.5.1 Locate the nucleus in the following. Each ends in a double-stressed compound.

Model: Would you 'like some Christmas 'pudding?

She wants a mink coat.   Go to Gordon Square.
Get me a ham sandwich.   I've bought a silver necklace.
Where's the Town Hall?   Go to Liberty Avenue.
I'd like a cinnamon danish.   She's won an academy award.
They're double-parked.   She opened the kitchen window.

E3.5.2 Pair-work practice.

   ○ 'What's her \name?

- • 'Mary \Johnson.
- • 'Alice \Peters.
- • 'Sophie \Wyatt.
- • 'Janice \Battersby.
- • I'melda \Staunton.

   ○ 'Where do they \live?

- • 'Melrose \Avenue.
- • 'Dorset \Road.
- • 'Richmond \Square.
- • 'Wimbledon \Park.
- • 'Clapham \Junction.

   ○ 'What's the ad\dress?

- • Vic'toria \Drive.
- • \Narrow Street.
- • Ja'maica \Road.
- • \Gower Street.
- • 'Chancery \Lane.

E3.5.3 Some of these sentences end in a single-stressed compound, some in a double-stressed one. Sort them out and locate the nucleus in each.

Call the fire brigade.   Over the garden fence.
Go to the police station.   Let's watch the ballroom dancing.
Wait for the Morden train.   I love winter sports.
What are the examination dates?   Come to my country cottage.
Get some plastic bags.   What's the weather forecast?

E3.5.4 Pair-work practice.

   ○ 'What shall we \play?

- • \Table tennis.
- • \Ice hockey.
- • 'Hide-and-\seek.
- • 'Beggar-my-\neighbour.
- • 'Happy \Families.

   ○ 'What are they \suffering from?

- • \Food poisoning.
- • 'Athlete's \foot.
- • \Whooping cough.
- • A \chest infection.
- • \Heat exhaustion.

E3.5.5 Lists of station names. Locate the nucleus in each IP. Read out each list, paying attention to correct tonicity.

> Euston, | Warren Street, | Goodge Street, | Tottenham Court Road, | Leicester Square, | Charing Cross.
> Paddington, | Edgware Road, | Baker Street, | Great Portland Street, | Euston Square, | King's Cross.
> Finchley Road, | Swiss Cottage, | St John's Wood, | Baker Street, | Bond Street, | Green Park, | Victoria.
> Harrison, | Journal Square, | Grove St, | Pavonia, | Christopher St, | 9th St, | 14th St.
> Bedford Avenue, | Lorimer St, | Graham Av, | Grand St, | Montrose Av.

E3.5.6 Lists of menu items. Locate the nucleus in each IP. Read out each list, paying attention to correct tonicity.

> Pea Soup, | Chicken Pie, | Green Peas, | Mashed Potatoes, | Fruit Cake.
> Orange Juice, | Mushroom Omelette, | Green Salad, | Banana Fritters, | Dundee Cake.
> Won Ton Soup, | Beef in Black Bean Sauce, | Prawn and Bean Shoots, | Special Fried Rice, | Chinese Tea.
> Chef's Salad, | Chicken Club Sandwich, | Grapefruit Juice, | Coffee Latte.
> Fruit Juice, | Veal Escalope, | Boiled Rice, | Mushy Peas, | Strawberry Pavlova.

E3.5.7 Locate the nucleus. Start at the end of the intonation phrase and consider each word in turn, moving leftwards towards the start of the IP. Stop when you encounter a word which there is no reason *not* to accent. That is probably the right place for the nucleus.

> *Model:*
>
> Has he brought his running shoes with him?
> him: *function word (pronoun)*
> with: *function word (preposition)*
> shoes: *the second element of a compound*
> running: *the item for the nucleus (on its stressed syllable)*
> tonicity: 'Has he brought his 'running shoes with him?

> I'll get some sugar lumps for you.
> The cushion's got some hard lumps in it.
> Please insert your credit card for me.
> This paper's got some dirty marks on it.
> I'm finding it hard to get a product number from them.

E3.5.8 Pair-work practice.

> o 'What shall I do with this \rag?   • 'Wipe the \floor with it.
> o 'Can I /help at all?   • You could 'warm up the \dinner plates for me.
> o 'What about the \children?   • I've got some \orange juice for them.
> o 'Is the report /ready now?   • I 'just need to add the per\ception tests to it.
> o 'What's the \matter?   • I 'haven't got my \Sainsbury's voucher with me.

E3.5.9 The following nucleus placements are impossible (or at least very unusual). Why?

× I'm 'just co'<u>ming</u>.	× It de'pends on the govern'<u>ment</u>.
× They're 'pretty unedu'<u>cated</u>.	× He's 'one of my col'<u>leagues</u>.
× I 'don't need any'<u>thing</u>.	× 'Would you like a cup '<u>of</u> tea?
× 'Put the money in '<u>the</u> box.	× 'What are you looking '<u>at</u>?
× 'She can paint better than I '<u>can</u>.	× I'm 'gradually getting used to '<u>it</u>.

THE OLD AND THE NEW

3.6   Information status

In English, the location of the nucleus is strongly affected by whether the words in the utterance contain **old** or **new** information. The general rule is that we accent new information, but not old information. That is, we **deaccent** (= remove potential accents from) old information.

If all the information in the utterance is new, then we can accent all the lexical items. So the nucleus is placed (as expected) on the last lexical item:

Yes madam?   • I'd 'like a 'gin and '<u>tonic</u>.

However, in practice we tend to downgrade potential accents between the first one and the last. (This is discussed in 5.9.) So in practice we often say:

Yes madam?   • I'd 'like a gin and '<u>tonic</u>.

and we apply this principle in the examples.

As long as the last lexical item contains new information, that lexical item is accented, and thus bears the nucleus. However, if the last lexical item contains **old** information (= something already mentioned), then it is not accented. Rather, it is deaccented. So the nucleus goes earlier, namely on the last item that *does* contain new information:

How about a gin and tonic?   • Oh I'd pre'fer a '<u>vodka</u> and tonic.

In this example, *tonic* has already been mentioned, and is therefore old information. As a result, it gets deaccented. Thus the place of the nucleus normally signals the **end of the new information** in an intonation phrase.

We generally avoid placing a nucleus on an item which repeats something that has been said earlier: we do not accent a **repeated** item (a 'given' item, old information). So we say, for example:

D'you object to dogs?   • No I a'<u>dore</u> dogs.
Who doesn't want to dance?   • '<u>Bill</u> doesn't want to dance.

It would sound strange to say:

D'you object to dogs?	(?) •	No I a'dore '<u>dogs</u>.
Who doesn't want to dance?	(?) •	'Bill doesn't want to '<u>dance</u>.

In the correct versions, we see that the **repeated** items (*dogs*, *want to dance*) are not accented. Rather, they are deaccented: they lose the accent they might otherwise have had. This is because the information they convey is not new.

We deaccent repeated words even if, strictly speaking, they contain new information. Thus we tend to say:

a 'green chair and a '<u>blue</u> chair
'Tina Rodman and '<u>Jane</u> Rodman
'72'<u>5</u>2 (= 'seven two '<u>five</u> two)

–where the final, deaccented, item would not actually be predictable from the context (even though the intonation, once we reach the nucleus, makes it predictable for the hearer). After all, the speaker might have been going to say:

a 'green chair and a blue '<u>curtain</u>
'Tina Rodman and Jane '<u>Stuart</u>
'725'<u>6</u> (= 'seven two five '<u>six</u>)

EXERCISES

E3.6.1 Locate the nucleus on the last item of new information.

Model:	
○ Like a gin and tonic?	• I'd pre'fer a '<u>vodka</u> and tonic.

○ Care for some ham and eggs?	• I'd rather have bacon and eggs.
○ Did you see Peter and Jackie?	• No, but I saw Floyd and Jackie.
○ Was that French and Spanish?	• No, German and Spanish.
○ I'll come at three thirty.	• Make it four thirty.
○ Do you like pasta?	• I adore pasta.
○ How d'you feel about smoking?	• I can't stand smoking.
○ Is the washing done?	• Most of the washing's done.
○ Look! A red shirt!	• It's an orange shirt.
○ Is my order ready?	• Only half of your order's ready.
○ Have you been to California?	• For three years, | I lived in California.

E3.6.2 Pair-work practice.

○ 'Shall we have the beef /<u>curry</u>?	• \No, | 'let's have the \<u>prawn</u> curry.
○ Would you 'care for some red /<u>wine</u>?	• I'd 'rather have some ∨<u>white</u> wine.
○ 'Are you studying 'physics and /<u>chemistry</u>?	• No bi\<u>o</u>logy and chemistry.
○ 'Do you drink your coffee with /<u>sugar</u>?	• No with\<u>out</u> sugar.
○ 'Would you like chicken and /<u>rice</u>?	• I'd pre'fer the ∨<u>lamb</u> and rice.

o Do you 'like /dancing? | • I just \love dancing.
o 'Ham and to/mato? | • No sa\lami and tomato.
o 'Was he wearing a 'brown /jacket? | • No a \blue jacket.
o I be'lieve you live in south \London? | • No in ∨north London.
o Are 'all the staff a/way? | • Well ∨most of them are away.

E3.6.3 Locate the nucleus in each IP.

> *Model:*
> 'Please 'welcome | 'David 'Crystal | and his 'son 'Ben Crystal.

May I introduce | Catherine Hughes | and her husband Jim Hughes.
I'd like you to meet Danny Alexander | and his wife Jenny Alexander.
Do you know Shaun Protheroe | and his wife Lucy Josephs?
This is Professor McCall | and Mrs McCall.
Over there | are Shaun McCleod | and his brother Rudi McCleod.

3.7   Synonyms

Old information is not necessarily a matter of repeated **words**. We can also repeat old information using **synonyms**, in which we express with different words a concept already mentioned. Such synonyms, too, are usually deaccented:

Shall we wash the clothes? | • Oh I 'hate doing the laundry.
Shall we walk there? | • Yes I 'like going on foot.

To *do the laundry* has the same meaning as *wash the clothes*. To *go on foot* is the same as to *walk*.

Alternatively, the speaker can preserve a degree of accenting on the repeated item or idea, while relegating it to secondary (minor) status by placing it in a separate IP, typically with a rising tone (see 2.24). So these examples might alternatively have a fall-plus-rise pattern:

Shall we wash the clothes? | • Oh I \hate | doing the /laundry.
Shall we walk there? | • Yes I \like | going on /foot.

(See also 3.32 and 5.12.)

If a word or phrase is a **hypernym** of a word or phrase already mentioned (= has a broader meaning), then it counts as given, and the nucleus goes elsewhere. We usually do not say:

(?) ma'laria | and 'other tropical di'seases

but rather:

ma'laria | and 'other tropical diseases

This is because the idea of 'tropical disease' was already present in the word *malaria*, just mentioned.

⊙   D'you 'like ╱<u>whist</u>?   • Oh I like ╲<u>most</u> card games.

Card games is a hypernym of *whist*.

But if a word or phrase is a **hyponym** of a word or phrase already mentioned (= has a narrower meaning), then it counts as new. In consequence, it is accented and attracts the nucleus:

⊙   D'you 'like ╱<u>ball</u> games?   • Well I'm 'quite fond of ╲╱<u>football</u>.

Here, *football* is one of various *ball games*. But by mentioning it explicitly the speaker adds new information, making the notion more specific: not basketball or baseball, but football.

New information merits accenting. This principle applies even in many cases where the 'new' information may be highly predictable:

          What's the time?   • It's 'five o' '<u>clock</u>.

The semantic content of the word *o'clock* is so small that we could omit it without any loss of meaning (*It's 'five.*). Yet, if present, *o'clock* receives the nucleus.

          How long did the concert last?   • 'Three '<u>hours</u>.
          What's the price?   • 'Fifty '<u>dollars</u>.

It may be obvious from the context that the concert could not have lasted three *minutes* or three *days*. It may be clear that the price could not be fifty *cents* or fifty *euros*. Yet the nucleus still goes on *hours* and *dollars* respectively.

          What d'you think of Brenda?   • She's a 'nice '<u>woman</u>.

This is the normal pattern even if we assume that both speakers already know Brenda, and must therefore be aware that she is a woman. The fact that information is 'given' by the context – by the set of assumptions shared by both speakers in an interaction – does not force us to deaccent a lexical item that is new as such.

          (*on seeing the sun shining*) What a 'lovely '<u>day</u>!
          (*at the end of a meal*) What a de'licious '<u>meal</u> that was!

If the sun is shining, we know that it is day rather than night: so why accent *day*? After you finish eating, you know you've had a meal: so why accent *meal*? Presumably, because the lexical items *day* and *meal* respectively have not previously been mentioned: they are not part of the **linguistic** context.

EXERCISES

E3.7.1 Locate the nucleus and choose an appropriate tone. Then supply an alternative intonation pattern with two IPs.

Models:

○ 'Shall we ⌐walk there?	• Yes I ⌐like going on foot.
or	• Yes I ⌐like | going on ⌐foot.
☎ ○ 'Will you have some ⌐punch?	• Oh 'actually I've already ⌐got a drink.
or	• Oh 'actually I've already ⌐got | a ⌐drink.

○ Have you applied to join?	• No, I don't want to become a member.
○ Have you washed the dishes?	• Oh, I hate doing housework.
○ Did you take the bus?	• No, I never use public transport.
○ Have you been to Brazil?	• No, I've never visited South America.
○ What d'you think of Jimmy?	• I'm not interested in footballers.

E3.7.2 Pair-work practice.

○ D'you 'like ⌐Roderick?	• No I 'can't ⌐stand | people like ⌐that.
○ 'Shall we meet on ⌐Tuesday?	• Well I'm ⌐busy | ⌐that day.
○ D'you 'like ⌐football?	• No I ⌐hate | ⌐games.
○ Do you 'ever go ⌐running?	• No I 'can't ⌐stand | ath⌐letics.
○ Shall we 'go and see Okla⌐homa?	• ∨Sorry, | I don't ⌐like | ⌐musicals.

E3.7.3 Insert an IP boundary and locate a nucleus in each IP.

Model: treating ma'laria \| and 'other diseases

studying phonetics and other useful subjects
showing spaniels and other breeds of dog
looking after cats and other similar animals
bring along Wayne and the rest of the boys
buying and selling phones and other electronic equipment

E3.7.4 Pair-work practice.

○ 'When does it ⌐start?	• 'Six o'⌐clock.
○ 'How long will it ⌐last?	• About 'two ⌐hours.
○ 'What does it ⌐cost?	• 'Ten ⌐dollars.
○ 'When'll it ⌐finish?	• 'Half past ⌐eight.
○ 'What time will we get ⌐home?	• 'Nine ⌐thirty.

E3.7.5 Locate the nucleus.

Model: What a 'beautiful '⌐day!

What a wonderful meal!
What a beautiful evening!
What a lovely house!
That was a marvellous meal!
What an attractive dress!

3.8   Prospective and implied givenness

It is not only repeated words that tend not to be accented, but also words that are **about to be repeated**. Compare (ii) with the unmarked pattern in (i):

(i)   a 'red 'triangle | and a 'blue 'square.
(ii)   a 'red triangle | and a 'blue triangle.

In (ii) the word *triangle* is deaccented on each occasion: the second time because it is a repeated word, and the first time because it is going to be repeated.

Accentuation and tonicity depend on the speaker's mental planning. The tonicity in (ii) implies that this sequence of two IPs was planned as a complete unit in advance. If, on the other hand, the speaker utters the first IP while he has still not yet planned the second IP, then for the same words we get an alternative pattern, (iii):

(iii)   a 'red 'triangle | . . . oh and a 'blue triangle.

If these words were uttered as a single IP rather than being spread over two, we would still have the difference between (i) and (ii):

(i)   a 'red triangle and a blue 'square.
(ii)   a 'red triangle and a 'blue triangle.

The speaker also has the option of deaccenting items that are *not* repeated and so objectively do represent new material. This can be a way of forcing on the hearer the view that this material is not new – that it is given, that it is part of the knowledge already shared by speaker and hearer (3.33).

> I'd like to speak to the manager.   (i) • She's 'much too 'busy.
> (ii) • She's 'much too busy.

Reply (i) has neutral tonicity, with *too busy* treated as new. In reply (ii), the speaker forces the hearer to accept (= treat as given) the fact that the manager is too busy; the emphasis is on the great degree of her being too busy, and we have marked tonicity with the nucleus on *much*. Intensifiers are often given nuclear accenting in this way.

Here is another example, one that I witnessed. A taxi-driver was picking up two passengers who had a lot of luggage. The driver loaded most of the cases into the boot (trunk) of the car, but could not find room for the last one. So he finally placed it on the back seat. One passenger said to the other:

🎧   We've 'solved ∨that problem.

The placement of the nucleus on *that*, leaving *problem* to go in the tail, can be interpreted as implying that life is a succession of problems. The speaker treats the notion of *problem* as given (and implies a contrast between *that* problem and other problems; see 3.10).

In this way the speaker can use nucleus placement to indicate what part of the information is to be taken as old, given, mutually agreed, and what part can be taken as new, fresh, additional. The speaker's decisions may not always agree with objective reality. This can be used for comic effect:

> The ∨Queen | said 'how de\lighted she was | to be in ∕Scunthorpe, ‖ and 'then the \Duke made a joke.

With this tonicity (deaccenting *made a joke*), the speaker implies that the Queen, too, was joking when she said how delighted she was to be in Scunthorpe. The further implicature is that Scunthorpe is agreed to be such a dull place that no one could truthfully claim to be delighted at being there. Compare the following, with neutral tonicity, where there is no such implicature:

> The ∨Queen | said 'how de\lighted she was | to be in ∕Scunthorpe, ‖ and then the 'Duke made a \joke.

Thus one participant in a conversation can use intonation to manipulate the conversation by imputing particular knowledge or views to the other participant or participants.

If someone has been doing a number of foolish things, you might greet the latest foolishness with:

🎧   \Now what's she done?

– which implies that you have already been querying her previous actions (what she's done), since by your intonation you treat them as given, not new.

EXERCISES

E3.8.1 Treating each example as a single IP, locate the nucleus. Assume that everything is fully planned in advance by the speaker.

> a big book and a small book
> the first exam paper and the second exam paper
> Andrew got drunk and Tom got drunk.
> Monica fell over and then Lucy fell over.
> The second edition was better than the first edition.

E3.8.2 Repeat E3.8.1, but now divide each example into two IPs.

E3.8.3 Pair-work practice.

> ○ Were you 'pleased with how we ∕did?   • Well ∨my performance | 'wasn't as good as \your performance.

○ So we've 'both done ˎwell.

• Yes but ˇyour score | was 'better than ˎmy score.

○ So the 'two of you have a lot in ˎcommon.

• Yes ˇMaddy's a Pisces | and ˎI'm a Pisces.

○ So you've 'both been in ˎFrance.

• Yes ˇLinda went to Paris | and ˎI went to Paris.

○ 'Did you enjoy the ˊmeal?

• ˎYes, | though the ˎsecond course | 'wasn't as good as the ˇfirst course.

E3.8.4 (i) Explain the tonicity in the following. (ii) Use them for performance practice.

The colˇlision | involved a ˊFord saloon | and a ˎRenault saloon.
ˇThis room | is occupied by 'Mr Smith and ˎMrs Smith.
The 'children reˇsponsible | were Fi'ona Green and ˎTina Green.
'James the ˇFirst | was suc'ceeded by ˎCharles the First.
At ˇthis point | 'King's ˊRoad | becomes ˎNew Kings Road.

E3.8.5 Practise saying the following examples aloud. What is implied by their tonicity?

Mr 'Mellish is ˎreally sorry about this.
'Jennifer's ˎawfully excited.
I'm inˎcredibly impressed.
Was she ˊdeeply affected?
They'll be ˎvery reluctant.

FOCUS

3.9   Broad and narrow focus

Another way of analysing the linguistic function of tonicity involves the notion of **focus**: the concentration of attention on a particular part of the message. When we utter a stretch of speech (an IP), we can either bring everything into focus (**broad** focus), or we can focus selectively on one part of it (**narrow** focus). The part of the IP that is placed in focus is called the focus **domain**. The nucleus marks the **end** of a focus domain.

Maximally **broad focus** means that the focus domain is the whole IP: every-thing in the IP is brought into focus. We would use broad focus, for example, in answer to the question *What happened?*:

'What happened 'next?   • 'Everyone burst out 'laughing.

To give a stretch of utterance broad focus, we use neutral tonicity. The nucleus goes on the last lexical item:

'What's going 'on here?   • Se'lena's had a 'heart attack.

In **narrow focus** only part of what we say is brought into focus. For example, if we are asked a question, and in our answer we repeat part of the material from the question, then that old information will usually not be brought into focus. That is, the lexical items in the old information will not be accented. The nucleus shows where the focus domain ends.

'Who brought the 'wine?	• 'Mary.
	• 'Mary did.
	• 'Mary brought the wine.
	• I think it was 'Mary.
	• I think it was 'Mary that brought the wine.

All five versions of the answer have narrow focus. The focus domain is just the item *Mary*. The intonation indicates that we are concentrating attention on the relevant part (*Mary*), and not on the old, given, repeated material that follows *Mary* in the longer versions.

What did 'Mary bring?	• The 'wine.
	• She brought the 'wine.
	• Mary brought the 'wine.
	• It was the 'wine that she brought.
	• What she brought was the 'wine.

The nucleus tells us where the focus domain ends, and the onset may tell us where it begins (though not very reliably: see 5.11). Consider these two possible 'turns' in a conversation:

(i)   'Tell me about her.
(ii)   'What kind of a 'car does she drive?

Both might elicit the answer:

• She drives a 'Ford Fi'esta.

The nucleus and nuclear tone could be the same, but the focus domains in the two cases would be different: in (i) it is *drives a Ford Fiesta*, but in (ii) just *a Ford Fiesta*. You cannot tell this from the intonation, only from the context. The focus is **ambiguous**.

EXERCISES

E3.9.1 Pair-work practice: narrow-focus answers, using various wordings. The nucleus stays on the same item.

○ What got broken?	• Her 'leg.
	• Her 'leg got broken.
	• It was her 'leg that got broken.

	• I think it was her 'leg.
	• Her \leg, | as far as I /know.
○ Who went with him?	• His 'brother did.
	• His 'brother went with him.
	• Just his 'brother.
	• It was his 'brother who went.
	• The one who went with him was his 'brother.
○ Who's coming to the party?	• 'Jack.
	• 'Jack is.
	• I think 'Jack's coming.
	• 'Jack's coming to the party.
	• Well ∨Jack's coming to the party, | and ∨Mary is, | and so's \Jill.

E3.9.2 Expand the following answers, maintaining the same focus and keeping the nucleus on the same word.

Model:	
○ Who's bringing the food?	• 'Mary.
	• 'Mary is.
	• 'Mary's bringing it.
	• 'Mary's bringing the food.
	• It's 'Mary that's bringing it.

○ Who'll answer the letter?	• 'Jimmy.
○ Who wrote to Mrs Smith?	• The 'secretary.
○ Who's going to win the prize?	• 'Kylie.
○ Who'll be ready first?	• 'Robert.
○ Who's doing the flowers?	• Mrs 'Jenkinson.

E3.9.3 Locate the nucleus, using narrow focus appropriate to the question asked.

Model:	
○ Who sent the invitations?	• 'Bill sent the invitations.

○ Who's going to cook the meal?	• I'm going to cook the meal.
○ Who'll be laying the table?	• The kids'll be laying the table.
○ Who's opening the wine?	• Dad's opening the wine.
○ Who's going to carve the meat?	• Mum's going to carve the meat.
○ Who'll be serving the dessert?	• Jane'll be serving the dessert.

E3.9.4 Each of the following could be either a broad-focus or a narrow-focus answer. Think of questions to which these answers would be appropriate.

> *Model:* • We 'painted the 'kitchen.
> BROAD FOCUS: What did you do today?
> NARROW FOCUS: Which room did you paint?

I've 'promised to o'bey him.
She's 'booked the 'plane tickets.
He en'rolled for the 'chemistry class.
You've 'written a 'novel.
I 'went to Hono'lulu.

3.10 Contrastive focus

A particular kind of narrow focus is **contrastive focus**. Here the nuclear accent draws attention to a contrast the speaker is making. Any following material within the same IP is unaccented and forms part of the tail of the IP:

You 'may have ∨started your essay, | but 'have you ∖finished your essay?

In this example the contrast is between *started* and *finished*. In such cases the repeated, non-contrastive material (here, the second *your essay*) is often replaced by a pronoun, or entirely omitted:

You 'may have ∨started your essay, | but 'have you ∖finished it?
You 'may have ∨started your essay, | but 'have you ∖finished?

In the next example, the contrast is between *Philip* and *Jim*:

'Philip | can run faster than 'Jim can run.
'Philip | can run faster than 'Jim can.
'Philip | can run faster than 'Jim.

The accent on the first item in the contrast is not necessarily nuclear. It is also possible for everything to be in one IP, thus:

'Philip can run faster than 'Jim can. *etc*.

Any word can be accented for contrast, including a function word. A pronoun, a preposition, virtually any word, can bear the nucleus, if it is contrastive:

∨I'm | 'writing a ∖letter. ‖ 'What are ∖you doing?
I 'know what ∨Peter wants, | but 'what do ∖you want?
It 'wasn't ∨under the table, | but 'actually ∖on it.
I can 'send a fax ∨to him, | but I 'can't receive one ∖from him.

Sometimes there is a double contrast. It is then the speaker's choice whether to make both contrasts nuclear, or just one of them:

🎧   ∨You've | got ˎbetter, ‖ but ∨I | ˎhaven't. *or*
🎧   'You've got ˎbetter, | but 'I ˎhaven't.

or, in a context where getting better is already an implicit or explicit topic of the conversation:

🎧   ∨You've got better, | but ∨I haven't.

When a radio or TV announcer reports the result of a football match, there is usually a double contrast. One contrast is between the name of the home team and the name of the away team. The other is the contrast between the two scores. So all four words are accented:

          'Arsenal | 'three, ‖ 'Fulham | 'one. *or*
          'Arsenal 'three, | 'Fulham 'one.

In the case of a drawn game, however, the score achieved by the second team is a repetition of that achieved by the first – so it is usually treated as repeated (old), and is not accented. So we get:

          'Arsenal | 'two, ‖ 'Fulham two. *or*
          'Arsenal 'two, | 'Fulham two. *or even*
          'Arsenal two, | 'Fulham two.

In the last version the speaker has to think ahead, in order to remove focus not only from the repeated item (here, the second *two*) but also from the item that is going to be repeated (the first *two* – see 3.8).

A contrast may be **explicit**, as in the above examples, or **implicit**. If it is implicit, the hearer is left to infer the other term in the contrast:

          I 'don't know what ∨you're complaining about.

Here there is an implicit contrast between the addressee (*you*) and some other possible complainant who may have better grounds for complaint than the addressee.

          Fruit's terribly expensive these days.   • ∨Apples aren't too bad.

Here there is an implicit contrast with other kinds of fruit, which the second speaker implicitly agrees is indeed expensive.

          I 'love your 'hair.

This example has ambiguous focus. It could be either (i) a broad-focus comment, perhaps initiating a new conversation:

          Hi, Jennifer! | How are you today? | I 'love your 'hair.

or (ii) a narrow-focus response, focusing on *hair*, in a situation where *love* or a synonym had already been brought into discussion. For example, it could be a narrow-focus response in the conversational exchange:

> What do you like about me?   • Well I 'love your 'hair.

If, on the other hand, the nucleus were on *love*, that could only be a narrow-focus response in a situation where *hair* was to be taken as given.

> But darling, don't you like my hair?   • I 'love your hair.

Sometimes a pattern of contrastive focus is **lexicalized**. In phonetics, for example, we have a technical term *monosyllable* (= word of one syllable), a word which would be expected to have the stress pattern ,mono'syllable (compare ,mono'mania). But in practice the only time we use this word is when we want to contrast it with *polysyllable* (= word of more than one syllable). Accordingly, we place a contrastive accent on *mon-*. But since this pattern is so usual, we tend to treat the word as having the basic lexical stress pattern 'mono,syllable. In this way contrastive focus has become the fixed stress pattern for the word.

In athletics two of the disciplines are the *high jump* and the *long jump*. Here, too, contrastive focus has been lexicalized, and these expressions – despite being grammatically phrases, adjective plus noun – have the fixed stress patterns 'high jump, 'long jump. This is maintained in metaphorical uses:

> 'John's in for the 'high jump. (= He'll be punished for what he's done.)

A similar explanation presumably applies to 'high school. Originally there was an implicit contrast with *primary school* or *elementary school*, but now this pattern is fixed. We see the same thing in 'high street. The same principle also applies to the phrase *the de'veloping countries*, now in fixed implicit contrast to *the developed countries*.

London Underground lines have lexicalized contrastive focus: the 'Central Line, the 'Northern Line.

EXERCISES

E3.10.1 Pair-work practice.

○ We 'bought it before \Christmas.	• 'Not be∨fore Christmas, | \after Christmas.
○ The 'towels are in the \cupboard.	• Not ∨in the cupboard, | \on the cupboard.
○ You 'say there's an application from the \Graduate Fund.	• ∨To it, | not ∨from it.
○ 'Have you written the ⁄letter yet?	• No but I ∨will write it.
○ 'Have you been ⁄smoking in here?	• I ∨do smoke, | but 'not in ∨here.
○ 'What did you think of the \Smiths?	• I a'dored ∨her, | but I 'couldn't stand \him.
○ 'How do you feel about Bob and \Nesta?	• I 'like ∨her, | but not ∨him.

○ 'What about Andrew and \Rosemary?   • I 'don't care for ∨her, | but ∨he's OK.
○ So 'that's what \Emma said.   • Well you've 'told me what ∨she said, |
    but 'what did \you say?
○ We 'need to sort out who does \what.   • Well 'Mary's bringing some ∨quiche, |
    but 'what can \I bring?

E3.10.2 Locate the nucleus in each IP.

Model: I 'know what 'Judith wants, | but 'what does 'Molly want?

I've got a small bottle, | but I want a large bottle.
I can see the top of the slide, | but where's the bottom of the slide?
He can come tomorrow, | but not today.
She'll have finished by twelve o'clock, | but not by eleven o'clock.
I can recognize the front row, | but who's in the back row?

I spotted the first mistake, | but didn't spot the second mistake.
She wasn't wearing a green scarf, | she was wearing a red scarf.
I don't like skate and chips. | I like plaice and chips.
D'you want a medium cola | or a large cola?
My son's a lawyer, | and I want my daughter to be a lawyer, | too.

E3.10.3 Suggest a question to which each sentence might be a response, with (a) broad and (b) narrow focus.

Model: • I 'm 'going to New York.
BROAD FOCUS: What are you doing tomorrow?
NARROW FOCUS: Where are you going next?

I'm riding a bike.
She's visiting her mother.
They're getting a new cooker.
I've bought some sunglasses.
He's teaching psychology.

E3.10.4 Locate the nucleus. (These are all examples of narrow focus.)

Model:
○ 'What d'you think of her \hair?   • I \love her hair.

○ D'you 'like my /paintings?   • I love your paintings.
○ 'Where's my \apple?   • I've eaten your apple.
○ Have you 'started the /ironing?   • Actually, I've finished the ironing.
○ 'Could I have twenty /cents?   • You can have fifty cents.
○ D'you 'like /jazz?   • No, I can't stand jazz.

     ◦ 'Was it just a /small mistake?   • In fact it was a pretty big mistake.

     ◦ He 'saw the ∨motorcyclist.   • Ah, but he didn't see the pedestrian.

     ◦ Will 'egg and /chips be OK?   • No, she wants sausage and chips.

     ◦ Was 'that with brown /bread?   • No, with white bread.

     ◦ 'Have you got a large /garden?   • No, we've got a really tiny garden.

E3.10.5 Locate the nuclei in these football scores. Create further examples from the names of the teams you love or hate.

Model: 'City 'one, | U'nited 'two.

                  'Wolves 'nil, | 'Tottenham nil *or*

                  'Wolves nil, | 'Tottenham nil.

Wimbledon one, | Aston Villa one.

Notts Forest three, | Sunderland nil.

Stenhousemuir three, | Queen of the South three.

Tranmere two, | Everton two.

Norwich City nil, | Manchester United five.

E3.10.6 Under what circumstances might you say the following? What is focused?

Model: • I'd like 'lamb and 'rice.

could be a broad-focus response to (for example)

          ◦ What about you?

or a narrow-focus ('rice') response to

          ◦ What would you like with your lamb?

or a contrastive-focus response to

          ◦ Would you like lamb and potatoes?

                              • I'd like 'lamb and rice.

could not be a broad-focus response, but only a narrow-focus response to (for example)

          ◦ What'll you have with your rice?

or a contrastive-focus response to

          ◦ Would you like beef and rice?

---

1   It was a 'very difficult 'problem.

        It was a 'very 'difficult problem.

        It was a 'very difficult problem.

        It 'was a very difficult problem.

2   Would you 'like to try my new com'puter?

        Would 'you like to try my new computer?

        Would you 'like to 'try my new computer?

        Would you 'like to try my 'new computer?

3   We're 'flying to Barce'lona tomorrow.
     We're 'flying to Barcelona tomorrow.
     We're 'flying to Barcelona to'morrow.
     'We're | 'flying to Barce'lona tomorrow.

4   'This train | will 'terminate at 'Morden.
5   'Some of them | have 'handed 'in their essays.
6   The 'next thing we shall be doing | is 'writing 'down what we hear.

E3.10.7 Locate the nucleus.

This is St Anne's High School.
She teaches in an elementary school.
You'd better take the Northern Line.
Is Bhutan one of the developing countries?
Are you sure *breathes* is a monosyllable?

3.11   Pronouns and demonstratives

As discussed in 3.3, we do not usually accent personal **pronouns**:

'Are you going to ⁄tell him?   • 'Just try and \stop me!

However, we do accent a pronoun if it is placed in contrastive focus. We frequently want to emphasize a contrast between one person and another:

'I'm as surprised as 'you are.
I 'know how ∨she feels, | but 'how do ∨you feel?
∨He was there, | but there was 'no sign of \her.
∨They've | all \had their food. ‖ 'When do ∨I get some?

Although this change of person can be made explicit (= expressed openly), it is often left implicit:

D'you ⁄both play tennis?   • Well ∨I do| but my ∨husband doesn't. (*explicit*)
                               • Well ∨I do. (*implicit*)

'What do people \think of the idea?   • I 'know what ∨I think.
Can we 'all go to the ⁄party?   • ∨You can.

If you 'ask ∨me, | . . .
If you 'want to know what ∨I think, . . .
As 'far as ∨I'm concerned | . . .

Pronominal **determiners** (*my, your, his,* etc.) may be made nuclear for the same reason:

In ∨my opinion | . . .
From ∨his point of view | . . .

In the case of *in my opinion* the implication is *but others may have other opinions* or *but you may disagree*. The speaker does not need to actually say this explicitly– the contrast is implied by the choice of tonicity.

> (*discussing where to go*) 'Let's go back to '<u>my</u> place.

In colloquial conversation the implications of marked tonicity are very frequently left without explicit expression:

> Did you 'see what '<u>I</u> got in the post?

– with some such implication as 'You're the one who usually gets interesting letters, but today things are different.'

The **complement** of the verb *to be* regularly receives the nucleus, even if it is a pronoun. This is another common reason to locate the nucleus on a pronoun, and can often (though not always) be analysed as involving narrow or contrastive focus:

'Who's ⁄<u>that</u>?	• It's \<u>me</u>.
'Who'll be on \<u>next</u>?	• It'll be \<u>you</u>, I think.
'Who took the \<u>milk</u>?	• It was \<u>him</u>.
'Who left the \<u>sugar</u> on the table?	• It wasn't v<u>me</u>.

The nucleus remains on the pronoun if *it* and the verb are ellipted (= omitted):

'Who's ⁄<u>that</u>?	• \<u>Me</u>.
'Who left the \<u>sugar</u> on the table?	• 'Not v<u>me</u>.
v<u>Some</u>one stole the money. ‖ 'Was it the \<u>sales</u> staff?	• I 'don't think it was v<u>them</u>.

> (*there is a noise at the door.*) ⁄<u>Peter</u>? | Is 'that ⁄<u>you</u>?
> The 'lucky v<u>winner</u> | could be \<u>you</u>!
> That's 'really \<u>it</u>. | There's 'nothing more we can \<u>do</u>.
> This is v<u>it</u>, boys, | the 'moment we've been \<u>waiting</u> for.

Alternatively, the same idea can be expressed with the pronoun as subject. It is still in focus, and bears the nucleus:

'Who's ⁄<u>there</u>?	• \<u>I</u> am.
'Who left the \<u>sugar</u> on the table?	• Well v<u>I</u> didn't.

The general rule is that pronouns are stressed only if they are contrastive. However, there are various more or less idiomatic usages in which we focus on a pronoun despite there being no obvious contrast with any other item:

'How can I get to the \<u>lecture</u> hall?	• 'Follow \<u>me</u>.
Hul⁄<u>lo</u>, Roger.	• \<u>Jim</u>!	'What are \<u>you</u> doing here?
The 'year after v<u>next</u>	is going to be \<u>difficult</u> for us.	• 'What do \<u>I</u> care? ‖ I'll be re\<u>tired</u>	by ⁄<u>then</u>.

English also has a number of **idioms** involving fixed tonicity: fossilized idiomatic expressions said with a particular intonation. In the following, a pronoun has a falling nuclear tone:

ଣ   'Good for \you! (*genuine congratulation*)
ଣ   'Bully for \you! (*sarcastic congratulation*)
         'Blow \me!   (= I am very surprised.)
         'Get \her!   (= Look at her putting on airs.)
         'Search \me! (= I don't know, I've no idea.) (*also* 'Search ∨me!)

In clause-final position the **possessive** pronouns (*mine, yours, his, hers, ours, theirs*) tend inherently to convey new information and so attract the nucleus. They are usually in implicit contrast with other possessive expressions:

> 'Which one is 'yours?
> 'Give me 'hers | and 'take 'his.
> Our 'washing machine broke 'down, | but our 'neighbours let us use 'theirs.

However, this does not apply to the post-modifier construction *of mine, of yours,* etc., where the possessive is usually not accented:

ଣ   I've 'just been talking to a 'friend of mine.

Final **demonstratives**, too, namely *this, that, these, those,* tend to convey new information, and attract the nucleus:

> 'Look at 'this!
> 'Who's 'that?
> I'd 'like some of 'those, please.

Final *there* usually attracts the nucleus if it refers to a place that is new (= not previously mentioned), but not if it refers to a place that is given (= already mentioned or obvious from the context). When it is a post-modifier, it is usually not accented:

> 'Hold it right 'there!
> 'London's | a 'long way a'way. ‖ 'How long will it take to 'get there?
> 'Look at that 'parakeet there.

EXERCISES

E3.11.1 Pair-work practice.

ଣ
○ I think \everyone would agree.	• ∨I'd be happy about it. | But 'not the ∨others.
○ Do you 'all like la∕sagne?	• ∨I do. | But I'm 'not sure whether ∨Barbara does.
○ So we can 'all stay \here.	• ∨You can. | But ∨I'm not going to.
○ The 'kids aren't going to be \happy with this.	• Well ∨they may not be. | But ∨I am.
○ 'What a nice \man!	• ∨You may think he's OK. | But ∨I don't.

E3.11.2 Locate the nucleus.

Model: ○ What's your name?   • \Jim. | What's \your name?

○ Where do you live?   • In London. | Where do you live?
○ How old are you?   • Twenty. | How old are you?
○ Who's your favourite singer?   • Oh Madonna. | Who's your favourite?
○ What's your favourite colour?   • Blue. | What's your favourite colour?
○ How many brothers and sisters have   • Two brothers. | How many \have you got?
  you got?

E3.11.3 In pairs, have a conversation along the lines of E.3.11.2. Add further similar questions and answers.

E.3.11.4 Locate the nucleus, placing it on the contrastive personal pronoun.

Model: 'Peter's told me what 'he wants, | but 'what do 'you want?

You like it when you win, | but not when I do.
I know what you like, | but what does she like?
John knows where I live, | but I don't know where he lives.
It's clear what she wants, | but not what he does.
You've told me where they went, | but where did you go?

The children want to go to Disneyland, | but what would we rather do?
Sheila | says Henry likes pop music, | but what does she like?
I'm happy to stay in, | but what would you prefer?
Emma and I are going for a walk.| What would you like to do?
I'll visit you on Monday, | but when will you visit me?

E3.11.5 Pair work. One person asks questions beginning *Do you think we should . . . ?*. The other person answers, with a nucleus on the contrastive personal pronoun.

 ⚏ *Model:* ○ Do you think we should buy a new sofa?
            • If you 'ask ∨me, | it would be a 'waste of \money.

○ Do you think we should . . . ?   • If you 'ask ∨me, | . . .
                                            • As 'far as ∨I'm concerned, | . . .
                                            • If 'I were ∨you, | . . .
                                            • 'What ∨I think is | . . .
                                            • 'Don't ask ∨me! | . . .

E3.11.6 Pair-work practice.

○ 'What about Professor \Jenkinson?   • In ∨my opinion | he's mis\taken.
○ And the /Smiths?   • Well ∨I think | they're \crazy.

○ 'What did Robert say about the \airlines? • In ∨his view, | they 'need to re\structure.

○ 'What do you want the \children to do? • As far as ∨I'm concerned, | they can do what they \like.

○ 'What shall we do \next? • Don't ask ∨me! | Ask \her.

E3.11.7 Locate the nucleus on the final possessive pronoun or demonstrative.

Model: 'This biscuit is 'mine.

Where did you put yours?
Mary's taken hers,| and Peter's got his.
I like our car better than yours.
I can't use mine.| Let me borrow yours.
He touched his mouth to hers.

Where's this?
Who are those?
Tell me what this is.
What are these?
Give me some of those.

Who's that?
Which one is yours?
That book's mine.
Ask him which is his.
Isn't it one of ours?

E3.11.8 Pair-work practice.

○ 'Who'll be on \next? • It'll be \me.
 • \I will.

○ 'Who's that \knocking? • \Us!
 • \We are!

○ 'Who's going to do the \dishes? • \You are.
 • It'll be \you.

○ 'Who asked for some \soap? • It was \me.
 • \I did.

○ 'Who took the milk? • It was \her, | the \secretary.
 • The \secretary did.

○ 'Who took the last \chocolate? • It wasn't ∨me.
 • Not ∨me.

○ 'Who's the one with the \map? • \Him.
 • \He's got it.

○ 'Who was stung by the \wasp? • It was \her.
 • \She was.

o 'Who was re\sponsible?

- It 'wasn't ∨them.
- 'Not ∨them.

o 'Who did they \choose?

- It was \me!
- They chose \me!

E3.11.9 Locate the nucleus on the pronoun in narrow focus. There are three possible answers each time.

⌒   *Model:*   o 'Who said \that?

- It 'wasn't ∨me.
- 'Not ∨me.
- Well ∨I didn't.

---

o 'Who made all this \mess? | Was it /Mark?

- I don't think it was him.
- Not him.
- Well he didn't.

o 'Who's going to wash the \dishes?

- Not me.
- Well I'm not.
- I don't think I am.

o 'Which of you are coming \with me?

- I think we are.
- We are.
- It's us.

o 'Who did the judges \choose?

- I'm pleased to say it was actually me.
- Well me, | actually.
- It was me!

o 'Who's going on \this bus?

- Actually you are.
- This time it's you.
- I think it's you.

E3.11.10 Explain the difference in intonational meaning in the following pairs or triplets. Think of appropriate contexts in which you might use each.

1   (i)   She was 'talking to me.
    (ii)   She was 'talking to 'me.
2   (i)   I'll 'see you 'next.
    (ii)   I'll 'see 'you next.
3   (i)   You'd 'better 'ask him.
    (ii)   You'd 'better ask 'him.
    (iii) 'You'd better ask him.
4   (i)   Are you 'going to 'follow us?
    (ii)   Are you 'going to follow 'us?
    (iii) Are 'you going to follow us?
5   (i)   I 'don't 'like her.
    (ii)   I 'don't like 'her.
    (iii) 'I don't like her.

3.12   Reflexive, reciprocal and indefinite pronouns

The most frequent use of a **reflexive pronoun** (*myself, yourselves,* etc.) is for emphasis, in which case, as you might expect, it is accented:

> I'll 'write to him my'<u>self</u>.
> He 'did it all by him'<u>self</u>.
> Will you be 'able to come your'<u>self</u>?
> She's 'not very enthusiastic about it her'<u>self</u>.
> The 'villa pays for it'<u>self</u>.

When, however, they are used as true reflexives – as the object of the verb or after a preposition – they are not usually contrastive, and therefore not accented. They usually form part of the tail:

> She feels 'rather '<u>pleased</u> with herself.
> 'Don't make a '<u>fool</u> of yourself!

🎧   Have you '<u>hurt</u> yourself?   • 'Yes I've '<u>cut</u> myself.

You use accented *myself* at the end of a comment, with a non-fall tone, to suggest that this is your opinion, but that others may not share it:

> I 'think that's \<u>right</u>, | my∨<u>self</u>. (= I 'think that's \<u>right</u>, | ∨personally.)
> I 'don't a\<u>gree</u>, | my⁄<u>self</u>.
> I'm not \<u>sure</u>, | my∨<u>self</u>.

> Do you 'know ⁄<u>Paris</u>?   • \<u>No</u>,| I've 'never \<u>been</u> there | my∨<u>self</u>.
🎧   'Like a cup of ⁄<u>coffee</u>?   • No I 'don't \<u>drink</u> coffee, | my⁄<u>self</u>.

In informal regional English of the north of England *myself* in this usage is replaced by *me*:

> I'm \<u>mad</u> about it, | ⁄<u>me</u>.

The **reciprocal** pronouns *each other* and *one another* are usually not contrastive, and therefore not accented:

🎧   I think we 'all ought to '<u>help</u> one another.
> At 'least 'Phil and Sue are '<u>talk</u>ing to each other.

The same applies to the **indefinite** pronouns *someone, somebody, something, anyone, anybody, anything*:[4]

> 'Can you '<u>see</u> anyone?
> I've 'just '<u>read</u> something | 'really '<u>funny</u>.
🎧   Can I '<u>get</u> you anything?
> I 'can't keep it quiet any '<u>longer</u>. | I've just 'got to '<u>tell</u> someone.

The spoken phrase *or something* (= or something similar) is unaccented when used at the end of a sentence. So are other indefinite pronouns following *or* in this usage:

☉   His name was 'Jimmy, | or 'Billy, or something.
                'Stop 'bothering me! | 'Ask 'Muriel or somebody.
                'Can I get you a 'drink or anything?

The indefinite pronouns can nevertheless exceptionally receive the nuclear accent
for emphasis. Compare:

          A: 'What's the 'matter?
          B: I 'thought I 'heard someone.
          A: But there's 'no one at the 'door.
          B: I'm 'sure I heard 'something. (= not nothing)

          I 'can't 'see anyone.   (*neutral*)
          I 'can't see 'anyone.   (*marked negative*)

          They 'didn't 'bring anything.   (*neutral*)
          They 'didn't bring 'anything.   (= They 'brought 'nothing.)
          I 'wouldn't go back there for 'anything.   (= I certainly wouldn't!)

Note also:

☉   We 'didn't hear a 'thing.   (= We 'heard 'nothing.)
                I 'won't tell a 'soul.   (= I 'won't tell 'anyone, | I'll 'tell 'no one.)
                I 'don't like 'either of them. (= I 'like 'neither of them.)

☉   I 'won't \tell anyone.   (*neutral*)
☉   I 'won't tell \anyone.   (*marked negative*)
☉   I 'won't tell vanyone.   (= I'll 'only tell a 'few people.)

EXERCISES

E3.12.1 Pair-work practice.

○ You 'seem very vsure of yourself.   • 'That's because I 'heard it my\self, | with
                                              my 'own \ears.

○ But 'can I be sure you'll de\liver it?   • If you 'don't vtrust me, | you'd 'better do it
                                                  your\self.

○ It gets 'terribly vcrowded.   • On a vweekday | you'll have it 'all to
                                        your\self.

○ 'Why do you \hesitate?   • I'm a'fraid I might \hurt myself.

○ 'Shall I have another /chocolate?   • 'Go /on, | \spoil yourself!

E3.12.2 Locate the nucleus. Think carefully about whether to put the nuclear accent on the
reflexive pronoun.

          Models: I've 'hurt myself.   *but*   I'll 'do it my'self.

          Have you cut yourself?
          Did you write it yourself?
          He calls himself Jim.

Could you come yourself?
I was all by myself.

Go on, | treat yourself! | Buy an ice cream.
We had the beach | all to ourselves.
Did she hurt herself?
You could always do it yourselves.
You don't seem yourself | today.

E3.12.3 Locate the nucleus. Do not accent a reciprocal or indefinite pronoun.

> *Models:*   They were 'tal<u>k</u>ing to one another.
> I 'want to 'te<u>ll</u> you something.

Can Peter and Jenny see one another?
The girls looked at each other.
I'm afraid Joseph and Kevin hate each other.
They were sitting on the floor, | facing each other.
Some of the witnesses | contradicted one another.

I feel I've just got to tell someone.
You could talk to a teacher or someone.
Sarah said something | about coming to see us.
Come here. | I want to show you something.
Don't just stand there, | do something!

3.13 Contrastive focus overrides other factors

We sometimes put the nucleus on a 'given' item because we need to place the item in contrastive focus. This arises particularly when we correct another speaker. Because it is in contrast, the repeated material nevertheless receives the nuclear accent:

He's a 'famous ⟍actor.   • Well 'not exactly an ⌄actor, | 'more a ⟍singer.
She had on a 'green ⟍dress.   • Oh 'not ⌄green. | It was ⟍blue.

Consider also the following example:

It's 'awfully hard to get up at   • Well if you're 'so late to ⌄bed, | you 'won't
⌄five.   be able to get ⟍up early.

In this example, *early* counts as information already given (since 5 a.m. is early in the day). Although *get up* is also given, the need to draw the contrast between it and *be late to bed* leads the speaker to accent it, indeed to place the nucleus on it.

If there is new information **following** a contrastive nucleus, it has to be made into a separate IP:

> She 'said it was \wrong, | but ∨he | said it was \right.

In this example there is a contrastive nucleus on *he*. But *right*, which follows, conveys new information, and must therefore have its own nucleus in a separate IP.

Contrastive focus may override lexical stress patterns, too. In particular, a regular early-stressed compound may get a late accent for reasons of contrast. For example, both '*birthday card* and '*birthday present* have lexical stress on the first element, *birthday*. Yet with contrastive tonicity you might say:

> I 'got her a birthday 'present, | but I 'didn't get her a birthday 'card.

Names of localities usually have lexical double stress: thus *Tra₁falgar 'Square*, *₁Raynes 'Park* (see 3.5). This pattern can be overridden under contrastive focus. A common case is in a list. Here we often see examples of the thinking-ahead principle mentioned above (3.8), namely that of removing accenting from an item that is about to be repeated as well as from the item that is actually repeated.

> We 'started in Tra'falgar Square | and 'then went to 'Leicester Square.
> 'This train calls at 'Raynes Park, | 'Motspur Park, | 'Malden 'Manor . . .

Occasionally we may even focus on **part** of a word only. This may mean that the contrastive accent goes on a syllable different from the one bearing the main lexical stress:

🎧 'How many 'were there?   • 'Fif'teen. (*normal pattern*)

🎧 Did you say 'fifteen | or 'sixteen?   • 'Fifteen! (*contrastive pattern*)

I'd say it was 'not so much 'democratic, | 'more 'autocratic.

🎧 They're 'not 'Chinese, | they're 'Japanese.

🎧 It 'wasn't really 'red, | 'just red'dish.

She'll 'talk to any'body | and any'thing.

'That's it for 'Schumann; | 'what about Schu'bert?

Prefixes and suffixes may receive contrastive focus:

I 'thought the villagers were pretty 'friendly.   • 'Surely not! ‖ 'I thought | they were 'rather 'unfriendly.[5]

'This stress is post-'primary.   • 'No | it 'isn't! ‖ It's 'pre-primary.

Note that the stress pattern of contracted negatives is never overridden. That is, we never emphasize negative polarity by accenting the *n't* part of *didn't*, *wasn't*, etc. (We do have the option of undoing the contraction and accenting *not*.)

'You took my 'stapler!   • I 'didn't!
                              • I 'did 'not!

Contrastiveness also overrides the usual rules about special function words such as the reflexives (3.12):

You'll 'hurt yourself.   *but*   You 'won't hurt '<u>me</u>, | you'll hurt your'<u>self</u>.
'Who taught you pho'<u>netics</u>?   • '<u>No</u> one, | I 'taught my'<u>self</u>.

EXERCISES

E3.13.1 Contrastive focus: nucleus on a repeated word.

- ○ They're ar'riving to∨<u>morrow</u>.
- ○ We're 'meeting on ∖<u>Tuesday</u>.
- ○ She 'lives in ∖<u>Caterham</u>.
- ○ ∖<u>Jack</u> was first.
- ○ He's from Vir∖<u>ginia</u>.

- • 'Not to∨<u>morrow</u>, | the 'day ∖<u>after</u>.
- • ∖<u>Wednesday</u> you mean, | 'not ∨<u>Tuesday</u>.
- • ∖<u>Purley</u>, | 'not ∨<u>Caterham</u>.
- • 'Not ∨<u>Jack</u>, | ∖<u>George</u>.
- • 'Not Vir∨<u>ginia</u>, | ∖<u>Delaware</u>.

- ○ She was wearing a 'green ∖<u>dress</u>.
- ○ I 'like your ∨<u>tie</u>.
- ○ 'I'll have the cour∖<u>gettes</u>.

- • 'Not ∨<u>green</u>, | ∖<u>blue</u>.
- • It's a cra∖<u>vat</u>, | 'not a /<u>tie</u>.
- • They're 'not cour/<u>gettes</u>, | they're zuc∖<u>chini</u>.

- ○ There were a 'whole lot of ∖<u>spiders</u> there. || I ∖<u>hate</u> | /<u>insects</u>!
- ○ 'Jason's just ∖<u>lazy</u>.

- • A 'spider's not an ∨<u>insect</u>, you know.

- • 'Not ∨<u>lazy</u>, | 'laid-∖<u>back</u>.

E3.13.2 Locate the nucleus. The lexical stress pattern is likely to be overridden.

> *Model:* ○ There are 'four'<u>teen</u> of them.   • 'Not 'four<u>teen</u>, | 'thir<u>teen</u>.

- ○ Five nines are fifty-five.
- ○ It's in Leicester Square.
- ○ She's at King's College.
- ○ D'you come from North Korea?
- ○ She's wearing a nylon blouse.

- • No, they're forty-five.
- • No, it's in Russell Square.
- • Not King's College, Birkbeck College.
- • No, South Korea.
- • It's a cotton blouse.

E3.13.3 Pair-work practice: contrastive focus overriding the lexical word stress.

- ○ We've 'done some psycholin∨<u>guistics</u>.
- ○ I 'need a ∖<u>dictionary</u>.
- ○ He's a 'psycho∖<u>therapist</u>.
- ○ I need 'ten ∖<u>milligrams</u>.
- ○ So ∨<u>this</u> plan | offers 'quite a few ad∖<u>vantages</u>.

- • But we 'haven't done any ∖<u>sociolinguistics</u>.
- • 'Monolingual or ∖<u>bilingual</u>?
- • No a ∖<u>physiotherapist</u>.
- • You mean 'ten milli∖<u>litres</u>.
- • But 'what about the ∖<u>disadvantages</u>?

3.14   Contrastive focus on polarity or tense

Sometimes the speaker wants to emphasize the **polarity** (= the quality of being either positive or negative) of a verb, or its **tense**. In both cases this may cause the nucleus to go on an auxiliary or modal verb.

When we deny the truth of an assertion made by the other speaker, we can focus on the negative word (if the thing being denied is positive). This is a **marked negative**. The nucleus goes either on the word *not* or on the word containing the negation, e.g. a contracted negative such as *won't*:

I think they'll just surrender.	• They ˯won't surrender!
Peter | could run a marathon.	• He ˯couldn't run a marathon!
You took my plate.	• I ˊdidn't take your plate!
Oops, | sorry, | you're busy.	• I'm ˯not busy.

To deny the truth of a negative proposition, we focus on the word that indicates positive polarity. This is a **marked positive**. The nucleus usually goes on a form of the verb *to be* or on a modal or auxiliary verb:

You're not inv<u>o</u>lved.   • Oh but I ˎ<u>am</u> involved!
If you 'can't see her ' now, \| 'when '<u>can</u> you see her?
You 'thought I hadn't 'fi<u>n</u>ished, \| but I '<u>had</u> finished.

The pro-form *do* receives the nucleus when it signals a change of polarity (positive to negative or negative to positive):

He 'promised he would 'fi<u>n</u>ish it, \| but 'actually he '<u>didn't</u>.
She 'said she wouldn't '<u>tell</u> them, \| but 'actually she '<u>did</u> tell them.

Or there may just be the restatement of an existing polarity:

He '<u>prom</u>ised he would finish it, \| and he 'actually '<u>did</u> finish it.

In the following example, an ambiguity in the written form is resolved by appropriate focus, shown in speech by intonation:

☊   I was thinking of organizing a collection for cancer research.
☊   (i) • Well, '<u>I'll</u> make a donation \| if you '<u>do</u>.
☊   (ii) • Well, '<u>I'll</u> make a donation \| if '<u>you</u> do.

Here, response (i) means 'if you organize a collection', while response (ii) means 'if you make a donation'.

If the assertion being denied is negative, so that our denial is positive, we focus on the auxiliary or modal verb (often a form of the emphatic *do*):

You didn't bring an umbrella.	• I '<u>did</u> bring an umbrella.
He hasn't opened his briefcase.	• He '<u>has</u> opened his briefcase.
You don't like rock, | ˎ<u>do</u> you?	• I '<u>do</u> like rock!

Note, however, that if the negation word is followed by a 'new' lexical item the nucleus goes (as normal) on that new lexical item, even though the speaker's main intent may be the negation:

Have some more milk.   • I 'don't '<u>want</u> any more milk.

Where there is a contrast involving the subject of the clause as well as one involving polarity, English often focuses on the subject while – illogically? –

not accenting the actual polarity word. This pattern usually involves a fall–rise tone (see 2.7 on correction):

> ˅Lawrence didn't pass the test, | though the ˅rest of us did.
> So ˅Mary's ready, | but ˅Rachel isn't.

I 'don't \like	/Beethoven.	• Well ˅I do.
I shall be 'singing \hymns.	• Well the ˅others won't.[6]

There is also another possible reason for placing the nucleus on the word that carries the indication of polarity: namely, as a device for adding emphasis to an exclamation. This is a kind of contrastive focus, though the contrast is implicit:

> You \have done well! | 'Daddy \will be pleased.
> 'Oh \no! | 'That was \not a good idea.
> 'That \is a nice hat you're wearing!

In the last example there may have been no previous mention of a hat or of what is being worn.

As with polarity, so with **tense**. We focus on an auxiliary or modal verb to emphasize that we are talking about the past not the present, or the future not the past:

Are you a vegetarian?	• Well I ˅used to be,	but 'now I eat \meat.
D'you play tennis?	• I ˅did play tennis	before my ope/ration.
Have you written back?	• No but I'm ˅going to write back.

> 'This ma˅chine | runs 'more slowly than it \used to run.
> I 'haven't done the ˅washing yet, | but I ˅will do it.

Notice that in these examples various repeated words could have been ellipted (= omitted). The same meanings could alternatively be expressed as follows:

Are you a vegetarian?	• Well I ˅used to be a vegetarian . . .
D'you play tennis?	• I ˅did	before my ope/ration.
Have you written back?	• No but I'm ˅going to.

> 'This ma˅chine | runs 'more slowly than it \used to.
> I 'haven't done the ˅washing yet, | but I ˅will.

Contrastive focus is the commonest reason for a function word to receive the nucleus . . . but not the only one.

EXERCISES

E.3.14.1 Pair-work practice: contrastive focus on polarity.

o You 'didn't \see me!	• I \did see you!
o You've for'gotten your \books!	• I have \not forgotten my books.
o You 'haven't done your \homework.	• I \have done my homework.

   o 'Have you ever been to /Edinburgh?   • Yes I \have been to Edinburgh.

   o You're 'not going to be able to \do it.   • Oh but I \am going to be able to.

   o You've for'gotten your \lines.   • I have vnot forgotten my lines.

   o We're 'losing \height!   • We're vnot losing height.

   o I'm 'going to \fall!   • You're vnot going to fall.

   o I 'don't think we're going to vwin.   • We vare going to win.

   o But 'gibbons are not \primates.   • 'Gibbons vare primates.

3.14.2 Locate the nucleus.

>   *Model:*   He 'thought I'd 'finished the essay,| but 'actually I 'hadn't finished it.

I was afraid I was going to fail, | but in fact I didn't fail.
She said she hadn't done the washing up, | but actually she had done it.
A horrible insect? | Actually, | a spider isn't an insect.
You expect me to believe it? | I don't believe it. | How can I believe it?
You'd think that Italian would be easy, | but actually it isn't easy.

3.14.3 Pair-work practice: focus on changed subject, not on polarity.

   o I don't \eat | /meat.   • Well vI do.

   o 'Tony could make seven \thirty.   • vWe can't, though.

   o vApparently | the 'ladies don't \like him. • Mrs vWalker says she does.

   o A 'lot of people say they won't be \at the • vWe'll be coming, | \won't we, Suzanne?
     concert.

   o vGiles | has \finished his homework.   • vDarren hasn't, though, | \has he?

3.14.4 Pair-work practice: focus on adverbial, etc., not on polarity.

   o Do you 'work /hard?   • Of \course I do.

   o Have you 'got your /passport?   • Of \course I have.

   o Will you 'come /with us?   • \Course I will.

   o Are you 'going to join /in?   • You \bet I am.

   o \God, | I was 'so \angry!   • I \bet you were.

   o I'm 'going to win the \prize.   • I'm \sure you are.

   o I 'guess you were rather disap\pointed. • Well \naturally I was.

   o 'Are you going to /fire her?   • Of \course not.

   o 'Do you still /love me?   • Of \course I do.

   o 'Will he get his /refund?   • Of \course he won't.

   o Do you 'ever eat /broccoli?   • Well vsometimes I do.

   o 'Have you ever written a /book?   • Not vyet I haven't.

   o She 'never works vlate.   • Oh on vFridays she does.

   o The 'shops are open all \day | on   • In vGermany they're not.
     /Saturdays.

   o 'UCL is \closed | in /Easter week.   • vCity University isn't.

3.14.5 Pair-work practice: contrastive focus on tense.

o Do you /smoke?	• Well I ˅used to smoke.
o D'you 'play /tennis?	• I ˅did play tennis | when I was /young.
o 'Do you eat /shellfish?	• Well, I ˅used to eat shellfish.
o 'Have you mown the /lawn?	• No but I'm ˎgoing to mow it.
o 'Does she write /books?	• No but she ˅used to write books.
o 'Can you see the /islands?	• No but I ˅have seen them.
o Do you ex'pect to finish /soon?	• I ˎhave finished, | alˎready.
o 'Are they going to make you /manager?	• I ˎam manager, | ˎnow.
o 'Are you going to learn I/talian?	• I've ˎbeen learning Italian, | for ˎmonths.
o 'Why don't you try ˎjogging?	• I've ˎbeen jogging, | ˎregularly.

3.15   Dynamic focus

Focus is not static but dynamic. As a conversation progresses, speakers constantly update what they are focusing on.

Consider a simple example. The family are sitting in a room at the back of the house when the doorbell rings. Dad says to his son:

'Vernon, | there's 'someone at the 'door. | 'Answer it, would you?

The boy does so, and comes back to report:

There's a 'man at the door. | He's col'lecting for a 'charity.

In the father's utterance, *door* was new information, and therefore placed in focus. In the son's reply, it is given, and so no longer in focus.

By **varying the tonicity** (= changing the accent pattern, altering the focus, putting the nucleus in different places) we make a particular IP pragmatically appropriate for the particular circumstances in which it is used. The most obvious reason for doing this is to express different kinds of contrastive focus.

Consider the utterance *she was trying to lose weight*. With broad focus, and therefore neutral tonicity, it would be said as:

She was 'trying to lose 'weight.

This might be a broad-focus answer to:

Why didn't she want any ice cream?   • She was 'trying to lose 'weight.

But we would have the same tonicity in a narrow-focus answer to:

What was she trying to lose?   • She was 'trying to lose 'weight.

. . . or in a contrastive-focus follow-on to:

She 'wasn't trying to lose 'money, | she was 'trying to lose 'weight.

What about focusing on some other element in the utterance? If we put contrastive focus on *lose*, we imply a contrast between *lose* and some other item:

> She 'wasn't trying to 'gain weight, | she was trying to '<u>lose</u> weight.

With contrastive focus on *trying*:

> She was '<u>try</u>ing to lose weight | though she 'didn't have much suc'<u>cess</u>.

With contrastive focus on *was* the contrast must be either one of tense or one of polarity:

> She '<u>was</u> trying to lose weight, | but she 'isn't '<u>now</u>.
> She '<u>was</u> trying to lose weight, | de'spite your claim that she '<u>wasn't</u>.

Contrastive focus on *she* implies a contrast with some other possible subject:

> '<u>She</u> was trying to lose weight, | though her '<u>friends</u> may not have been.

In lively conversation speakers constantly deploy contrastive focus, shifting the place of the nucleus around appropriately. Always keeping the nucleus on the last new lexical item can sound very dull.

EXERCISES

E3.15.1 Vary the tonicity in the following sentences. Say under what circumstances each nucleus placement might be appropriate, as the focus changes.

Model:

She was 'trying to lose '<u>weight</u>.	(broad focus, neutral; *or* not lose money)
She was 'trying to '<u>lose</u> weight.	(not gain weight)
She was '<u>try</u>ing to lose weight.	(though without much success)
She '<u>was</u> trying to lose weight.	(despite what you say; *or* but she isn't now)
'<u>She</u> was trying to lose weight.	(though others may not have been)

> We were walking down Melrose Avenue.
> The boys have finished all the yoghurt.
> Is Peter ready to show his pictures?
> Do you want to order the risotto?
> Try to keep singing quietly.

E3.15.2 Use the same words, but with different focus (manifested as different tonicity), in answering the various questions.

> • The students want to dance on Saturday night.

> Which night do the students want to dance?
> What do the students want to do on Saturday night?

> Who wants to dance on Saturday night?
> What's the latest news?
> When on Saturday do the students want to dance?
>
> E3.15.3 Construct similar sets of questions to elicit these answers, with varying focus and tonicity.
>
> - I'm planning to fly to Edinburgh.
> - The judge found James Chartwell not guilty.
> - That's a very great disappointment to us.
> - All the competitors have finished their tests.
> - We'll try to finish the roof next Monday.

NUCLEUS ON A FUNCTION WORD

3.16   Narrow focus: yes–no answers and tags

A yes–no question is a query about **polarity** (see 3.14). A direct answer to a yes–no question involves narrow focus on polarity and the word that indicates it.

To give a direct answer, we can say *yes* or *no* (or use a synonymous adverb or adverbial phrase, such as *sure*, *definitely* or *no way*). The nucleus goes on this word or phrase:

Have you finished?	• 'Yes.
	• 'Definitely.
	• Oh 'sure.
	• 'No.
	• 'Not 'really.

The word *yes* or *no* (or its equivalent) may be followed by a short sentence fragment (or indeed a longer sentence) involving a verb. Less commonly, we use the sentence fragment without the *yes* or *no*. It, too, bears a nuclear accent. In a sentence or sentence fragment used in this way, it is the operator (= auxiliary or modal verb) that shows whether the sentence is positive (*yes*) or negative (*no*). The focus is on the polarity, so we put the nucleus on the verb:

Have you finished?	• 'Yes, | I 'have.
	• 'Yes, | I 'have finished.
	• I 'have.
	• 'No, | I 'haven't.
	• 'No, | I 'haven't finished.

It is also possible to deaccent the initial *yes* or *no*:

Have you finished?	• Yes I 'have.
	• No I 'haven't.

Although the word *not* is accentable, the *n't* of a contracted form is not: instead, the accent goes on the stressed syllable of the word containing *n't*:

Is that a firearm?	• 'No, | it's 'not.
	• 'No, | it 'isn't.
Can she manage Wednesday?	• 'No, | she 'can't.

Notice the difference between narrow focus on polarity in answer to a yes–no question and narrow focus on a noun phrase in answer to a wh question:

Is Peter coming?	• 'Yes, | he 'is.
	• 'Yes, | Peter 'is coming.
Who's coming?	• 'Peter is.
	• 'Peter's coming.

There are various other elliptical constructions which likewise have narrow focus on the word that indicates polarity:

D'you think they'll appeal?	• I'm a'fraid they 'might.
Is she going to reply?	• I 'don't think she 'will.
Are you coming out with us?	• I'm a'fraid 'not.

We also get a nucleus on the polarity word in tag-like questions consisting of a verb plus a pronoun. These, too, involve narrow focus on polarity:

We're nearly ready.	• 'Are you?
They haven't taken their vouchers.	• 'Haven't they?
You're quite wrong, you know.	• 'Am I?

And the same applies to tag questions if (as is usually the case) they have their own IP:

It's a 'beautiful 'day, \| 'isn't it?
We could 'go to 'Chichester, \| 'couldn't we?
They've for'gotten all a'bout it, \| 'haven't they?
'Wayne didn't 'call, \| 'did he?

EXERCISES

E3.16.1 Pair work: in the answer, place the nucleus on the auxiliary or modal verb. Make longer and shorter answers. Use a rise for the question and a fall for the answer.

Model:	○ Have you finished?	• (Yes) I have (finished).
	○ 'Have you ⁄finished?	• ⟍Yes, | I ⟍have finished.
		• ⟍Yes, | I ⟍have.
		• Yes I ⟍have.

○ Did you feed the cat?	• (Yes) I did (feed it).
○ Are you going to watch the film?	• (Yes) I am (going to watch it).

○ Have you tried asparagus?	• (Yes) I have (tried it).
○ Will you write to Mary?	• (Yes) I will (write to her).
○ Can you speak German?	• (Yes) I can (speak German).

E3.16.2 Answer the same questions in the negative.

Model:	○ Have you finished?	• (No) I haven't (finished).
	○ Have you /finished?	• \No, | I \haven't finished.
		• \No, | I \haven't.
		• No I \haven't.

○ Did you feed the cat?	• (No) I didn't (feed it).
○ Are you going to watch the film?	• (No) I'm not (going to watch it).
○ Have you tried asparagus?	• (No) I haven't (tried it).
○ Will you write to Mary?	• (No) I won't (write to her).
○ Can you speak German?	• (No) I can't (speak German).

E3.16.3 Construct and perform similar answers, positive and negative, to the following questions.

Have you taken your medicine?
Are you going to answer those e-mails?
Do you know how to cook steak?
Are you trying your best?
Did you hear what I said?

E3.16.4 Pair-work practice: minimal response, encouraging further conversation (see 2.15).

○ She 'told me she \liked me.	• /Did she?
○ It was 'awfully ˅boring.	• /Was it?
○ They can 'have \my suitcase.	• /Can they?
○ It'll be 'ready to˅morrow.	• /Will it?
○ I 'can't stand ˅prawns.	• /Can't you?

E3.16.5 Pair-work practice: short response, surprised or sceptical, perhaps hostile (see 2.15).

○ \Jason was to blame.	• \Was he?
○ 'Jack's not \free.	• \Isn't he?
○ They're 'not \speaking to one another.	• \Aren't they?
○ I 'don't believe it's ˅true.	• \Don't you?
○ I'll 'bring it with me to\morrow.	• \Will you?

E3.16.6 Make your own short response. Decide whether to be encouraging (rise) or hostile (fall).

○ It's 'terribly un˅comfortable.	• . . . ?
○ She's for'gotten her um\brella.	• . . . ?
○ I 'won't be \here | to/morrow.	• . . . ?
○ It's 'quite in\credible.	• . . . ?
○ ˅Mary's | 'feeling rather \ill.	• . . . ?

E3.16.7 Performance practice: tag questions with a falling tone. You are not asking a real question (see 2.14).

It's \quiet | in /here,| \isn't it?
'Linda looks \beautiful,| \doesn't she?
The 'room's been nicely \decorated,| \hasn't it?
There are 'quite a lot \left,| \aren't there?
The 'onions look bit \tired,| \don't they?

We 'can't allow ∨cheating,| \can we?
She 'hasn't done very ∨well,| \has she?
I'm 'not going to be able to \finish on time,| \am I?
Tom's 'not very ∨satisfied,| \is he?
They 'didn't re∨member,| \did they?

E3.16.8 Supply your own tag question. Remember to change the polarity from positive to negative or from negative to positive. Use a falling tone on the tag.

It's a beautiful day,| . . .?
The play was marvellous,| . . .?
Brighton was rather a disappointment,| . . . ?
The train was awfully hot,| . . . ?
There's a lot of work to do,| . . . ?

The food's not bad,| . . . ?
He just doesn't bother,| . . . ?
We haven't heard from them for ages,| . . . ?
You haven't got any paper,| . . . ?
I'm not going to doubt your word,| . . . ?

E3.16.9 Locate the nuclei in this dialogue, and suggest suitable tones.

A: I've just bought some new shoes.
B: Have you?
A: Yes, and Anna says she thinks they're very smart.
B: Oh does she?
A: Look, I'm wearing them now. What do you think?
B: I don't think I'd have chosen them myself.
A: Oh wouldn't you?
B: Sorry, no.

E3.16.10 Devise a suitable context in which each of the following might be said.

Model:
(i) I \do.   (ii) ∨I do.   (iii) \I do.

(i) ∘ Do you /smoke?   • I \do.
(ii) ∘ 'I don't like \bacon.   • ∨I do.
(iii) ∘ 'Who likes \spinach?   • \I do.

1	(i) I \am.	(ii) vI am.	(iii) \I am.
2	(i) vWe have.	(ii) We \have.	(iii) \We have.
3	(i) You \did.	(ii) \You did.	(iii) vYou did.
4	(i) \She can.	(ii) vShe can.	(iii) She \can.
5	(i) I \will.	(ii) vI will.	(iii) \I will.

3.17 Prepositions

We have seen that prepositions are usually not accented unless they are brought into contrastive focus. However, there are two circumstances where in broad focus the nucleus is located on a preposition. Both involve wh questions in which there is no lexical material (= content words).

The first is when the preposition (the stranded remnant of a prepositional phrase) functions as the complement of *to be*:

> Look at this button. | 'What's it 'for?
> That's Mary. | 'Who's she 'with?

There is a difference between these examples and the corresponding sentences containing a lexical subject rather than a pronoun. If there is lexical material, the default is for the nucleus to be located on the last lexical item, following the usual rule:

> 'What's that 'button for?
> 'Who's 'Mary with?

The second involves a preposition immediately following a wh word:

> I've scored sixty.   • 'What 'of it?
> You know my essay?   • 'Yes, | 'what a'bout it?

Compare, with lexical material:

> You know my essay?   • 'What d'you want to 'say about it?

EXERCISES

E3.17.1 Locate the nucleus: on lexical material if there is any, otherwise on the preposition.

> *Models:*   'What's it 'for?   *but*   'What's that 'button for?

> What's this knob for?
> What's the lecture on?
> Who's your friend with?

Who's she with?
What's it about?

What's your book about?
(*in a library*) What'll it be under?
What was it for?
Who's Barbara with?
What was all the fuss about?

3.18   Wh + *to be*

A sentence such as *How are you?* consists of function words only. There are no lexical items. Yet the nucleus must go somewhere. So where does it go?

If a direct or indirect wh question has the pattern wh word – *be* – pronoun, then the nucleus goes on the verb *to be* itself. This need not involve narrow or contrastive focus of any kind.

(*greeting someone*)	'How 'are you?
	'Tell me how you 'are.
(*being shown something*)	'What 'is it?
	'Tell me what it 'is.
(*hearing someone at the door*)	'Who 'is it?
	I 'wonder who it 'is.

'How would it 'be | if we 'met for 'lunch?
That 'man over there, | 'who 'is he?
'When 'was it | that you 'came back from 'Canada?

If a speaker answers the question *How are you?* by repeating the same words back, there is normally a change of tonicity. The answer has contrastive focus on *you*:

🎧   'How 'are you?   • 'Fine thanks. ‖ 'How are 'you?
🎧   'Mr 'Smith! | 'How 'are you?   • I'm 'fine Miss Jones. ‖ And 'you?

If the verb *to be* consists of more than one word (e.g. *has been*, *will be*), the nucleus goes on the second of them:

'Welcome 'back! | 'How's it 'been?
Waiter: 'What'll it 'be?
🎧   We're 'going to get 'married.   • 'When's it to 'be?

The same applies in the corresponding indirect questions:

I 'asked her how she 'was.
They 'told us who they 'were.

🎧   (*talking about a forthcoming event*)   I 'wondered when it would '<u>be</u>.
🎧   (*talking about a mysterious noise*)   'What do you think it '<u>was</u>?

'This '<u>wedd</u>ing – | 'when do you think it will '<u>be</u>?

If the word following *be* in a wh question of this type is a demonstrative rather than a pronoun, then the nucleus tends to go on the demonstrative. This applies whenever the demonstrative throws focus onto something (treated as) new:

🎧   (*hearing someone at the door*)   'Who's '<u>that</u>?
              (*picking up an unknown object*)   'What's '<u>this</u>?
              She 'comes from Penmaen'mawr.   • 'Where's '<u>that</u>?

Alternatively, a demonstrative can be used like a pronoun, referring to something already given. In that case, the nucleus reverts to the verb:

🎧   (*knocking at the door continues*)   'Who '<u>is</u> that?

Conversely, a pronoun can be used like a demonstrative, focused and referring to someone new:

              (*pointing surreptitiously at a stranger*)   'Who's '<u>she</u>?

Again, note the difference between these examples and the corresponding sentences containing lexical material instead of pronouns. Here the nucleus follows the usual rule of being located on the last lexical item.

              When '<u>was</u> it | that you came back from Canada? *but*
              Which '<u>day</u> was it | that you came back from Canada?
              'How '<u>are</u> you?   *but*   'How '<u>old</u> are you?

There are other cases involving accenting of the verb *to be* in which the tonicity is not easily explained. They can be considered **intonational idioms**.

🎧   The 'trouble ('problem, 'thing, 'difficulty, 'snag) '<u>is</u> | that we're broke.

Here you are!

The usual pattern when you hand or show something to someone is:

'Here you /<u>are</u>.

o Would you 'pass me the /<u>milk</u> please?	• 'Here you /<u>are</u>.
o 'Could I see my ac/<u>count</u> please?	• Of \<u>course</u> sir.	'Here you /<u>are</u>.
o I'd like a 'pound of \<u>apples</u> please.	• 'Here you /<u>are</u> sir.
o I 'want a \<u>taxi</u>.	• 'Here you /<u>are</u> madam.	There's 'one \<u>waiting</u>.
o We 'need a new \<u>sofa</u>.	• 'Here you /<u>are</u>.	There's 'one advertised in this \<u>paper</u>.

When at last you see something you have been looking for or waiting for you can say:

'Here it /<u>is</u>.

or, more emphatically:

> \Here | it /is.

This pattern can also be used with *There . . .* and with other pronouns:

> 'Where's my \book? || Oh \here | it /is.
> I 'can't find my \keys. || Oh \there | they /are! || 'On the \table.

With a falling tone, the speaker is announcing something new:

> Now 'here he \is, || the 'one and /only | 'Mister \Magic!

EXERCISES

E3.18.1 Pair-work practice.

o Oh Mr vSmith?	• /Yes,	what \is it?
o Hul\lo,	/George!	• \Hi Peter.	How \are you?
o 'Could you pass me the /stapler?	• Er . . . 'where /is it?
o I 'went to see \Mary	in \hospital.	• And 'how /is she?
o 'That was \Gwen	on the /phone.	• Did she 'say where she /was?
o I've 'just come back from the \gig.	• 'How \was it?
o 'Bring me the \keys.	• 'Where \are they?
o There's 'someone on the \phone.	• 'Who \is it?
o Can I 'go to the /concert?	• 'When \is it?
o There's 'someone at the \door!	• 'See who it \is.

E3.18.2 Locate the nucleus on a form of the verb *to be*.

Model: 'How 'are you?

Tell me how you are.
Ask her how she is.
I wonder who they are.
Who do you think it was?
This party – | when do you think it'll be?

E3.18.3 Practise these short dialogues, being careful about nucleus placement.

A: Hul\lo, Mr Robinson. | 'How /are you?
B: \Fine, thanks,| Mrs /Davies. | 'How are \you?
A: I'm 'very \well.

C: There's 'someone at the \door. | 'Find out who it /is, would you, please?
D: It's a de\livery man.
C: \Oh, | vthat's all right. | I \wondered | who it /was.

D: He's 'brought a \parcel.
C: 'How ex\citing! | 'I wonder what it'll \be.

3.19   Other function words that attract the nucleus

There are a few words that regularly attract the nucleus despite being function words: notably *too* and *anyhow* and their synonyms.

When used in the meaning 'also', *too* is usually accented. In this meaning it often comes at the end of a sentence or clause, and thus attracts the nucleus. Sometimes it is attached to the same IP as the preceding words, but sometimes it has its own IP:

Mary wants some ice cream, | and 'Peter wants some, 'too. *or*
Mary wants some ice cream, | and 'Peter wants some, | 'too.

I'm going to the library.   • Oh, 'I'll come, 'too.
                      or • Oh 'I'll come, | 'too.

Exactly the same rules apply to its synonym *as well* (and the non-standard variant *an' all*), and to the negative equivalent *either*:

We're 'going to the \beach.| 'Why don't \you come along | as \well?
(*or, non-standard*) . . . | 'Why don't \you come along | an' \all?
I 'don't like vJim, | and I 'don't like \Tammy, | \either.
'Could you give /me some please, | as /well?
I 'can't vsing very well.   • \I can't, | \either.   (= Nor can I.)

The *too* refers to the accented item that immediately precedes it:

'I'm singing, | 'too. (= not only are other people singing, but so am I.)
I'm 'singing, | 'too. (= I am not only doing something else, but also singing.)

(i)   'Mary's going to invite Peter, | 'too. (narrow focus on *Mary*: not only will someone else invite him, but so will Mary)
(ii)   'Mary's going to in'vite Peter, | 'too. (narrow focus on *invite*: not only will she do something else to him, but she will also invite him)
(iii)   'Mary's going to invite 'Peter, | 'too. (narrow focus on *Peter*: not only will she invite someone else, but also Peter; or broad focus: not only will something else happen, but also Mary will invite Peter)

The sentence adverb *anyway* and its synonym *anyhow* are almost always nuclear. They are said with a reinforcing fall (see 2.23):

This i'dea may not vwork, | but let's 'try it \anyway.
or: . . . but let's \try it, | \anyway.

She 'doesn't ˇsmoke – | 'not ˇnowadays, | \anyhow.
\Anyhow, | I've 'got to be \going | /now.
\Anyway, | 'why were you looking at my \letters?

EXERCISES

E3.19.1 Pair work: vary the response sentences as in the model.

> *Model:*
> ○ 'Mum's very \worried about her.
>   - \Dad is, | \too.
>   - \Dad's worried, | \too
>   - \Dad's worried about her, | \too.
>   - 'So's \Dad.
>   - 'Dad is \too.

○ \Gavin's | going to the /party.   • \Rachel is, | \too.
○ ˇIngrid's | fond of \pizza.   • The \children are, | \too.
○ I 'managed to \finish the essay.   • \I did, | as \well.
○ ˇPeter hasn't called.   • Ni\cole hasn't, | \either.
○ I 'don't think ˇDebbie will agree.   • \Jake's not going to, | \either.

E3.19.2 Contextualize each of these.

> *Model:*
> 'We're taking umbrellas, | 'too.   (=we're not the only ones)
> We're taking um'brellas, | 'too.   (=not just coats)

I 'feel dreadful, | 'too.
I feel 'dreadful, | 'too.
'I feel dreadful, | 'too.

You 'ought to 'type the letters, | 'too.
'You ought to type the letters, | 'too.
You 'ought to type the letters, | 'too.
You 'ought to type the 'letters, | 'too.

'We play football, | as 'well.
We 'play football, | as 'well.
We play 'football, | as 'well.

I 'haven't seen 'Chloë, | 'either.
I 'haven't 'seen Chloë, | 'either.
'I haven't seen Chloë, | 'either.

'We're not going to pay you, | 'either.
We're not 'going to pay you, | 'either.
We're 'not going to 'pay you, | 'either.
We're 'not going to pay 'you, | 'either.

FINAL, BUT NOT NUCLEAR

3.20 Empty words and pro-forms

There are various categories of word and phrase that tend not to receive the nucleus, even though they may be the last lexical item in an IP.

Some nouns, for example, have a very little meaning of their own: particularly vague general nouns such as *things*, *people*. Such **empty words** are usually not accented.

I 'keep 'seeing things.
'What are you going to 'tell people?
They're 'really 'going places.

(With these, compare:

I 'keep hal'lucinating.
'What are you going to 'say?
They're 'really suc'cessful.)

Sometimes expressions such as *the man*, *that woman*, etc. mean little more than *he*, *she*. Like pronouns, therefore, they are not accented when used in this way:

'Have a 'word with the guy. (= 'Have a 'word with him.)
I 'can't 'stand that woman. (= I 'can't 'stand her.)

There are several idiomatic expressions in which *some* is accented (often bearing a fall–rise nuclear tone), while the following noun is not. (The same pattern is lexicalized in the word '*sometimes* and various other words beginning *some-*.)

For vsome reason, | I keep forgetting to do it.
In vsome cases | the answer is obvious.
vSome days | I feel very depressed.

This represents a kind of fossilized implication, namely a contrast with *other* reasons, cases, days, times, etc.

Numerals (*one*, *two*, *three*...) tend to be accented, since they have considerable semantic content. However, when *one* is used as a pronoun – a pro-form, a kind of function word – it is not accented and so does not take the nucleus:

'Can I borrow your 'ruler? | 'I haven't 'got one.

With a plural or a mass noun, the pro-form corresponding to *one* is *some* or *any*. When used in this way, *some* and *any* are not accented:

'Could I borrow some 'sugar? | 'I haven't 'got any.
We 'need some 'cards. | 'Can you 'see any?
I've got 'lots of 'milk left – | 'would you 'like some?

Other words are sometimes used as virtual pro-forms, more or less synonymously with *one*, *some* or *any*. They too do not get accented.

> ᴠThat looks like a nice wine. | I'll \buy a bottle.   (= I'll \buy some.)

When *one* is used after an adjective, it is not accented.

> I'll 'take 'this one.
> ᴖ   The 'train was 'crowded, | so we 'caught a 'later one.
> Would you like a 'green one | or a 'red one?

Against this general principle, *one* is usually accented in the expressions *the one*, *the right|wrong|first|last|only one*, *which one*:

> (*seeing an empty box of chocolates*) You took the 'last 'one!
> (*to someone who has just picked up a key*) Have you 'got the right 'one?

The word *so* is normally not accented when it is used as a pro-form (to refer back to an idea, situation etc. that has just been mentioned):

> ᴖ   If you're 'feeling un'well, | just 'say so.
> The 'band is 'popular, | and 'likely to become 'more so.
> Is he 'still going to 'college?   • I 'think so.

As we saw above, when a form of *do* is used as a pro-form (= as a substitute for another verb), it is not accented:

> 'Martin got better marks than 'Wayne did.
> 'Peter smokes, | and his 'sister does, | 'too.
> 'Will you go to 'Brighton tomorrow?   • I 'may do.

Likewise, *there* is usually not accented when used as a pro-form.

> 'China? | I've 'always wanted to 'go there.

EXERCISES

E3.20.1 Pair-work practice.

o 'What d'you think of \Maggie?	• 'Can't \stand the woman.
o 'How do you rate \George?	• I 'quite \like the chap.
o We're 'so excited about our enᴠgagement.	• 'When are you going to \tell people about it?
o Have you 'fixed the /date yet?	• We've got to 'take our time and \plan things.
o 'Will you be inviting /Steve?	• \No,	I 'can't a\bide the man.

E3.20.2 Locate the nucleus.

| *Model:* | I just 'don't under'stand people. |

Where's that handle thing?
The Government | has a duty to protect people.
If the salesman hasn't told you the answer, | go and ask the guy.
This is where we keep our pens and things.
I think I must be seeing things. | I could have sworn that was Martin.

Among other things | it meant we were late.
You mustn't annoy people.
Would you like to come back to my place?
I've got something to say to you guys.
Rather than issue orders, | it's better to try and persuade people.

E3.20.3 Pair-work practice.

o 'Have you got a /notebook?　　　• \No, | I'll 'have to \buy one.
o 'Where's your \passport?　　　　• 'I haven't \got one.
o 'Is there a /key on the table?　　• I 'can't ⌄see one.
o Have we 'got any /sugar?　　　　• \No, | I'll 'go and \buy some.
o 'Care for some /coffee?　　　　　• I've al'ready \had some, | /thanks.

o 'Is there some /milk there?　　　• I 'can't ⌄see any.
o We'll 'need some ⌄tools.　　　　• I'll 'get Adrian to \lend us some.
o Have you 'got a large /screwdriver? • No but I'll 'tell you if I \need one.
o Is there 'any /tea there?　　　　　• No but I'm 'just going to \make some.
o Have we 'got any /apples?　　　　• I 'can't ⌄see any.

E3.20.4 Locate the nucleus.

| *Models:* | Can I 'borrow your 'ruler? | 'I haven't 'got one. |
| | 'Mine's a 'large one. |

You know those funny Renault cars? | I've just seen one.
I've been saving up for a laptop, | and now at last I can buy one.
I was planning to use new ones, | but I can't find any.
I can't give Jimmy any money, | because I haven't got any.
We've got plenty of paper. | D'you need some?

Have they got an old one?
Would you like a blue one | or a green one?
I've got large ones and small ones.
This is a story for the little ones.
That's an awfully old-fashioned one.

E3.20.5 Pair-work practice.

○ Is she 'satisfied with the /outcome?   • I vthink so.
○ 'Will they be back /later?   • I exvpect so.
○ I've been 'ready for \ages.   • 'Why didn't you \say so?
○ Is 'Jeremy going to get the /job?   • I 'don't vthink so.
○ Are they /happy together?   • I 'do vhope so.

3.21   Vocatives

Vocatives – calling the name of the person or persons you are talking to – stand outside the grammatical structure of a sentence. Are they accented or not? This depends partly on where they stand. A vocative at the beginning of an utterance is accented, and normally has its own IP, thus becoming nuclear:

\Humphrey! | 'Lovely to \see you again.
Luvcille, | 'are you going to be a/vailable?

We also accent a vocative when we want to indicate who we are talking to, perhaps when there are other people within earshot:

'Hi, \Peter!
\Morning, | Mrs /Robinson!

But usually it is already clear who we are talking to. Perhaps we are looking at them, holding eye contact with them. Perhaps there is no one else present. Then a **final vocative** is usually not accented but attached to the preceding IP as (part of) the tail:

'Nice to \see you again, Humphrey.
'Are you going to be a/vailable, Lucille?
\Hi, Peter!
\Morning, Mrs Robinson.

\Yes, dear. | I'll do it 'right a\way, dear.
/Chocolate, anyone?
'Here's my \essay, Dr Smith.

Even if a final vocative appears to include new information directed towards the known addressee, it remains unaccented. (Or it may be uttered as a separate IP in low key; see 5.16.)

I 'love you, my little dimpled one.
You've 'missed it, you fool.
'Stop, you blithering idiot!

EXERCISES

E3.21.1 Locate the nucleus. Make sure the vocative is in the tail.

Model: Good 'morn<u>ing</u>, John.

Yes, dear.
Certainly, my sweet.
Of course, darling.
Hullo, boys.
Good evening, doctor.

Morning, everyone.
Is this your pullover, Jim?
Where's your handbag, Mary?
You've got it wrong, you fool.
Have you brought an umbrella, Mike?

E3.21.2 Pair or group work. Practise the following first without and then with a final vocative. (Use the name of the person you are talking to.)

Hul\<u>lo</u>.
'This is my \<u>father</u>.
That was 'quite an ex\<u>per</u>ience, | \wasn't it?
'What would you like to do \<u>next</u>?
I 'think there's one more muffin \<u>left</u>.

I 'like your v<u>shirt</u>.
I 'don't think we're v<u>read</u>y yet.
It 'isn't very v<u>nice</u>, you know.
We were 'pretty surv<u>prised</u>.
We 'don't need v<u>all</u> of them.

'Have you seen my /<u>news</u>paper?
'Did you know /<u>I</u> would be here?
Have you 'ever been to Jo/<u>hannes</u>burg?
Would you 'like some more /<u>rum</u>?
Are you 'going to come here a/<u>gain</u>, do you think?

E3.21.3 Pair work. Replace xxx and yyy by the name of the person you are speaking to.

o Do you 'come here /<u>often</u>, xxx?
o 'Where do you \<u>come</u> from, then, xxx?
o 'Have you been here /<u>long</u>, xxx?
o 'How long do you plan to \<u>stay</u>, xxx?
o 'When are you going to come and visit \<u>me</u>, xxx?

• 'Nearly every \<u>day</u>, yyy.
• \<u>Edin</u>burgh, | /<u>act</u>ually, yyy.
• 'Only a few v<u>min</u>utes, yyy.
• 'Two \<u>weeks</u>, | I /<u>hope</u>, yyy.
• 'All in good \<u>time</u>, yyy.

3.22   Reporting clauses

When reporting clauses (= words such as *he said*, *she asked*) follow quoted words, they are usually out of focus. The nucleus goes on the appropriate item among the quoted words, and the reporting clause forms a tail to the IP:

> ''How are you 'doing?' he asked.
> 'I 'don't be'lieve it,' she explained.

There is often a rhythmic break between the quoted words and the reporting clause, as shown by the mark ¦:

> 'How are you 'doing?' ¦ he asked.
> 'I'm 'fine,' ¦ she replied.

This means that reporting clauses present a certain problem of analysis. Do we have two IPs in each of these examples, or just one? Rhythmically, the reporting clause may indeed be separated from the preceding reported matter, so that it seems to be like a separate IP. But tonally it is part of the same IP: in its pitch pattern it is indeed like a tail. So if we were to treat a reporting clause as a separate IP, we would have to say that the IP was anomalous in having no nuclear tone.

The problem is shown by the following potentially minimal pair. There may be a clear rhythmic difference between (i) and (ii):

🎧   (i) ''Where are you 'from, Bill?' asked Jim.
🎧   (ii) ''Where are you 'from?' Bill asked Jim.

The rhythmic difference may involve a stress (beat) on *Bill* when it is the subject of the reporting clause, but not when it is a vocative. There is also a break in the rhythm at the boundary point, shown below. There may also be a silent beat (°) at this point, in addition to the usual expected rhythmic beats on lexically stressed syllables (shown by ' and °):

(i)   ''Where are you 'from, Bill?' °¦ asked °Jim.
(ii)   ''Where are you 'from?' ¦ °Bill asked °Jim.

The material after (¦) is intonationally tail-like: low level after a nuclear fall on *from*, or continuing the rise after a nuclear rise or fall–rise on *from*.

Longer reporting clauses may need to be broken up into more than one IP. Any additional nuclei copy the same nuclear tone as the tone on the quoted material, but usually in low key (See 5.16).

> 'She's \crazy,' Peter insisted, | ↓ with a 'bitter \sound to his voice.
🎧   'Are you /sure?' she asked, | ↓ 'looking at him /strangely.

Exceptionally, where a reporting clause is immediately followed by further material, it may have its own IP, usually with a rise to indicate non-finality:

'What a 'great i\dea,' | said /Billy, | and 'jumped out of the \car.
''What can we do to\day?' | he /asked, | but there was 'no re\ply.

– though alternatively these reporting clauses could follow the usual pattern:

'What a 'great i\dea,' said Billy, | and 'jumped out of the \car.
''What can we do to\day?' he asked, | but there was 'no re\ply.

For reporting clauses that precede the quoted words, see 5.13.

EXERCISES

E3.22.1 Performance practice.

'I 'wonder where he \is,' ¦ she said.
''Have you got any /money?' ¦ she asked.
'It's 'awfully vdark,' ¦ she complained.
'I'm \sixty, | /actually,' ¦ he admitted.
'Vengeance is \mine, ¦ saith the Lord.

E3.22.1 Locate the nucleus. Make sure the reporting clause is in the tail.

> *Model:* ''What's the 'matter?' ¦ he enquired.

'What does she want?' he asked.
'We'll just have to try our best,' said Mary.
'It's up to the manager,' declared the secretary.
'Who are you?' asked Alice.
'The future lies before us,' he said sententiously.

'I wonder who that is,' he said, | hearing the doorbell.‖ 'I expect it's the postman,' said Mary. |
'Why don't you answer it? | Perhaps he's got a parcel.' ‖ He opened the door. ‖ 'Mr Silcott?' |
said a gruff voice. | 'I've got a delivery for you. | Sign here, please.' ‖ James did so. | It was
indeed a parcel. ‖ 'What is it?' called Mary.

3.23 Adverbs of time and place

Although adverbs in general are usually accented, adverbs and adverbial phrases of **time** and **place** are often not accented (= unfocused) when at the
end of an IP, even if they contain new information. They therefore form part of
the tail:

I had an 'unexpected 'letter yesterday.
She's 'coming to 'dinner tomorrow.
The 'trade balance was in the 'red last month.
Does a 'Mr 'Pomfrey live here?

🎧   'Did you see Big 'Brother on television last night?
            He's 'got a tat'too on his arm.
            There's a 'fly in my soup.[7]

This does not apply in sentences where the sense of the verb would be incomplete without the final adverbial. Such adverbials are typically in focus, and therefore bear the nucleus:

            'Put it on the 'table.
            'Write the details in the 'book.

Alternatively, in statements, final adverbs and adverbials of time and place may bear the nucleus in a separate IP, typically making with the preceding IP a fall-plus-rise pattern (see 2.24):

🎧   I had an 'unexpected \letter | /yesterday.
            She's 'coming to \dinner | to/morrow.
            The 'trade balance was in the \red | /last month.
            I 'went to \London | on /Sunday.[8]

Naturally, there are also many cases in which final adverbs and adverbial phrases of time and place are important to the message, and are therefore brought into focus and receive a nuclear accent:

            He's got a tat'too on his 'arm (| 'not his 'leg).
            'O/K, | 'that's a∨greed: | we'll 'come round to\morrow.

EXERCISES

E3.23.1 Pair-work practice.

o 'Why are you ex\cited?	• I'm 'seeing \Tom today.
🎧 o 'Why are you looking \worried?	• I've 'got an e\xam this afternoon.
🎧 o 'Everything O/K?	• It's a 'bit \hot in here.
o 'What have you got to \tell me?	• Well I 'spoke to Mrs ∨Jones yesterday	and she's 'worried about \Hugo.
o Shall we /go?	• No I'm 'not \ready yet.
o 'What's the \matter?	• I've 'got a bit of \grit in my eye.
	• 'Doreen's spilt some \wine on her dress.
	• There's a \man at the door.
	• I've found an \insect in my salad.
	• 'Billy's got \ink on his fingers.

E3.23.2 Locate the nucleus. (i) Treat the final adverb or adverbial as non-contrastive (out-of-focus), and therefore make it part of the tail. (ii) Alternatively, give the final adverb(ial) a separate IP. Practise saying the sentences aloud both ways.

🎧   *Model:*   We're 'going to \Brighton tomorrow.
              or   We're 'going to \Brighton | to/morrow.

I'm seeing Melissa this morning.
The trade balance improved last month.
I'm meeting Jack tonight.
It's a bit chilly in here.
I saw the doctor yesterday.

It's pretty wild out there.
They had lots of paintings in the house.
He's got a splinter in his thumb.
There's a flaw in your argument.
You must put a cedilla under the letter.

E3.23.3 Locate the nucleus. Place it on the final adverbial only if you think it should be the topic.

> *Model:*   'Are you going to 'Bright̲o̲n̲ tomorrow?

Going to the football on Saturday?
Are you watching television tonight?
Are there any decent pubs nearby?
Have you read the papers today?
Did you go to Jim's lecture yesterday?

Where are you planning to eat this evening?
What are your plans while you're here?
What are we doing tomorrow?
What are you going to put here?
Where can we eat today?

E3.23.4 Performance practice.

I'm 'going to take the \d̲o̲g̲ for a walk.
I 'need to \s̲p̲e̲a̲k̲ to you for a minute.
I'm 'going to let \y̲o̲u̲ do the cleaning for a change.
There's a 'funny \m̲a̲r̲k̲ on your back.
'Would you like some /m̲u̲s̲t̲a̲r̲d̲ with your ham?

3.24   Other unfocused adverbs and adverbials

In keeping with the general rule that the nucleus goes on the last in-focus lexical item, **descriptive** adverbs, i.e. adverbs of manner that modify the verb, do tend to bear the nucleus if they are at the end of the clause.

You've 'answered the questions very 'w̲e̲l̲l̲!
She ex'pressed her views 'h̲o̲n̲e̲s̲t̲l̲y̲.
He per'formed 'b̲r̲i̲l̲l̲i̲a̲n̲t̲l̲y̲.

> You should ap'proach 'cautiously.
> She 'walks with a noticeable 'limp.

However, there are several types of adverbs and adverbial phrases that – contrary to the general rule – do not get accented when at the end of a clause. They remain out of focus. Like adverbs of place or manner, they go in the tail, with the nucleus on some earlier word.

We will divide them into two lists. Those in the first list are straightforward:

then (inferential, meaning 'in that case', not 'at that time')
though
or so, even
sort of (thing), as it were
a bit
you know

> We'll 'see you on 'Tuesday, then.
> 🎧 He had a 'heart attack last year. ‖ It 'hasn't stopped him 'smoking, though.
> The 'bride looked 'beautiful – | 'radiant, even.
> We could 'just 'stay here | and 'pass the 'time, sort of thing.
> 🎧 You've 'got to slow 'down a bit.
> Her 'health's pretty 'poor, you know.

Those in the second list (following) tend to behave in the same way, although alternatively they can be accented, taking the nucleus in their own IP (usually a rise):

if necessary, of course
please, thanks, thank you
in a way
or thereabouts
for a change, for . . .'s sake
in fact, as a matter of fact
I would/should have thought, I imagine
enough

> She was 'rather an'noyed, in fact. *or*
> She was 'rather an'noyed, | in 'fact.
> 🎧 I'd like 'four 'tickets, please.
> 'How about dinner at 'home for a change?
> 🎧 He'll be 'off soon, I imagine.

The adverb *enough* is usually unaccented when it follows an adjective. As an adjective or noun, though, it attracts the nucleus in the usual way:

> 'These shoes are not 'big enough.
> 🎧 It's 'just not 'good enough.
> You 'haven't promised e'nough.

In general, the adverb *indeed* is accented:

>'Thank you very much in'<u>deed</u>.

However there is one spoken idiom in which it is not accented, namely when it is used in a short response question with a fall, to show that you are surprised or annoyed by something someone has just told you:

>Quentin's won a prize.   • \<u>Has</u> he, indeed?

   The word *again*, when at the end of a clause, is usually accented if used in its basic sense of 'one more time', since in that sense it is often contrastive. However, it is not accented when it means 'back to a previous state', nor in other more or less idiomatic uses:

>'Could you say that a'<u>gain</u>?
>'This is how to '<u>close</u> it, | and 'this is how to '<u>open</u> it again.
>'What did you say your '<u>name</u> was again?

Et cetera and its synonyms (*and so on, and so forth, and whatnot, and stuff, and things, and the like, and such like*) are usually kept out of focus:

>They sell '<u>cards</u>,| '<u>cal</u>endars, etc.

EXERCISES

E3.24.1 Locate the nucleus. Relegate the unimportant words at the end to the tail.

> *Model:*   I 'wouldn't go my'<u>self</u> of course.

He's quite clever, you know.
Do you find intonation a problem, then?
We could just chat, sort of thing.
The outcome was antithetical, as it were.
His death must have been a big shock, though.

It must be twenty miles or so.
Isn't it rather dangerous, though?
We have to leave in five minutes or so.
Good, | that's settled then.
I'd say it was pretty bad – | disastrous, even.

E3.24.2 Pair-work practice.

o So you \<u>finished</u>!   • It was 'disap\/<u>point</u>ing, though.
o 'Why are you \<u>bleeding</u>?   • Well I \<u>stumbled</u>, sort of.

o ∨Jocelyn's not looking well.
o He ＼hit me!
o 'How many people turned ＼up?

• She's had a 'hard ＼time, you know.
• 'Hit him ＼back, then.
• ＼Oh, | ⁄fifty or so.

E3.24.3 In the following, the final phrase may either form part of the tail or be given its own IP.

> *Model:*   It's 'pretty ＼dangerous, I should imagine.
> *or*   It's 'pretty ＼dangerous, | I should i⁄magine.

We can connect in Newark if necessary.
It was pretty upsetting, of course.
That was rather worrying, I should have thought.
She's Portuguese, I imagine.
Bring the cheese rolls, please.

I can do without your help, thank you.
They thought it was a triceratops, | but it was a brontosaurus, in fact.
Let's go to Worthing for a change.
She can't stand him, as a matter of fact.
I want to rest for a bit.

E3.24.4 Performance practice.

'Could I have some ⁄more, please?
It was 'pretty up∨setting, of course.
'Why ＼not, for goodness' sake?
'What's the ＼point, I'd like to know.
Is ⁄Mary at home, by any chance?

We 'finished quite ＼early in fact.
It's ＼obvious, I would have thought.
I'm 'OK on my ＼own, thank you.
'Try to re＼lax a bit.
It 'needs re＼newing, of course.

E3.24.5 Pair-work practice.

o 'What were the ＼essays like?
o Do you re⁄member it?
o These are 'very important i＼deas.
o 'Why would Bill have left so ＼suddenly?
o He 'said he was too ＼busy.

• ∨Most | were 'very good in＼deed.
• 'Very clearly in＼deed.
• They 'are in＼deed.
• 'Why in＼deed?
• ＼Did he, indeed?

E3.24.6 Some of the following are likely to have the nucleus on *again*, some are not. Which are which?

He's away at present. | Could you try again, | next week?
I had to do my essay | all over again.
She nursed him back to health again.

It's great to have you home again.
I've told you again and again, | don't do that!

E3.24.7 Locate the nucleus. Make sure final *et cetera* and its synonyms are out of focus.

> *Model:*   I'll 'buy some 'drinks et cetera.

There were a lot of pictures and posters and so on.
She had downloaded | a whole lot of clipart and stuff.
He had a collection of pressed flowers and whatnot.
They've found a stash of drugs and things.
You'll need screwdrivers and so forth.

PHRASAL VERBS

3.25   Verb plus adverbial particle

A **phrasal verb** consists of a verb plus a **particle**, which may be an adverb (*away*, *back*, *together*) or a preposition that can also function as an adverb (*by*, *down*, *on*, *up*). The general rule is that phrasal verbs are lexically **double-stressed**, with the primary stress going on the particle. Thus ˌstand 'up has the same stress pattern as ˌun'known or ˌquite 'good. If the nucleus comes on a phrasal verb, the word on which this nucleus is located is therefore typically the particle:

'How are you getting 'on?
The 'prisoner | 'broke 'down.
The 'next 'month | she 'passed a'way.
I'll 'get something to bring 'back with me.
'Let the children run a'bout a bit.
I'll 'leave you to carry 'on, then.

There are a few exceptions, such as 'pour down (= rain hard):

It was 'really 'pouring down.

EXERCISES

E3.25.1 Pair-work practice.

o Good \morning, Mr Morson.
o So 'what did the enemy /do?
o I 'don't \know | how much ˅wallpaper I need.
o I'm 'wearing too many \clothes.

• 'Come \in, | 'sit \down.
• They 'ran a\way.
• Well 'work it \out.
• 'Take some of them \off.

o 'Were you /<u>born</u> in Devon?

o Are we 'landing at /<u>Gatwick</u>?

o Can we 'stay a bit /<u>longer</u>?

o The com'puter screen's \<u>blank</u>.

o I've 'dropped my \<u>papers</u>.

o I'm \<u>going</u> | /<u>now</u>. | 'Good/<u>bye</u>!

• \<u>Yes</u>, | but I 'wasn't brought ᵥ<u>up</u> there.

• \<u>No</u>, | that's 'where we took \<u>off</u> from.

• \<u>No</u>, | it's 'time to drink \<u>up</u>.

• Well 'switch it \<u>on</u> then!

• 'Just pick them \<u>up</u> again.

• 'O/<u>K</u>, | 'look /<u>after</u> yourself.

E3.25.2 Locate the nucleus.

Model: They 'all ran a'<u>way</u>.

How long can they hold on?
When will we be coming back?
Stop pushing in, you oaf!
It's time to get up, you know.
The car was just pulling out.

The plane's | just taken off.
Put it down carefully, | or it might fall off.
The treasurer says | we've got to cut back.
She's very ill. | D'you think she's going to pull through?
So where do they expect the space shuttle to splash down, then?

3.26   Verb plus prepositional particle

A **prepositional verb** consists of a verb plus a particle which is clearly a preposition: for example, *look at, send for, rely on*. These are mostly lexically **single-stressed**, with the primary stress going on the verb. Thus '*look at* has the same stress pattern as '*edit* or '*borrow*. The second element, the preposition, being unstressed, does not get accented (unless for contrastive focus). If the nucleus comes on a prepositional verb, the word on which this nucleus is located is typically the verb itself.

Here are the photos.   • 'May I '<u>look</u> at them?

This happens particularly in certain constructions which leave the preposition stranded (= without any following noun phrase). Typical cases are passivization, relative clauses and wh questions. The preposition then goes in the tail, although phonetically it retains its strong form:

It 'needs to be thoroughly '<u>looked</u> at. (*passive*)
Are 'these the books I '<u>sent</u> for? (*relative*)
I 'haven't got anyone to '<u>go</u> with, though. (*relative*)
'Which of them can you really re'<u>ly</u> on? (*wh question*)

Again, there are a few exceptions. In particular, prepositions of more than one syllable tend to be stressed: ˌlook 'after is (for most speakers) double-stressed, and so is ˌdo with'out. So we say:

> Is there 'anyone you want me to look 'after?
> 'What can you do with'out?
> 'Guess who I bumped 'into the other day.

In any case, when there is contrastive focus, implicit or explicit, the nucleus can readily go on the preposition:

> We 'can't leave Mary be'hind. | 'Let's ask her to come 'with us.
> 'What shall I do with my um'brella?   • Oh 'bring it 'with you.

There are also phrasal verbs that include both an adverbial particle and a preposition, e.g. *go along with*, *look down on*. These are double-stressed, e.g. ˌgo a'long with. When one of these is the last lexical item in focus, the nucleus goes on the adverbial particle, as expected:

> 'That argument | is one I 'really can't go a'long with.
> She 'felt that her 'mother-in-law | 'always looked 'down on her.
> The 'maze | was 'quite difficult to get 'out of.
> 'HTM'L | is 'something I need to find 'out about.

EXERCISES

E3.26.1 For these questions, use the strong form of the final preposition (since it is 'stranded' without a following noun or pronoun).

> 'Who are you ⟍waiting for?
> 'Who was she ⟍talking to?
> 'Who can we ⟍count on?
> 'What does this ⟍call for?
> 'Where does she ⟍come from?

> 'What are you ⟍looking at?
> 'Who are you ⟍coming with?
> 'What did you ⟍ask for?
> 'What is it ⟍based on, then?
> 'Where are they ⟍travelling to?

E3.26.2 Repeat the questions in E3.26.1, but now answer them with a suitable sentence or phrase. In your answer the preposition (if present) should have its weak form (since it is no longer stranded).

| *Model:*   ∘ 'Who are you ⟍waiting for?   • I'm 'waiting for ⟍Stan. |
| • For ⟍Stan. |
| • ⟍Stan. |

E3.26.3 Pair-work practice.

🎧
- o Have you got the /butter?
- o Is 'that the /birthday cake?
- o 'Care for some /whisky?
- o 'What's a \guillotine?
- o I 'liked the intro∨duction.

- • ∨Yes, | but I 'need something to \put it in.
- • \Yes, | but I 'haven't got anything to \cut it with.
- • 'What have you got to \mix it with?
- • 'Something to cut \paper with.
- • \Yes, | it 'gave us something to \build on.

E3.26.4 Performance practice.

'Why are you \staring at him?
'When were you \talking to her?
'Could I have a /look at them?
'Are you going to /chat with them?
'When will you be \calling for them?

E3.26.5 Locate the nucleus in the middle IP.

Model: Good'bye, then. || I'll be 'waiting for you | next 'Thursday.

'There's 'Bill. || I've been talking to him | about his 'project.
'Thanks for the 'essay. || I'll look at it | to'morrow.
I've got 'dia'betes. || But I can live with it. | I 'have to.
There's 'plenty of 'money in the account. || You can draw on it | as you 'need.
I'll 'use the 'minibar, | and sign for things | as I 'take them.

E3.26.6 Locate the nucleus. These phrasal verbs include both an adverb and a preposition.

Model: He 'always looked 'down on her.

How long are you going to be away for?
Stop dithering, | and get on with it!
Is Michael someone you look up to?
I don't think I can go through with it, | after all.
Don't let her get away with it!

3.27   Adverb or preposition?

Whereas adverbs and adverbial particles are usually accented (with the exceptions discussed in 3.23–4), prepositions and prepositional particles are not. English has several words that can function both as prepositions and as adverbs, for example *in, on, by*. The EFL learner may face uncertainty over whether or not they are to be accented.

As you might expect, they are typically accented when used as adverbs but not when used as prepositions. If they are at the end of the clause, adverbs attract the nucleus but prepositions repel it.

Adverbial particle:

> A 'workman was walking 'by.
> They in'tend to carry 'on.
> The 'children were running a'bout.
> 'Granny felt rather left 'out.
> The 'plane was about to take 'off.

Preposition:

> I 'haven't got enough light to 'see by.
> He's someone I can 'always 'count on.
> 'What are you 'talking about?
> 'This matter | 'needs to be 'dealt with.

Note the contrast between double-stressed *ˌcarry 'on* and single-stressed *'count on*. In *carry on* the *on* is an adverb and can have no complement. In *count on (someone)* the *on* is a preposition and requires a complement (= object).

Compare the verbs *sit in* and *take in*, as in the examples *she sat in a comfortable chair* and *she took in the information*. There are various tests we can apply to make it clear that the first *in* is prepositional, the second adverbial. The constituents in the first example are *she sat* and *in a comfortable chair*, but those in the second are *she took in* and *the information*. Replacing the lexical noun phrase by a pronoun, we get *she sat in it* (not ×*she sat it in*) but *she took it in* (not ×*she took in it*). Lexically *sit in* is single-stressed, but *take in* is double-stressed. When in final position, the first does not attract the nucleus, but the second does:

> 'What did she 'sit in?
> 'How much did she take 'in?

It is best for the learner to learn each new phrasal verb with its appropriate lexical stress pattern. There are certain useful guidelines. Those phrasal verbs that need no following object are double-stressed: *come in, fall off, crop up*. If the particle can be moved to after the object (see 3.28), then again the phrasal verb is double-stressed: *take out, bring up, put back*.

As mentioned in 3.26, phrasal verbs that have two particles are double-stressed: *put up with, go along with*.

EXERCISES

E3.27.1 Pair-work practice.

- o You've left 'this line \blank.
- • Well 'those details weren't \asked for.
- o 'How do the de\liveries work?
- • I 'don't \know, | my/self. | You'll 'have to ask a\round.

○ So they're 'all in a bit of a \mess.
○ So 'who's \this?

○ 'Make a note of the ad\dress.

○ 'Victor's doing \better | than /you.

○ There 'used to be a \cherry | /here.

○ So 'how are we going to \tackle this project?
○ I 'wonder if I could have your sup\port.
○ I must go to the ∨bank | and 'get some \money.

• 'Josie's the one ∨I feel sorry for.
• Oh, 'this is \Norman. | I'd 'like you to keep an \eye on him.
• 'Could I have something to /write with, please?
• He's a'head at the ∨moment, | but I'm de'termined to catch ∨up.
• It was a \lovely tree. | 'Why was it chopped \down?
• We must 'work as a \team. | Let's 'all pull to\gether.
• 'Which scholarship are you ap\plying for?

• You'll 'have to de∨cide | 'which account to \draw on.

E3.27.2 Decide where the nucleus should go. These phrasal verbs (etc.) are of mixed types: consider each one carefully.

Models: 'Which dish shall we bring 'in ?
        but   'Which room can we 'wait in?

Tell me where you come from.
I need someone to go with.
What are you looking for?
They warned us to stand back.
Suddenly she drew back, | startled.

The cold water gets heated | as it's drawn off.
Who do you feel more sorry for, | Pat or Kim?
Beverley | is someone we've got to keep an eye on.
How long will you be away for?
It's a difficult problem to deal with.

E3.27.3 Explain the difference in the following. The context is foreign currencies and a bank account.

(i)   'What currency did you pay 'in?
(ii)   'What currency did you 'pay in?

3.28   Separated particles

There is one important case where (in neutral tonicity) the nucleus does *not* fall on the adverbial particle of a phrasal verb. This is when the particle has been separated from the verb (= 'extraposed', moved to a position after the object). When this happens, the **object** bears the nucleus if it is lexically filled (= if it is or contains a noun or other lexical material).

Rule: in the case of **a lexical object and a separated particle**, the nucleus goes by default on the object:

    🎧   'Take your 'shoes off.
                I 'want my 'money back.
                She 'got her 'handkerchief out.

However if the object is a **pronoun** (i.e. not lexical), the nucleus goes on the adverbial particle in the regular way:

    🎧   'Take them 'off.
                I 'want it 'back.
                'Did you get it 'out?

This also applies if the object is lexically filled but is already given, and therefore out of focus.

        (*to someone who has just heard a good joke*)   You ought to 'write these jokes 'down.

Some other constructions involving adverbs behave in a rather similar way. For example, the adverb may well *not* be accented after a lexically filled subject in sentences such as:

        Is the 'television on? (*or*   Is the 'television 'on?)
        'What's Peter's 'book about? (*or*   'What's Peter's book a'bout?)
        She's got a 'red 'dress on.

– but is inevitably accented after a pronoun:

        (*talking about the television*) 'Is it 'on?
        (*discussing a book*) 'What's it a'bout?

        Where's the dress? • She's 'got it 'on!

– which shows that *be on*, *be about*, *have (got) on* behave in this respect like phrasal verbs.

We see a similar pattern in certain combinations of verb and prepositional phrase:

    🎧   'Bring your um'brella with you.   but
    🎧   'Bring it 'with you. (*not*: ×'Bring it with you.)

Where there is contrastive focus, the separated particle can readily be accented even after a lexical object:

He 'took the plug 'out, | then 'put it back 'in again.
I said, 'turn the television 'off! | And 'leave it off.
(*police to gunman*) 'Put the gun 'down!

EXERCISES

E3.28.1 Pair-work practice.

○ I'm 'not going to ⟍stand for it. • 'Keep your ⟍voice down!
○ ⟋Yes sir? • 'Could you take these ⟋plates away?
○ 'What is there still to ⟍do? • We must 'take the ⟍books back.
○ 'What shall I do ⟍next? • Oh 'get your ⟍notebook out.
○ And ⟋then? • 'Write these ⟍words down.

○ 'What's the ⟍next stage? • We'd 'better draw some ⟍plans up.
○ It's 'rather ⌄gloomy in here. • Well 'switch the ⟍lights on.
○ ⟋Yes madam? • 'Bring the ⟍guests in, please.
○ 'What must I do ⟍next? • 'Take your ⟍hat off, | if you ⟋would.
○ 'How can I get it ⟍level? • 'Fill the ⟍holes in, | of ⟋course.

E3.28.2 Performance practice.

ᐰ   'Pick the ⟍boxes up. ‖ I ⌄said, | 'pick them ⟍up! ‖ 'Now put them ⟍down again.
'Put your ⟍toys away. | 'Put them a⟍way!
I 'wish they'd stop messing us a⌄round.
'O⟋K, | I 'made a mi⟍stake. | 'Don't rub it ⟍in!
'Next ⌄Friday | I'm 'going to take the ⟍boys out.

E3.28.3 Locate the nucleus.

Models: 'Take them 'off.
    but   'Take your 'shoes off.

Get your handkerchief out.
Pick your pencil up.
She wrote the details down.
It's time to take the plates away.
They brought the meeting forward.

Take it out.
Pick it up.
She wrote them down.
Take them away.
They brought it forward.

Would you fill the form in, please?
Will you put the chairs out?
You must write your report up.

> Don't forget to take the bottles back.
> We must keep the momentum up.
>
> I don't know how you put up with it.
> When do we have to hand our essays in?
> Which chair was she sitting in?
> At last the candidates were led in.
> I'm looking for a nice hill to run up.

E 3.28.4 Choose the appropriate intonation pattern for each response. Why is the other pattern implausible?

A: 'Why did you ring the \bell?   B: (i) Cos I'm \getting off at the next stop.
                                        (ii) Cos I'm 'getting \off at the next stop.

A: You 'saw a \coin on the ground. ‖   B: (i) I 'picked it \up.
   'What did you do \next?   (ii) I \picked it up.

A: 'Mary stood \up. ‖ 'What did   B: (i) I 'stood \up, | \too.
   \you do?   (ii) \I stood up, | \too.

A: Good\/bye.   B: (i) I'll 'soon be /back.
                                        (ii) I'll 'soon /be back.

A: He 'doesn't a\/gree with us.   B: (i) Oh he'll 'come /round.
                                        (ii) Oh he'll /come round.

NUCLEUS ON LAST NOUN

3.29   Final verbs and adjectives

The examples just given illustrate a more general tendency: we put the nucleus on a **noun** where possible, in preference to other word classes.

This is seen in various constructions which involve having a **verb** at the end of a sentence or clause. A final verb is usually deaccented, and the nucleus goes on a preceding noun:

'How's the 'homework going?
I've 'still got an 'essay to write.
'Which 'book did you choose?
We've 'got to get the 'car fixed.
I 'wonder where 'Mary went.
A'long the sides of the 'road | there were 'several 'cars parked.[9]

This applies in particular to final defining relative clauses:

Just 'look at the 'tie he's wearing!
'Where's that 'salad I was eating?
I 'don't like that 'cheese you've bought.[10]

In the following example, the nucleus is likely to be on *Helen* or *children* (nouns), depending on focus, but not on the verb *bringing*:

> D'you 'know how many '<u>chil</u>dren Helen's bringing?
> D'you 'know how many children '<u>Hel</u>en's bringing?
> × D'you 'know how many children Helen's '<u>bring</u>ing?

The same deaccenting applies to the final **adjective** in sentences such as:

> We're 'going to get the '<u>ta</u>ble ready.
> He 'ought to keep his '<u>mouth</u> shut.
> Is the '<u>win</u>dow open?
> You 'need to keep the '<u>brush</u> wet.[11]

and to the *up* in:

> I 'wonder what '<u>Elea</u>nor's up to.

Compare the following, where there is no preceding noun to attract the nucleus – so the nucleus goes on the last lexical item (the verb or adjective), as expected:

> Just 'look at what he's '<u>wear</u>ing!
> 'What did she '<u>say</u>?
> 'How's it '<u>go</u>ing?
> I've 'still got something to '<u>write</u>.
> 'What did you '<u>choose</u>?
> We've 'got to get it '<u>fixed</u>.

> He 'ought to keep it '<u>shut</u>.
> Is it '<u>o</u>pen?
> I 'wonder where she '<u>went</u>.
> We're 'going to get it '<u>rea</u>dy.
> You 'need to keep it '<u>wet</u>.
> I 'wonder what she's '<u>up</u> to.

In set (i) below, the NP is lexical, so the nuclear accent goes on the noun. In set (ii), the NP is a pronoun or empty word (see 3.20), so the nucleus goes on the verb:

> (i)   I've got some '<u>work</u> to do.

> We 'haven't '<u>fin</u>ished: | there's 'still some '<u>wash</u>ing to do.
> He's 'got some '<u>writ</u>ing to do.

> (ii)   'Tell me what to '<u>do</u>.

> I'm '<u>bu</u>sy: | I've 'got things to '<u>do</u>.
> 'Give him something to '<u>do</u>.

The constructions in question mostly involve a syntactic movement of some kind, taking a noun phrase (or other type of phrase) that would otherwise follow the verb and moving it to an earlier position. This leaves the verb at the end.

Several **idiomatic** or **fossilized** expressions have a fixed tonicity that can be explained by the tendency to place the nucleus on a noun rather than a verb.

> 'Onions make my 'eyes water. (= make me shed tears)
> You're 'going to get your 'fingers burnt. (= suffer unpleasant consequences)
> She's 'got a 'screw loose. (= is crazy)
> Let's 'wait for the 'dust to settle. (= till things calm down)
> 'Wait and see which way the 'wind is blowing. (= what's going to happen)

> She looked like 'something the 'cat had brought in. (= very untidy)
> 'Keep your 'fingers crossed! (= let's hope something good happens)
> We can 'go on 'asking | till the 'cows come home. (= for ever)
> It 'made my 'hair stand on end. (= frightened me)
> They 'got on like a 'house on fire. (= quickly established a good relationship)
> He'll 'have his 'work cut out! (= it will be difficult for him to do)

Further examples of idiomatic tonicity:

> 'What's 'that supposed to mean? (used when you are annoyed at what someone has just said)
> You can 'say 'that again! (= I completely agree with you)
> 'There's a good girl! 'There's a clever dog! etc. (to compliment a child or an animal)
> 'What 'of it? (= I don't care. It doesn't concern me.)
> to be 'at it (= be busy; be arguing; be having sex)
> 'throw a 'spanner in the works (= unexpectedly disrupt something)
> 'What's 'that when it's at home? (= what does that word mean?)

Note the difference in default accenting in pairs such as the following:

> (i) a 'wish to 'please (= a wish that we should please people)
> (ii) an 'audience to please (= an audience that we must please)

> (i) He has a 'duty to per'form. (= He must perform, that is his duty.)
> (ii) He has a 'duty to perform. (= He must perform a duty.)

> (i) She 'gave him directions to 'follow. (= She said he must follow her.)
> (ii) She 'gave him di'rections to follow. (= He had to follow her directions.)[12]

EXERCISES

E3.29.1 Locate the nucleus on the last noun rather than on the verb that follows it.

> *Model:*   'Look at what she's 'wearing!
>   *but*   'Look at the 'shoes she's wearing!

Did you hear the lecture he gave?
What about the book you were writing?

I wonder how the project's going.
I've got two essays to write.
Where's that report I wrote?

How often do you have the house painted?
I've got to get my room tidied up.
He needs to have his clothes washed.
Keep the engine running.
This is the book I mentioned.

E3.29.2 Locate the nucleus on the wh phrase if it contains lexical material, but not otherwise.

Model:　　　'Which 'co<u>lour</u> do you prefer? 　　　　*but*　'Which do you pre'<u>fer</u>?

Which dress did you choose?
How much sugar should I add?
Whose books have you borrowed?
What car do you drive?
Which route shall we take?

Which did you choose?
How much should I add?
Whose have you borrowed?
What do you drive?
Which shall we take?

E3.29.3 Locate the nucleus on the subject if it is lexical, otherwise on the verb (= the last lexical item).

Model:　　　'What did '<u>Ma</u>ry do? 　　　*but*　'What did she '<u>do</u>?

What does Rodney think?
What will he say?
When will Janice finish?
When will she finish?
Why do they keep complaining?

Where is Martin going?
How are the students doing?
How can she stand it?
What does C, A, T spell?
What kind of car does William drive?

E3.29.4 Locate the nucleus on the last noun rather than on the adjective (etc.) that follows.

> *Model:*   I'll 'get the '<u>ta</u>ble ready.
> *but*   I'll 'get it '<u>rea</u>dy.

Could we have the window open, please?
We need to keep the wine cool.
How can we keep the salad fresh?
We must get the classroom ready.
You must get the length right.

Keep your head down!
He held his hands up.
We'll have to have that tree pruned.
You must get your room tidy.
Would you like the car washed?

3.30   Events

We see the same preference for placing a nuclear accent on a noun rather than a verb in so-called **event sentences**. These are sentences describing an event, where the verb is intransitive. The nucleus tends to be located on the subject, provided it is lexically filled, even if the verb contains apparently new information:

> The '<u>phone's</u> ringing.
> The '<u>car</u> won't start.
> The '<u>handle's</u> fallen off.
> There's a '<u>train</u> coming.
> The '<u>brakes</u> have failed.

Compare the corresponding sentences with a non-lexical (pronoun) subject:

> It's '<u>ring</u>ing.
> It 'won't '<u>start</u>.
> It's 'fallen '<u>off</u>.
> There's 'one just '<u>com</u>ing.
> They've '<u>failed</u>.[13]

Some event sentences involve an adjective as well as a verb, and we again see the noun receiving the nuclear accent, rather than the verb or the adjective:

> Your '<u>zip's</u> come undone.
> The '<u>door's</u> open.

Compare the equivalent sentences with a pronominal subject:

It's 'come un'<u>done</u>.
It's '<u>open</u>.

Descriptions of the weather count as event sentences of this type:

It's a 'funny '<u>day</u>: | the '<u>sun</u> is shining, | but there's a '<u>wind</u> springing up.

So do statements relating to unpleasant bodily sensations:

My '<u>arm's</u> hurting.
My '<u>nose</u> is all red.

Less easy to categorize is:

We've got some '<u>bed</u> linen for sale.

which nevertheless corresponds to:

We're 'selling '<u>bed</u> linen.

The tonicity of event sentences is paradoxical in that they can apparently involve very broad focus, being uttered for example as a response to *What's happened?* or *What's the matter?*. Yet their nucleus is not located on the last lexical item adding (apparently) new information. One possible explanation is that the verb (or adjective) in an event sentence is predictable from the context, so does not need to be in focus. In the case of *The 'phone's ringing*, we know that what telephones typically do is ring. Compare a possible sentence:

The 'phone's ex\<u>ploded</u>!

– where the verb *exploded* is truly not 'given' and thus demands the nucleus.[14]

In written English, there is an ambiguity in sentences such as *Dogs must be carried* (a public notice in the London Underground). The intended reading, 'if you have a dog with you, you must carry it', has the focus on *carried* and would be spoken as:

'Dogs must be '<u>carried</u>.

The other possible reading, 'everyone must carry a dog', has the focus on *dogs* and would be spoken as:

'<u>Dogs</u> must be carried.

EXERCISES

E3.30.1 Pair-work practice.

    ○ 'What's \<u>happened</u>?   • The \<u>ceiling</u>'s collapsed!
                                  • Your \<u>mother</u> called.
                                  • The \<u>train</u>'s late.

          • The \road's blocked.
          • 'Queen \Anne's dead.

  ○ 'What's the \matter? • The \baby's crying.
          • The \kettle's boiling.
          • There's a \storm coming.
         • My \arm hurts.
          • The ex\haust's gone.

E3.30.2 Locate the nucleus.

Model:	My 'tooth is hurting.

My knee's got something wrong with it.
The baby's hands feel cold.
My ankle's hurting again.
You've spelt 'friend' wrong.
Her long-lost son's turned up!

E3.30.3 Locate the nucleus.

Model:	'Watch 'out!	There's a 'train coming.

Can't you stop the tap dripping?
Before I buy, | I'm waiting for the price to fall.
I think there's rain coming.
You've got your collar turned up.
Next door, | there was a baby crying.

E3.30.4 Explore the implications of varying the tonicity in the following.

When's the sun going to come out?
Did you find out who the credit card belonged to?
When d'you think the pizza'll be ready?
She said there were some students waiting.
Why is her hair green?

Let's hope the dog hasn't eaten it.
I think the children may have broken them.
Look what the cat's brought in!
What does Mary say?
What did Rosemary tell you?

At that moment a car drew up.
Has a new plan been agreed?
They waited for months. | At last a ship came over the horizon.

The screen's gone blank.
Two cars have collided.

E3.30.5 Introduce yourself as if on the telephone, using this formula, with the nucleus on your name:

☏   Hel'lo, | this is 'Jimmy speaking.

ACCENTING OLD MATERIAL

3.31   Reusing the other speaker's words

Sometimes one person in a conversation echoes back words that another speaker has just used. Since the second speaker wishes to comment on this material, or to query it, naturally he accents it:

I 'can't \stand | /whisky.   • You 'can't stand /whisky?
We're having \strawberries | for /tea.   • \Ooh, | \strawberries!

See discussion above, 2.16 (pardon questions, second-order questions, please-repeat wh questions).

Sometimes the echoed word, although repeated, nevertheless clearly conveys new information:

You 'say your name's /Smith?   • \Yes, | \Smith.
Would you like 'coffee or \tea?   • \Tea, please.
Was the thief 'tall or \short?   • \Oh, | 'definitely \tall.

In these examples the first speaker asks the second for information. Supplying that information involves repeating a word just used by the first speaker. Thus the same word is reused by the second speaker, and the information it conveys is new. So it has to be brought into focus. Compare:

Was the thief 'tall or \short?   • Well ∨fairly tall.

Here, instead, the second speaker takes tallness as given and puts contrastive focus on the qualification *fairly*.

We can also echo the other speaker's words and comment on them:

'What's three times \five? | 'Fif/teen?   • 'Fif\teen, | 'that's /right.
So you're 'going to \emigrate.   • \Emigrate, | \yes.

In the next example, there are two possibilities for the second speaker:

∨Sorry, | I'm 'on a \diet.   (i) • But if you 'eat ∨chocolate, | 'how can you be on a \diet?
                              (ii) • But if you 'eat ∨chocolate, | 'how \can you be on a
                                       diet?

One possibility, (i), is to repeat the first speaker's accent pattern, placing the nucleus on *diet*. The other, (ii), is to deaccent *diet* as given, and to place the nucleus on *can*.

EXERCISES

E3.31.1 Pair-work practice.

- ○ 'Red or \white? — • I'll 'have the \white, | /please.
- ○ 'Would you like /coffee | or \tea? — • \Tea, | /please.
- ○ D'you prefer 'Oxford or \Cambridge? — • Oh \Cambridge, | myˇself.
- ○ I thought the 'cellos were \marvellous. — • The /cellos? | ˇI didn't.
  ○ 'Where's the con\necting plug? — • The con/necting plug? | \Here.

- ○ It was a 'terrible ˇaccident, | \wasn't it? — • \Yes, | \terrible.
- ○ That was an 'excellent ˇlecture! — • \Yes, | \excellent.
- ○ 'I'd give it \seven. — • No 'not ˇseven. | 'More like \six.
- ○ It's called \Spacetrek or something. — • Not ˇSpacetrek – | \Star Trek!
- ○ They've been to 'Monte Cas\sino. — • \Carlo, | not Casˇsino. ‖ 'Monte \Carlo.

3.32   Reusing your own words

We can also repeat ourselves for emphasis, giving the same information more than once, and presenting it afresh each time, focusing on it anew:

> It's \true, | it's \true!
> I 'can't ac\cept it, | I just 'can't ac\cept it.

This may involve reaccenting the same words, as in the examples just given, or reaccenting the same **ideas** while expressing them differently, e.g. by using synonyms:

> I \hate her, | I de\test her, | I 'can't \stand her.
> I \love you, | I a\dore you, | I 'think you're \wonderful.

We may also need to reaccent words already used in cases such as

> 'When I say ˇstop, | \stop!
> 'First things \first.
> Sur'prise, sur\prise!

There are also several idiomatic expressions, with the typical structure *X and X* or *X-preposition-X*, in which a repeated word is accented on each occasion. Examples include *more and more, hours and hours, again and again, (to meet someone) face to face, from day to day*:

The 'tremors | got 'worse and 'worse.
We 'walked | for 'miles and 'miles.
The 'noise got louder and 'louder.
'Profits in'creased | from 'year to 'year. | They just 'grew and grew and 'grew.

Some instances of a speaker accenting repeated words do not seem to have a logical explanation, and must be regarded as idiomatic. For example, we might complain about a speaker's voice quality or intonation by using the cliché:

It's 'not what he ˇsaid, | it's the 'way that he ˌsaid it.

Logically, you would expect contrastive focus on *what* and *way* rather than the repeated focusing on *said*.

On saying goodbye we can use the idiomatic expression:

I'll 'see you when I 'see you.

EXERCISES

E3.32.1 Pair-work practice.

- o 'How was the paˌrade?
- o 'Did you enjoy the ˊconcert?
- o 'How do you feel about ˌBetty?
- o 'How was your ˌholiday?
- o Are you ˊsure about that?

- o Am I ˊright?
- o 'What ˌcolour is it?
- o 'What was the ˌweather like?
- o 'What d'you fancy for this ˌevening?

- o 'What's the ˌmatter?

- • It was ˌbrilliant, | 'quite ˌbrilliant.
- • Yes it was ˌgreat, | 'really outˌstanding.
- • I 'don't ˌlike her, | I 'can't aˌbide her.
- • ˌWonderful, | 'just ˌwonderful.
- • Yes I'm ˌsure. | I'm ˌpositive.

- • No you're ˌwrong, | 'thoroughly ˌwrong.
- • A sort of ˌblue, | 'greeny ˌblue.
- • ˌDamp. | 'Definitely ˌdamp.
- • We could 'try a ˌrestaurant. | It's ˌages | since we 'went to a ˇrestaurant.

- • 'When I say ˇ'start', | you're sup'posed to ˌstart.

E3.32.2 Pair-work practice.

- o 'Did you sort it out ˊquickly?
- o 'How do you find the ˌcourse?
- o 'How are ˌgrocery prices here?
- o 'What was the ˌservice like?
- o 'Tell me about these different kinds of ˌflowers.

- • We had to ˇqueue | for 'hours and ˌhours.
- • It gets 'better and ˌbetter.
- • They go 'up and ˌup.
- • The ˇsermon | went 'on and ˌon.
- • I 'don't know which is ˌwhich, I'm afraid.

E3.32.3 Locate the nucleus.

Model: Things are getting 'worse and 'worse.

I warned her again and again.
I was waiting for days and days.
Jake's getting bigger and bigger.
They talked and talked | all night long.
She rang and rang, | but in vain.

The noise grew louder and louder.
I don't know which is which.
You must introduce me to people. | Tell me who's who.
Numbers are increasing | from year to year.
The result is about fifty-fifty.

WHAT IS KNOWN?

3.33   Knowledge: shared, common and imputed

Material is often placed out of focus because it is 'given' by the context in which it is uttered, even if the deaccented words have not themselves already been used. That is to say, the ideas expressed are implicitly treated as already known by both speaker and addressee (**shared** knowledge) and perhaps by people in general (**common** knowledge).

Train announcements on the London Underground are a good example. Between stations, you may hear a recorded voice announce:

'This train | 'terminates at 'Edgware.

The word *train* is not accented, because the announcement is made in a train, and you, the hearer, know you are in a train. Hence, *train* is not new information: it is shared knowledge. It can be left out-of-focus. As you approach a station you may hear:

The 'next station | is 'Oval.

Here, *station* is not accented. Why? Because everyone knows that the train stops at stations. So *station* is not new information: it is common knowledge. It can be left out-of-focus. After a short time, as the train comes to a standstill, you hear:

'This station | is 'Oval.

You know you have reached a station: so again *station* is shared knowledge, which does not need to be accented. On the other hand you may well have forgotten or not noticed the previous announcement, so the actual name of the station, *Oval*, counts as new and is placed in focus, so attracting the nucleus for a second time.

It must be admitted that there are various cases where an item which might logically be supposed to be common knowledge is nevertheless focused on by the speaker. For example, the speaker and the hearer might already know that Mary was a girl, and yet the speaker could say:

> '<u>Ma</u>ry's | a 'very nice 'girl.

On hearing some report or news item, we can comment:

> That's 'not good '<u>news</u>.

As a comment on the weather we can say:

> It's a 'beautiful '<u>day</u>.

We suggested above (3.6) that the explanation is that the final noun in the above examples is not part of the linguistic context. Alternatively, rather than seek a logical explanation for this tonicity, perhaps we should regard such cases as merely idiomatic.

A speaker may locate the nucleus in such a way as to imply that something is shared or common knowledge or given information, even if there is no evidence that that is the case. For instance, someone might say:

> It 'won't make the '<u>slight</u>est difference, | but I shall 'write and com'<u>plain</u>.

This seems to imply that the hearer already knows that it won't make a difference. The speaker **imputes** this knowledge to the hearer. This follows from the fact that the word *difference* is out of focus. The focus is on *slightest*, implying that the only matter at issue is the extent of the difference. The speaker forces this implication on the hearer.

Alternatively, without this implication, it is equally possible to say:

> It 'won't make the slightest '<u>diff</u>erence . . .

Accenting thus makes it possible for the speaker to impute knowledge and opinions to the addressee – to involve the addressee in a conspiracy, as it were – and thus manipulate the direction of the conversation without ever putting the implications directly into words.

In certain styles of conversation the nucleus is readily placed on an **intensifying word**, even though there may be further ostensibly new material to follow. By 'intensifying words' we mean not only adverbs of degree (*very*, *extremely*) and their equivalents (*awfully*, *remarkably*) but also various other expressions whose effect is to heighten the emotion of what is expressed. Arguably, by focusing on an intensifying word, as with *slightest* above, the speaker is imputing to the hearer implicit knowledge of the out-of-focus material located in the tail of the intonation pattern – or at least treating it as background material that can be left out of focus.

> 'That's '<u>ve</u>ry interesting!
> I was ex'<u>tre</u>mely annoyed with them.
> He had a 'quite in'<u>cre</u>dible piece of luck.

I 'know e'xactly what you mean.
They 'come in 'all shapes and sizes.

Ironical exclamations such as:

⌒   'That's \all I need! (= I wish that hadn't happened.)

can perhaps be seen in this light.

It is of course also possible (and perhaps more usual) to place an additional nuclear tone in the usual place, namely on the last lexical item. This alternative version does not impute to the listener the knowledge expressed in this item.

'That's 'very | 'interesting!
I was ex'tremely | an'noyed with them.

EXERCISES

E3.33.1 Account for the location of each nucleus in the following passage.

⌒   ∨Welcome | to 'Bellamy's \Restaurant, Ladies and Gentlemen! | 'I'm your ∨waiter this
evening, | and I'd 'like to go through the \menu with you. ||
The ∨first course | offers a 'wide \choice of starters. || I'd par∨ticularly recommend |
the 'angels on ⁄horseback, | the 'pumpkin ∨soup | or the \celery soup. ||
For the ∨main course | we have 'steak, 'lamb or ⁄fish, | or 'also a vege\tarian
alternative. || I believe the ∨rump steak | is par\ticularly good tonight. ||

E3.33.2 Pair-work practice.

○ ∨You're looking tired.   • Well it's been a 'busy \day.
○ 'Did you en⁄joy yourselves?   • We've had a 'great \time.
○ 'How's \Paul these days?   • He's a 'sick \man, I'm afraid.
○ 'How's \Maggie?   • She is 'not a happy \woman.
○ 'How was your \stay?   • ∨Peter's | a 'wonderful \guy.

E3.33.3 Pair-work practice.

○ I've de'cided to re\sign.   • Oh I \am sorry to hear that.
○ 'Doreen's got sci\atica.   • Oh 'that's \very unfortunate.
○ She's 'finding it a bit \difficult.   • I know \just what you mean.
○ So you've 'not been se\lected.   • 'That's the \least of my worries.
○ 'What do you think of the \Lake District? • I 'just \love the mountains.

3.34   Difficult cases of tonicity

An addressee can reject the supposed common knowledge that has been imputed to him or her by the other speaker. The second speaker can deny

something the other person has said or implied. This, too, may involve the reaccenting of old information:

'Which kind of 'whisky do you like best?	• I 'don't 'like whisky. | I 'don't like 'any kind of whisky.
'Why are we going to 'Scotland again?	• We're 'not 'going to Scotland! *or* • We're 'not going to Scotland!
They 'want you to apologize.	• But I've 'nothing to apologize for. *or* • But I've 'no reason 'to apologize.
'That's 'typical | of 'footballers.	• But 'I don't 'play football. *or* • But 'I'm not a 'footballer.

In an argument about modernizing procedures someone might say:

> Well it vis the twenty-first century, | so . . .

where the unspoken implication is that the other person in the argument has
overlooked this fact, and is making the wrong assumption that it is still the twen-
tieth century. The speaker's tonicity choice is designed to oppose ('counter') this
unspoken assumption ('presupposition'). It does so by placing the nucleus on the
bearer of positive polarity (see 3.14).

Alternatively, without conveying this counterpresuppositional meaning, the
speaker might say, with neutral tonicity:

> Well it 'is the twenty-first vcentury, | so . . .

Now consider the following exchange.

> 'Never /mind. | 'Worse things happen at /sea.   • We're 'not \at sea.

In response to the cliché *worse things happen at sea*, the second speaker rebuts
the supposed implication that they are on a ship. You might expect the nucleus to
go on *not*, the bearer of negative polarity; but in practice we usually place it on
at, as shown.

From about 1980 people in Britain – not only phoneticians – have been noticing
a tendency for speakers to accent function words where there seems to be no
pragmatic reason for doing so. For example, an announcement heard on a railway
station ran as follows:

> 'Customers waiting vfor this service | vare advised | that the service vwill
> be arriving | in a 'few \minutes.

It is hard to explain this accenting of apparently unimportant function words (*for,
are, will*) at the expense of apparently more important lexical items.

In-flight safety announcements are read aloud from a fixed script. But the
flight attendant making them has discretion over the intonation used. One chose
the following tonicity pattern:

> vIn the event | vof an emergency | there vwill be emergency lighting | \in
> the aisles | . . .

Perhaps the attendant made these tonicity choices as a result of having to repeat the same formulaic words over and over again on successive occasions. The effect on this occasion was to imply that the existence of possible emergencies, the provision of lighting, and the location of lighting, were common knowledge shared between crew and passengers and therefore 'given'.

People complain about the same phenomenon in the speech of radio and television newsreaders:

> 'Under these circumstances | the 'minister 'has decided | . . .

Another explanation might be sought in the speaker's wish to sound lively and avoid boringness, so that the listener is spurred into listening more closely.

There is always a strong pressure not to accent repeated words. Yet the nucleus has to go \somewhere. This may lead to its being placed on a function word, even one that may appear to be utterly lacking in semantic content. A leading American public figure recently remarked:

> We will use 'all the tools available 'to us.

Logic would seem to have required:

> We will use 'all the tools a'vailable to us.

Here are further examples, collected over a few days of listening to people talk:

> She 'didn't do 'anything, | because there 'wasn't anything 'to do.
> (*a speaker addressing a meeting*) We've had e'normous difficulties 'getting here this evening, | but it 'is a great pleasure | 'to be here.
> (*about someone's forthcoming wedding*) He's taking 'no interest in the prepa'rations. | You'd 'almost think | he 'didn't want to 'get married.
> (*a financial commentator*) 'Faced with 'news of | yet a'nother company collapsing | 'how worried should investors 'be?
> (*a radio reporter*) We're 'here in 'Somerset, | in 'southwest 'England, | one of the 'most beautiful parts 'of the country.
> I 'don't like | 'football, | and I'm 'not good 'at it.

It is appropriate to finish this chapter on a note of humility. Although we have made great strides in the study of focus, accenting and nucleus placement, we do not yet have all the answers. Examples like these exhibit patterns of tonicity that still resist logical explanation.

EXERCISES

E3.34.1 Can we explain the tonicity of the following responses?

- ○ 'Pork or \beef?
- ○ 'Which brand of ciga\rettes do you smoke?

- • ∨Sorry, | I 'don't \eat meat.
- • \None. | I 'don't \smoke. | I 'think it's a \filthy habit.

○ 'Which \fruit do you like best?	• I 'don't \like fruit.
○ 'What kind of \car do you drive?	• I 'don't \drive.
○ 'Which \subjects do you like best?	• I'm 'not \at school, | /actually.
○ I 'want you at your \best for the match.	• I'm \at my best.
○ 'What are you going to \do, then?	• There's 'only one thing \to do.

Notes

1. In a corpus of about 1,200 IPs, Altenberg (1987) found that the nucleus went on the last word in 88% of cases.
2. In other Germanic languages, virtually all compounds are written as single words. From this perspective, it is an idiosyncrasy of English spelling that we write so many of them as two words:

'living room	*German* 'Sitzkammer	*Swedish* ''vardagsrum
'table lamp	*German* 'Tischlampe	*Swedish* ''bordslampa

3. Corresponding to an English late-stressed compound or phrase, other Germanic languages may have a regular, single-stressed compound. This is a source of possible learner error.

,church'warden	*German* Ge'meinde,vorsteher	*Swedish* ''kyrkvärd
,scrambled 'eggs	*German* 'Ruhr,ei	*Swedish* ''äggröra
,red 'wine	*German* 'Rotwein	*Swedish* ''rödvin

4. Compare Spanish, in which indefinite pronouns typically bear the nucleus: *Se le debe haber caído algo* (= *She must have dropped something*); *Preguntémosle a alguien* (= *Let's ask somebody*) (Ortiz-Lira, 1995: 260).
5. Speakers of Germanic languages must guard against putting the nucleus on *un-* where there is no contrastive focus. We do not normally say *I'm feeling 'unhappy.*
6. Compare the usual pattern in German: *Karen ist ja /fertig | aber Helga \nicht.*
7. Other languages may not deaccent in the same way. With English *There's a 'fly in my soup* compare Italian, *C'è una mosca nella mi'nestra* (Ladd, 1996).
8. Cruttenden points out (1997: 155) that this very frequent English pattern is 'virtually impossible' in German. One can say (i) or (ii), but not (iii):

(i)   Ich ging nach \London am Sonntag.
(ii)   Ich ging nach \London | am \Sonntag.
(iii) × Ich ging nach \London | am /Sonntag.

I think the most natural way of expressing this meaning in German would be *Am /Sonntag | bin ich nach \London gefahren.*
9. With English *'Which 'brand do you buy?* compare Spanish *¿Qué 'marca 'compras?* However both languages place the nucleus on the noun in *¿'Cómo van las ta'reas?* = *'How's the 'homework going?*, where the word order differs (Ortiz-Lira, 2000: 61).
10. With *'Where's that 'sweater I gave you?* compare Spanish: *¿'Dónde está ese suéter que te rega'lé?* (Ortiz-Lira, 1995: 261). With *'Where's that 'book you borrowed?* compare *¿'Dónde pusiste el libro que sa'caste?* (Ortiz-Lira, 2000: 62). In Spanish, the nucleus goes on the last lexical item even if it is a verb.

11. Again, Spanish is different. With English *'Keep your 'eyes shut* compare Spanish *Man'tén los ojos ce'rrados* (Ortiz-Lira, 2000: 62).

12. Other languages may not deaccent in the same way. With English *I have a 'book to read*, compare Italian, *Ho un 'libro da 'leggere*; *I 'don't like the 'shirts he wears*, but *Non mi 'piacciono le camicie che 'porta*. (Ladd, 1996.) In German, though, this principle works as in English, and applies even more widely, given the wider range of German constructions that place the verb at the end: thus *'Hast Du meine 'Tasche gesehen?*, where the nucleus is located on the last noun, just as in the English equivalent *'Have you seen my 'bag?* (And equally *'Hast Du was ge'sehen? = 'Did you 'see anything?*, where the object is not lexical.) The tendency to accent nouns ('arguments') rather than verbs ('predicates'), where both are in focus, is at the core of Gussenhoven's (1984) Sentence Accent Assignment Rule, which he plausibly claims is a rule common to all the Germanic languages.

13. With *The 'brakes have failed* compare Spanish *Me fa'llaron los 'frenos*, where the noun comes at the end (Ortiz-Lira, 2000: 60).

14. Compare Spanish, in which the word order is usually different, with the subject at the end, where it naturally receives the nucleus: *Se me e'chó a perder el 'auto* (= *My 'car broke down*). If the same word order is used as in English, the nucleus goes on the verb: *El 'auto se me echó a per'der*. Spanish would not use the English-style tonicity ×*El 'auto se me echó a perder* (Ortiz-Lira, 1995: 261).

4 Tonality: chunking, or division into IPs

4.1 Signalling the structure

How does the speaker break the material up into intonation phrases (IPs)? Where do the boundaries between successive IPs go? What determines the number of words that go into a single chunk of tune, a single IP?

To a large extent, the answers are a matter of common sense. Essentially, the intonation structure reflects the grammatical structure. An **intonation break** (= the boundary between two successive intonation phrases) generally corresponds to a syntactic (= grammatical) boundary. We regularly place an intonation break between successive sentences, usually between successive clauses, sometimes between successive phrases, and occasionally between successive words. We can even break within a word – though this is unusual and only used for special emphasis. Typical examples:

> 'Milk comes from '<u>cows</u>. ‖ 'Wool comes from '<u>sheep</u>.
> 'Milk comes from '<u>cows</u>, | and 'wool comes from '<u>sheep</u>.
> '<u>Milk</u> | 'comes from '<u>cows</u>.

Less typical examples:

> De'<u>licious</u>, | '<u>cool</u> | '<u>milk</u>.
> I '<u>don't</u> | '<u>like</u> it.

Even less typical examples:

> 🎧　　'Abso|'<u>lutely</u> | 'de|'<u>licious</u>!
> 🎧　　'<u>Bor</u>|'<u>ing</u>!

We also use intonation breaks to signal the boundaries of parenthetic material within a larger structure:

> '<u>Milk</u>, | I be'<u>lieve</u>, | 'comes from '<u>cows</u>.

Chunking (tonality) appears to function in much the same way in all languages, and does not seem to give much difficulty to learners of EFL.

The presence or absence of intonation breaks, and their location, signals to the hearer the syntactic structure of the sentence. Sometimes this structure is potentially ambiguous, and the tonality can disambiguate it. An intonation break signals a syntactic boundary:

(i)	'Help keep the 'dog off! (= Help to keep the dog off.)
(ii)	'Help!	'Keep the 'dog off! (= I ask for help! Keep the dog off.)

(i)	'What's that in the road a'head?
(ii)	'What's that in the 'road?	A 'head?!

ဂ	'Do you like 'pawpaw?	(i) • I'm 'sorry,	I 'don't 'know. (= I've never tried it.)
		(ii) • I'm 'sorry,	I 'don't,	'no. (= I don't like it.)

Versions (i) have a single IP where versions (ii) have two. The difference in meaning is obvious, and signalled phonetically by the use of two shorter intonation patterns rather than one longer one.

ဂ	(i) You can have 'cheese	'salad	or 'quiche.
ဂ	(ii) You can have 'cheese 'salad	or 'quiche.
ဂ	(iii) You can have 'cheese salad or 'quiche.

Here, version (i) offers a list of three possibilities. In version (ii) the list equally clearly consists of two possibilities. Version (iii) is ambiguous: it is not clear whether there are two items in the list or three.

(i)	'This will give teachers 'time	to pre'pare and mark 'work.
(ii)	'This will give teachers time to pre'pare	and 'mark 'work.

Here, version (i) is ambiguous. Do the teachers get time to prepare work and to mark work, or to prepare (in general) and to mark work? That is, is *work* the grammatical object of *prepare* as well as of *mark*, or just of *mark*? In version (ii) the intonation break after *prepare* makes it clear that the second interpretation is intended.

(i)	I was 'talking to a chap I met in the 'pub.
(ii)	I was 'talking to a 'chap I met	in the 'pub.

Here, in version (i) *met in the pub* goes together: I met the chap in the pub. In version (ii) the listener is pushed towards a different interpretation, in which *in the pub* goes with *talking*: I was talking to him in the pub.

(i)	I'll 'talk to the students in the 'garden.
(ii)	I'll 'talk to the 'students	in the 'garden.

Here, version (i) is ambiguous. It could mean either 'I'll talk to those students who are in the garden' or 'I'll talk to the students. I'll do so in the garden.' With version (ii), the second interpretation is more likely.

(i)	'Look at that dog with one 'eye!
(ii)	'Look at that 'dog	with 'one 'eye!

This is also ambiguous, but – differently from the previous cases – the ambiguity cannot be resolved by intonation. Only common sense tells us that it means 'There's a dog with one eye. Look at it!', not 'Use one eye to look at that dog.'

It is not only the presence or absence of an intonation break that can resolve a possible ambiguity, but also its location.

(i) The com'petitors who 'finished | 'first received a 'goody bag.
(ii) The com'petitors who finished 'first | re'ceived a 'goody bag.

Here, the adverb *first* goes with *finished* in (i), but with *received* in (ii). In (i) all the competitors first got a goody-bag (and then perhaps were given a sandwich or offered a massage). In (ii) only the front runners got the goody-bag, not those who finished later. The intonation break marks the end of the relative clause and hence the end of the noun phrase that is the subject of the verb *received*.

In the case of simple **lists**, grammarians differ over how many commas should be used (*A, B, and C* or *A, B and C*). Intonationally, all the list items tend to be treated equally: either none of them is followed by an intonation break (*A B and C*), or they all are (*A | B | and C*). There is in any case usually an intonation break at the end of the list.

(i)   The flags are 'red, white and 'blue.
(ii)   The flags are 'red, | 'white, | and 'blue.

Version (i) favours the interpretation that each flag has three colours. With version (ii), the interpretation might be that some flags are red, some white, and some blue. The intonation does not actually resolve the ambiguity – both versions remain ambiguous – but it does push the hearer in one direction or the other.

(i)   On 'Mondays Tuesdays and 'Wednesdays | it's at 'six.
(ii)   On 'Mondays, | 'Tuesdays, | and 'Wednesdays | it's at 'six.

In all these cases, the intonation break signals the presence of a syntactic boundary at the same place. Intonation parallels syntax.

Thus tonality in speech plays a role similar to the role of punctuation in writing. Intonation breaks often correspond to punctuation marks. However, the two do not always go in parallel.

There are many cases where a punctuation mark is used, but an intonation break is optional or even unlikely. In particular, little words such as *well*, *yes*, *no*, *oh* at the beginning of a sentence, although set off by a comma in writing, are not usually followed by an intonation break in speech:

Oh, I 'quite under'stand.
Well, I'm 'not 'sure.
No, I 'love it.

Sometimes an optional punctuation mark corresponds to an optional intonation break:

(i)   In 'August I come in 'late.
(ii)   In 'August, | I 'come in 'late.

Both versions are equally possible and perhaps equally probable.

Some of the final adverbials given in the first list at 3.24 are preceded by a comma in writing but have no intonation break in speech: *then*, *though*, *even*, *you know*:

> We'll 'see you on 'Tuesday, then.
> It 'hasn't stopped him 'smoking, though.
> The 'bride looked 'beautiful – | 'radiant, even.
> Her 'health's pretty 'poor, you know.

Conversely, there are many circumstances (some of them discussed below) where an intonation break can occur but there is no punctuation mark:

> The 'late Mrs 'Jenkinson | 'didn't a'gree.

EXERCISES

E4.1.1 Locate suitable intonation breaks in the following passage. Put double marks ‖ at the end of each sentence, and single marks | where appropriate within each sentence.

> When we got to the top we paused for a rest. Fortunately we had some chocolate with us and some bottles of water, and Nell had some raisins, which were very welcome. After we'd rested there for a few minutes we were ready to continue our journey, which we did with a new spring in our steps.

E4.1.2 Pair-work practice. In performing the responses, be careful to incorporate the initial interjection into the same IP as what follows, as shown. Ignore the orthographic comma.

☊	o 'Will you be staying /long?	• Well, I'm 'not \sure.
☊	o 'Will you be leaving on /Thursday?	• Oh, I 'haven't de\cided yet.
☊	o 'Are you ready to hand in your /essay now?	• No, I 'haven't quite \finished it yet.
	o 'Did you enjoy your /stay?	• Yes, I've 'had a \wonderful time.
	o 'Will you be coming /with us?	• Well, it 'all depends on my \wife,	/actually.

E4.1.3 Dialogue practice. Be careful to incorporate the final adverbials into the same IP as what precedes, as shown. Ignore the orthographic comma.

> A: So you've 'broken /up with Mary, then?
> B: /Mhm. | I 'don't rev\gret it, though.
> A: And she's 'left you for /good?
> B: I'm 'quite rev\laxed about it, you know.
> A: You're 'quite /happy, then?
> B: \Sure, | I'm \thoroughly happy – | de\lirious, even.

E4.1.4 Would the following pairs always be distinct in speech? Could they sometimes be ambiguous? Show the relationship between tonality and interpretation in each case.

1 (i)   What did you see on the way across?
  (ii)   What did you see on the way? A cross?

2 (i)   She washed and ironed her blouse.
  (ii)   She washed, and ironed her blouse.

3 (i)   You can have tropical, Neapolitan or pistachio flavour.
  (ii)   You can have tropical Neapolitan or pistachio flavour.

4 (i)   There's chicken-fried steak or ribs.
  (ii)   There's chicken, fried steak, or ribs.

5 (i)   What would you like on your toast, honey?
  (ii)   What would you like on your toast? Honey?

6 (i)   It's all over my friend.
  (ii)   It's all over, my friend.

7 (i)   What have you got on? Your sweater?
  (ii)   What have you got on your sweater?

8 (i)   Those who spoke quickly | got an angry response.
  (ii)   Those who spoke | quickly got an angry response.

9 (i)   What is this thing called love?
  (ii)   What is this thing called, love?

10 (i)   The Swedes, say the Danes, drink too much.
   (ii)   The Swedes say the Danes drink too much.

4.2   Choosing the size of the chunks

Each intonation phrase presents one piece of information. The speaker has to break the message up into chunks of information – into IPs – and has considerable freedom of choice in how to do so. Typically, an IP lasts for between one and two seconds (Tench, 1996: 31). An utterance, or a speaker's turn in a conversation, may consist of one or many such IPs.

The chunks also reflect the speaker's decisions about focus. Each IP covers a single focus domain (culminating in the nucleus, as seen in 3.9) and the associated out-of-focus material.

> I 'think you've made good 'progress this year.

In this example, the focus domain might typically be *good progress*. The associated out-of-focus material would be *I think you've made* and *this year*. The whole thing would be said as a single IP.

In an alternative spoken version of the same words, the speaker might decide to place an additional focus on *this year*, perhaps wishing to imply that there is a difference between this year and last year. Dividing it into two chunks, with an intonation break after *progress*, gives:

> I 'think you've made good 'progress | 'this year.

The speaker might also wish to place focus on *I*, perhaps to imply a contrast between what he or she thinks and other people might think. To do this, the speaker would accent *I* and might make *I think* into a separate chunk:

> 'I think | you've made good 'progress | 'this year.

The size of an IP is linked to the decisions the speaker makes about how many words, and therefore how many syllables, to accent. An IP usually contains only one or two accents (onset and nucleus, or just nucleus). Less commonly, it may have three accents (with, therefore, a complex head), and rather rarely four or more. Five is probably the absolute upper limit. See 5.1–5.

IPs tend to be longer, and have more accents, in scripted material and in material read aloud. In spontaneous conversation they tend to be shorter, with fewer accents. This may be because the IP is not only the basic chunk for intonation purposes but also the basic chunk for mental planning. In our minds as we speak we plan one IP at a time. Reading from a script, we can look ahead and plan ahead; in ordinary conversation we may not have decided what we are going to say until just before we say it.

Tonality thus varies considerably according to the **style** of speech. In some styles IPs may be very short, with nearly every accent being nuclear. Here is a genuine, if extreme, example. At a church concert the choral conductor, a tall man, apologized for fussing about a footstool to stand on. He said:

> 'Six foot /two | v isn't | e\nough.

By using such short IPs he was able to pack a lot of tone meaning into this short sentence. After the performance the person publicly thanking the singers began, rhetorically:

> 'Have /you | 'ever /heard | v such | a v marvellous | \anthem?

and ended by saying:

> ω   \Thank you | \very much | in\deed.

But in a private conversation this gushing style – the use of so many IPs, each as small as these – would probably be out of place.

EXERCISES

E4.2.1 Divide this passage into IPs, using (i) a style typical of reading aloud from a written text, and (ii) a style typical of unscripted speech.

> The first thing we have to consider is the earthworm and its relation to the condition of the soil. In autumn, falling leaves cascade onto the ground and accumulate there. If there were no earthworms the leaves would rot down into a solid viscous mass which would suffocate the soil beneath. But what the earthworms do is to drag down pieces of decomposing leaf into the soil, bringing with them air and moisture, so that the soil is rendered lighter and less compact. The result is a good friable tilth which is the gardener's delight and in which plants grow well. Without the earthworm nothing much would grow at all.

4.3   Chunking and grammar

As we have just seen, the speaker has considerable discretion over the size and therefore the number of intonation phrases into which to divide the spoken message. Nevertheless, there are some strong tendencies exerted by the grammar over tonality. Some components of syntactic structure are more likely than others to be made into separate IPs, set off by intonation breaks.

First, there is normally an intonation break at every **sentence** boundary. This is a major break (‖), more important than the intonation breaks within a sentence:

> Now 'here is the 'news. ‖ It has 'been an'nounced | that . . .
> 'That's the end of Part 'One. ‖ In 'Part 'Two, | we shall . . .
> 'Stop! ‖ You're 'going to hit the 'wall.

A second basic rule is that each **clause** tends to be said as a separate IP. So if a sentence consists of several clauses, there will usually be an intonation break at each clause boundary:

> 'When I 'cough, | it 'hurts my 'throat.
> 'First take the 'lid off, | and 'then unscrew the 'base.
> I'll tell you, | but you must 'keep it a 'secret.

In general, the speaker can insert an intonation boundary anywhere where it will make the grammatical structure clearer. An intonation boundary signals a boundary between syntactic constituents. In the next example, version (i), pronounced as a single IP, is ambiguous:

> (i) He was 'looking up the 'street.

This can mean either 'his gaze was directed up the street' (like *he was gazing up the street*, where *up* is a preposition) or 'he was searching for the street in a list' (like *he was looking up the name*, with *look up* as a phrasal verb). The speaker can resolve the ambiguity by placing an intonation boundary as appropriate, (ii) or (iii):

> (ii) He was 'looking | up the 'street.
> (iii) He was 'looking 'up | the 'street.

In a very mannered version, however, with intonation boundaries in both places, the ambiguity returns:

> (iv) He was 'looking | 'up | the 'street.

If a new sentence involves a change of grammatical subject, the subject (particularly if it is not a pronoun) tends to have its own IP:

> We'll ar'rive at about 'ten. ‖ The 'children | can 'come along 'later.

There is usually an intonation break between coordinate clauses:

> He 'turned 'round, | and a 'strange 'sight confronted him.

If, however, the subject of coordinate clauses is ellipted, there is usually no intonation break:

> She was 'sitting and 'thinking.
> Peter 'likes him and 'trusts him.
> (*less usual*) 'Peter 'likes him | and 'trusts him.

Where the object or some other complement is ellipted, again there is usually no intonation break after the first verb, providing the subject is unchanged:

> Peter 'likes and 'trusts him.
> I've 'washed and ironed the 'clothes. (= I've washed them and ironed them.)

Inserting an intonation break in the last example would suggest the reading with no ellipted object:

> I've 'washed | and 'ironed the 'clothes. (= I've got washed, *or*
> I've done the washing and I've done the ironing.)

In coordinate clauses with different subjects and verbs but an ellipted object, as in the next example, an intonation break after each of the verbs is virtually compulsory:

> Mary's pre'pared, | and we've 'all just 'eaten, | a de'licious 'meal.

The structure here is that Mary prepared a delicious meal, and we've all just eaten it. The NP *a delicious meal* is the object of both verbs.

Simple structures like the following count as a single clause, and are usually said as a single IP.

> I want to apologize.
> I think he's wrong.
> He said he was sorry.
> I hope you haven't forgotten.

EXERCISES

E4.3.1 Decide what has been ellipted in each of the following. In which is an intonation break necessary?

> James has been walking and cycling.
> Henry has written and performed a new monologue.
> Nick has written, and Jeremy has revised, an account of the events.
> I'm going to clean and repaint the bathroom.

E4.3.2 Pair-work practice: no intonation break in the responses.

○ 'What have you got to \say to me?
• I 'want to tell you I'm \sorry.
○ But 'Garry says it won't \work.
• I 'don't think he's \right.
○ So 'Rose has \gone.
• ∨Yes, | but she 'says she'll be back \soon.
○ I 'think the weather's going to im\prove.
• I 'hope you're ∨right.
○ We'd 'better buy some more \bread.
• I expect ∨Linda will get some | on her 'way \home.

4.4   Vocatives and imprecations

(See also 3.21.) The basic structure of a clause is subject, verb and one or more objects or complements. Vocatives are not an essential part of the clause structure (the clause would be grammatically complete even without them). This explains why under some circumstances they are given their own IP.

Vocatives are treated differently depending on where they come. In initial position, they tend to form a separate IP:

'Linda, | could I have a 'word?
'Jenny and 'Peter, | I want 'you to take the 'left side.
'Ladies and 'gentlemen! | 'Please be up'standing!

When not initial, they are usually attached to what precedes, forming part of the tail of the IP:

'This, Mr Roberts, | is the 'young man I was 'telling you about.
'Don't 'do it, Mrs Worthington.
'Have you got your 'passport, Mother?
'You, Jimmy, | have 'made a mi'stake.

In greetings, however, a final vocative often has its own IP:

Good 'morning, Andrew. *or*
Good 'morning, | 'Andrew.

Imprecations (= calling on God, or an equivalent euphemism or expletive) can form a separate utterance. But if part of a larger utterance, they usually have their own IP when initial, but otherwise are attached to the preceding IP.

In 'heaven's 'name!
In 'heaven's 'name, | 'why 'not?
'Why in heaven's name 'not? *or* 'Why in heaven's name | 'not?
'Why 'not, in heaven's name?

EXERCISES

E4.4.1 In which of the following would the vocative be spoken as a separate IP?

> Here, colleagues, are my suggestions.
> I'd like you to organize the flowers, Mrs Jeffers.
> Mr Kenyon, could you be responsible for the tickets?
> You, Ms Sanderson, can look after the financial arrangements.
> And perhaps you could liaise with the police, Andrew.

See further exercises on vocatives in 3.21.

E4.4.2 Pair-work practice.

○ You 'can't sit ˅there.   • 'Why ˎnot, for Christ's sake?
○ You're 'not allowed to do ˅that.   • 'Why on earth ˎnot?
○ We 'can't go ˅that way.   • 'Why ˎnot, for goodness' sake?
○ You'll 'have to park on the other ˎside.   • For 'crying aˏloud, | ˎwhy?
○ They 'mustn't put it ˅there.   • 'Bloody ˏhell, | 'why ˎnot?

4.5 Adverbials

Adverbials, too, often stand apart from the basic clause structure (the clause would be grammatically complete even without them). This explains why they, too, are frequently given their own IP. Their behaviour varies depending on their relationship to the rest of the clause.

Ordinary adverbs and adverbials – those that modify the verb or an adjective – are typically not given their own IP:

> She 'quickly picked up the 'pencil.
> We were 'really 'pleased with it.

However, adverbials at the **beginning** of the clause are usually followed by an intonation break and thus form a separate IP:

> On 'Thursday 'evening | I'm having 'dinner at 'Patsy's.
> 'Under the 'circumstances | we've got 'no 'choice.
> 'Technically | we 'have to re'ject it.
> Un'fortunately | we're 'not going to be able to 'make it.
> During the 'last three 'years | our 'budget hasn't increased at 'all.
> 'Only 'now | can we be'gin to see a so'lution.

In the **middle** of a clause, an adverbial is often a kind of parenthesis. It may have its own IP, with separate IPs before and after:

> Well we 'could | 'this year | 'do something 'different.
> (*compare:*   'This year | we could 'do something 'different.
>   We could 'do something 'different this year.
>   *or*   We could 'do something 'different | 'this year.)

> The 'rest of us, | un'fortunately, | will 'have to ac'cept it.

Adverbs at the **end** of a clause may be adverbs of manner that modify the verb and thus be integrated closely into the clause structure. In keeping with the general rule that the nucleus goes on the last in-focus lexical item, such adverbs tend to bear the nucleus.

> She 'dances 'beautifully.
> I 'just can't take him 'seriously.
> She 'spoke very 'frankly.
> I'll 'pay you back 'soon.

Sentence adverbials (adjuncts), that modify the whole clause or sentence, typically have their own IP. (For their tones, see 2.23.) They are set off from the surrounding material by an intonation break:

> Apⱽparently, | she's 'getting diˎvorced.
> ˎSeriously, | 'when do you think you'll be able to ˎfinish it?
> The ofⱽficials, | surⱽprisingly, | 'raised no obˎjections.
> I've been 'given a second ˎchance, | ˏfortunately.

> I've been 'talking to ˎRobert, | as a matter of ˏfact.
> I'm 'rather disapˎpointed, | ˏfrankly.
> I'll 'pay you ˎback, | ˎobviously.

Thus there is typically a difference of tonality in the following pair:

(i)   The ⱽking | 'treated his enemies ˎmercifully.
(ii)   We 'managed to ˏget her | 'straight to ˎhospital, | ˏmercifully.

In (i) *mercifully* modifies *treated*, and counts as an ordinary part of the clause, both grammatically and intonationally. In (ii) *mercifully* modifies the whole clause *we managed to get her to hospital*, and is set off as a separate IP.

If there are several final adverbials, they are usually separated by intonation breaks:

> 'What do you adˎvise?   • 'Take it 'slowly, | with'out 'rushing, | 'calmly.

> a. The water evaporated naturally. (= not through human intervention)
> b. The water evaporated, naturally. (= as you would expect)

4.6   Heavy noun phrases

A noun phrase (NP) is particularly likely to have its own IP if it is **heavy** (= long, consisting of several words). Since the grammatical subject of a sentence is often just such an NP, there is often an intonation break between the subject and the rest of the clause or sentence:

> The 'head of a large 'school | has a 'lot of responsi'bility.
> The 'people I've been 'talking to | were 'quite 'definite about it.
> 'London and the south'east | will have 'showers. || The 'rest of the country | will be 'dry.

The speaker has considerable discretion about this. A separate IP for the subject of a clause is more frequently found in reading aloud and in formal speeches to an audience than in everyday conversation (Cruttenden, 1997: 70).

The grammatical subject is particularly likely to have its own IP if it is different from the subject of the preceding sentence or clause, i.e. if there is a change of subject:

> I thought the 'food was \excellent. || And 'salmon vquiche | is 'something I a\dore.

Making the subject NP into a separate IP has the advantage of allowing the speaker to place contrastive focus on it by locating a nucleus there. Even very light (= short) NPs can be made into separate IPs to allow this:

> The vchildren | say they don't \like her. || But vI | think she's \wonderful.
> 'Cats and vdogs | can make \wonderful companions.

Objects, too, are followed by an intonation break if they are heavy:

> I 'gave the 'book you asked about | to the 'girl at the 'checkout.

EXERCISES

E4.6.1 Pair-work practice.

🎧	o 'How are you getting on at \school?	• The 'subject I like vbest	is 'I\T.
🎧	o 'Where's your \wife?	• 'Mary and the vchildren	will be 'joining us \later.
	o \Tell me,	'who's \that?	• 'Andrea \Levy,	the \novelist. || 'One of her vrecent books	'won the \Whitbread Prize.
	o 'Where do you like to go on \holiday?	• 'Some of our vbest holidays	have been in \Spain.

> ∘ 'What happened ˍnext, Dad? • The 'big Billy Goat ⌁Gruff | 'poked his ˍeyes out.
>
> E4.6.2 Put an intonation break after each heavy NP subject.
>
> The people of our country want an improved standard of living.
> My friends and I are ready to offer our help.
> The books in the reference section are not available for loan.
> The boxes at the back of the shelves are older stock.
> These new computing facilities are available for everyone.

4.7 Topics

The first element in a clause is typically the **topic** (or 'theme'), while the remainder is the **comment** (or 'rheme'). This first element is most often the grammatical subject. We can signal its status as topic (i) in various syntactic ways, (ii) by choosing an appropriate tone (see 2.21) and (iii) by giving it a separate IP:

> 'As for ˅Jeremy, | he 'can do what he ˍlikes.
> ˅Martha | will 'have to ˍwait.

We can also topicalize other clause elements. A topicalized object or complement is usually followed by an intonation break.

> His ˅rudeness | I shall igˍnore. ‖ But his ˅actions | I 'cannot forˍgive.
> 'Rather good ˍmeals | they serve at the ⌁Carvery.
> I 'loved the ˅singing, | but the ˅acting | I thought was aˍtrocious.
> On the 'question of ⌁guilt, | we must sus'pend ˍjudgment.
> 'More im˅portant | is the 'question of what we do ˍnext.

In **cleft sentences** one constituent of the sentence is fronted and introduced by *it is* (or *it was*, etc.). This topicalized constituent must include focused material and therefore an intonation nucleus. If there is further focused material to follow, then there must be an intonation break.

Any of the following could be an answer to *Who did you choose?*:

(i) I chose Ve'ronica. (*not cleft*)
(ii) It was Ve'ronica that I chose. (*cleft*)
(iii) It was Ve'ronica | that 'I chose. (*cleft, with focus on* I)

Version (iii) would be appropriate if the speaker was making a contrast between his own choice and someone else's choice.

Pseudo-cleft sentences involve *what*. There is usually an intonation break between the two halves of the construction:

> 'What they 'didn't like | was the 'noise.
> 'What I'm 'looking for | is a 'saucepan.
> 'Getting 'caught | is e'xactly what I am trying to a'void.

I sup'pose you'll criticize his \callousness?

• No his ⌄callousness | is 'what I shall ig\nore. (*with refocusing on* callousness)

I sup'pose you'll ig\nore | his /slowness?

• No his \callousness | is what I shall ig⌄nore. (*with refocusing on* ignore)

EXERCISES

E4.7.1 Pair-work practice: topic, comment.

○ 'Where are we going to \put them all?

• Well ⌄Emily | can 'sleep in the \guest room. || 'As for the ⌄others, | we'll 'have to \think of something.

○ 'What did you make of the per\formance?

• The ⌄choir | 'wasn't too \bad. || But the ⌄soloists | were a \great disappointment.

○ 'How are we going to e\valuate this?

• The 'presen⌄tation | wasn't too \bad. || But it 'lacked origi\nality.

○ 'What do you think of Julia's \cooking?

• Her ⌄fruit cake | is 'out of this \world.

○ 'Will you accept a lift from /Tom?

• His ⌄driving's | a\trocious.

E4.7.2 Pair-work practice: topicalized non-subject.

○ 'How was the \food?

• 'Marvellous fish and \chips | they do at Harry /Ramsden's.

○ 'Did you enjoy the /dance?

• The ⌄music | I can \take. || But the ⌄people, | \no.

○ 'What are we going to do about \Miriam?

• 'More to the ⌄point, | 'what are we going to do about her \brother?

○ 'What are the arrangements for the \rest of the week?

• On ⌄Thursday | we've got the \orals. || And on ⌄Friday | there's a com\mittee meeting.

○ We 'need to get some \money.

• Oh the ⌄bank | we can 'go to \later.

E4.7.3 Pair-work practice: cleft, further focus follows.

○ I 'don't like ⌄Betty's behaviour.

• It's her \attitude | ⌄I can't stand.

○ 'Who are you going to the \dance with?

• It was \Victor | whose invi⌄tation I accepted.

○ 'How are you coping with the \weather?

• It's the \heat | ⌄I find hard to take.

○ 'How have the \children been?

• It's \Marvin | who's been 'causing all the ⌄trouble.

○ Your ⌄tickets are ready.

• It wasn't ⌄me | who \wanted them.

○ And 'after /that?

• It was \Brenda | who came in /next.

○ What \size are you, sir?

• No it's my \sister here | who wants the /t-shirt.

○ 'One lobster /Thermidor.

• No it was the 'lady \there | who ordered the /lobster.

○ So we 'ought to look at /gibbons?

• It's \chimps | that are our closest /relatives.

○ 'Can we do /algebra, sir?

• Well it'll be Miss \Fenton | that'll be taking you to/day.

E4.7.4 Pair-work practice: cleft, no further focused material.

○ 'Here's the para\cetamol.

• But it was \aspirin I wanted.

○ Your \pizza, sir.

• But it was 'cannel\loni I ordered.

○ Your 'prawn \cocktail, madam.

• But it was \soup I asked for.

○ 'Have you got the /raspberries?

• But it 'wasn't vraspberries we were going to have.

○ It's 'next to an \aisle.

• But it was a \window seat you were supposed to get me.

E4.7.5 Pair-work practice: pseudo-cleft.

○ \Now madam: | 'how can I \help you?

• What I vwant | is a 'spring \break | in \Holland.

○ 'How are you getting on in \England?

• What I vmiss | is 'proper Czech \beer.

○ 'How's life in the Middle \East?

• What I vdon't like | is the way they \shout such a lot.

○ 'Soon be off to the Caribvbean.

• 'What I'm looking vforward to | is a 'daily dip in the \pool.

○ 'Getting on well with your /essay?

• What you've 'failed to vnotice | is that I 'finished vmine | \yesterday.

○ I 'don't like \having them here.

• 'What my vfather always said | was 'live and \let live.

○ The \bathroom needs repainting.

• What vI always say | is a 'stitch in time saves \nine.

○ 'What about these dirty \marks?

• What vgranny always did | was 'soak them in \vinegar.

○ I 'love that vtree.

• What my vneighbours want | is for me to 'cut it \down.

○ I'll 'see if there's somewhere further down the \road.

• What vyou need | is your 'own \parking space.

E4.7.6 Create sentences beginning in one of the following ways:

'What I vlike about . . . | is . . .
'What I vdon't like | is . . .
'What I vwant | is . . .
'What I vdon't want | is . . .
'What I can't vstand | is . . .

'All you need vnow | is . . .
The 'only thing I want vnow | is . . .
'What I want from v . . . | is . . .
'What he wants from vyou | is . . .
'What we need vnext | is . . .

4.8   Defining and non-defining

There are two kinds of relative clause: defining and non-defining. The first type usually does not have its own separate IP, the second does:

🎧   'Who's \Nikki?   (i) • She's my 'sister who lives in \Canada.
                          (ii) • She's my \sister, | who 'lives in \Canada.

Version (i), defining, implies that I have more than one sister; I am singling out the particular one who lives in Canada; it is that sister I am talking about, not my other sister(s). Version (ii), non-defining, is consistent with my having only one sister; I throw in the additional information about where she lives.

(i)   He 'used a comma that was 'wrong.
(ii)   He 'used a 'comma, | which was 'wrong.

Here, version (i) has a defining relative clause (= the type of comma that was wrong). Version (ii) has a non-defining relative clause, but is ambiguous: it may mean either 'he used a comma, and the comma was wrong' or 'he used a comma, and his using it was wrong' – i.e. the antecedent of the relative may be either the NP *a comma* or the whole clause *he used a comma*.

Defining relative clauses are much more frequent in conversation than non-defining ones. In typical cases such as the following, there is *no intonation break* before the defining relative clause:

       'Where's that 'pen I was using?
       'That's my 'coat you've taken!

There may well, however, be an intonation break *after* the relative clause, since the whole NP is now rather heavy:

       This 'new 'car I've bought | has a 'special 'locking device.
       The 'point you must re'member | is that . . .

The distinction between defining and non-defining applies to certain other constructions as well:

       'Look at that house near the 'bus stop. (= not the other houses)
       'Look at that 'house, | near the 'bus stop.
       'Bicycles chained to the 'railings | will be re'moved.
       'Outside the 'courthouse | there were some 'bicycles | 'chained to the 'railings.

In particular, it applies to phrases in **apposition**.

(i)   'This is my colleague 'Charles.
(ii)   'This is my 'colleague, | 'Charles.

Version (i) identifies as Charles this particular one of my various colleagues. Version (ii) does not necessarily imply that I have only one colleague, but it does involve presenting the person's status (*colleague*) and name (*Charles*) as two separate pieces of information. There is also a third version, a single IP with *Charles* not accented.

(iii)   'This is my 'colleague, Charles.

Version (iii) offers two possibilities: either that *Charles* is a vocative, the name of the person I am speaking to; or that I have mentioned several people called Charles, and that this is my colleague Charles rather than, say, my cousin Charles.

EXERCISES

E4.8.1 Pair-work practice: defining relative clauses, etc.

- ○ 'Who's \that?
- ○ 'What's that \book?

- • 'That's the man I was \talking about, | \Graham.
- • It's the 'one I'm \reading, | the de'tective story I \told you about.

- ○ 'What's for \dinner?
- ○ 'Where's \Malcolm?
- ○ 'What's the \problem?

- • The \salmon I bought.
- • In the 'room next to the \library.
- • The vcar I'm driving | has 'broken \down.

- ○ 'What are you \looking for?
- ○ 'What can I \get you?

- • 'Where's the \newspaper I was reading?
- • One of those de'licious \cakes you make, | /please.

- ○ 'What's the \matter?
- ○ 'How can I \help you?

- • 'This is the station we \change at.
- • We 'want to go to \Tottenham. || Is 'this the /bus we need to get?

- ○ 'How do we get to the /airport?

- • It de'pends which \route you want to travel.

E4.8.2 Pair-work practice: NPs in apposition.

- ○ 'Who were you /talking to?

- • Oh 'that's \Winston, | the 'man I was \telling you about.

- ○ 'What's /that?
- ○ 'Where do we go \next?
- ○ 'Which /channel are we on?
- ○ 'Why are you de\leting it?

- • It's a \spatula, | for 'cleaning the \bowl with.
- • To Mont\gomery, | the county \town.
- • 'BBC\7, | the \music channel.
- • It's 'all \spam, | 'stuff we don't \want.

E4.8.3 Show how the following can be disambiguated by intonation.

The difficulty(,) I predict(,) will be in the finances.
The problems(,) James saw(,) were mainly technical.

4.9   Parallel structures

As we saw in 2.22, the items in a **list** are sometimes separated by into-nation breaks, sometimes not. This applies more generally to parallel grammatical structures, including (i) parallel words or phrases, whether or not coordinated, and (ii) strings of letters or numbers.

With parallel words or phrases, there is likely to be an intonation break after each component if there are more than two components or if the components are heavy:

> I 'come in on 'Mondays, | 'Wednesdays | and 'Fridays.
> I want to buy some 'fruit, | some 'milk | and some 'bread.
> I can 'see a sort of 'tree, | and the 'outline of a 'person.
> You could do it on 'Tuesday after'noon | or on 'Wednesday 'morning.

If the parallel words or phrases are placed in contrast by the speaker, then they too are likely to be separated by an intonation break:

> I'm 'not going to repeat the mistake I made ∨last time | ＼this time.

The speaker has discretion to omit the intonation breaks, for example when speaking fast:

> 'When do you come in? • 'Mondays, 'Wednesdays and 'Fridays.

Some coordinated structures are potentially ambiguous, and can optionally be disambiguated by the insertion of an intonation break. For example, the phrase *old men and women* may be analysed either as [*old*] [*men and women*], or alternatively as [*old men*] and [*women*]. The issue is whether *old* applies to both nouns, or just to the one that immediately follows it. The phrase would usually be said without an internal intonation break, in which case it remains ambiguous. If, however, it is said as '*old* | '*men and* '*women*, the hearer is forced towards the first interpretation. If it is said as '*old* '*men* | *and* '*women*, the hearer is forced towards the second.

With a string of letters or numbers there are equally two possibilities. If we think they will be familiar to the hearer, or if there is no need to be particularly explicit, we run them together in the same IP. If we think they may be unfamiliar to the hearer or need to be made especially clear, we can make the message easier for the hearer to process by placing an intonation break after each item.

> A: 'How do you spell to ⁄*seize*?
> B: 'S, E, I, Z, ＼E.
> A: ⁄What was that again?
> B: ⁄S, | ⁄E, | ⁄I, | ⁄Z, | ＼E.

Longer strings typically get broken up into manageable chunks:

> My ∨phone number | is 'oh two ⁄oh | 'seven six seven ⁄nine | 'seven one seven ＼five.
> ∨Your reference | 'A L ⁄W | '2 0 0 ⁄4 | '3 9 6 ＼J.

EXERCISES

E4.9.1 Can these potentially ambiguous expressions be disambiguated by intonation? If so, how?

> empty cases and boxes
> six times three plus four
> an alveolar or labial-velar approximant
> a noun or verb phrase
> thirty five hundredths
>
> Henry and Rebecca Lynch
> fifty minus twenty times two
> red and blue shirts
> lazy boys and girls
> stewed fish or meat

E4.9.2 Dialogue practice.

> A: 'What's \Eve's number?
> B: 'Four six one \eight.
> A: /Sorry?
> B: /Four, | /six, | /one, | \eight.
> A: ∨That's not a proper number.
> B: Well it has 'four nine one ∨first, of course.
> A: So 'what's the \full number?
> B: 'Give me \strength. ‖ /Four, | /nine, | ∨one, | /four, | /six, | /one, | \eight.
> A: \Thank you. | You've 'got a /problem?

4.10   Tag questions

Tag questions tend to have their own IP (see 2.14). This applies particularly to **reverse-polarity** tags (also known as **checking** tags). In them the tag is negative if the main clause is positive, positive if the main clause is negative.

> *Positive–negative*
> We 'could do it to'morrow, | 'couldn't we?
> They've 'got their 'books, | 'haven't they?
> 'Mary'll be pleased, | 'won't she?
>
> *Negative–positive*
> It 'wasn't a di'saster, | 'was it?
> It's 'not 'finished, | 'is it?
> The boys 'can't have for'gotten, | 'can they?

Question tags have sharply different meanings depending on whether their tone is a fall or a rise (see 2.14).

A tag is sometimes incorporated as a tail into the IP of the main clause, if it has a rising tone. This does not happen with reverse-polarity tags after a fall:

> The boys 'can't have for∨gotten, can they?

In **constant-polarity** tags it is quite usual for the tag not to have its own IP. These are also known as **copy** tags, and are normally positive–positive. (If a constant-polarity tag does have its own IP, the tone must be a rise, as seen in 2.14.)

You're 'ready to 'go, are you? *or*
You're 'ready to 'go, | /are you?

'Close the 'window, would you, please? *or*
'Close the 'window, | /would you, please?

EXERCISES

E4.10.1 Pair-work practice: reverse-polarity tag in tail.

- o We 'ought to be \going | /soon.
- o We could 'set off at about \seven.

- o 'Let's try and \estimate | 'how long it'll \take.
- o I'll 'go and buy something to \eat.
- o 'Now for making the \sauce.

• There's 'plenty of /time, isn't there?
• We 'don't need to be there /early, do we?
• There 'aren't any special /problems, are there?
• We've got 'plenty of /bread, haven't we?
• You've 'done it be/fore, haven't you?

E4.10.2 Pair-work practice: constant-polarity tag in tail.

- o Mr \/Forton | 'offered me his congratu\lations.
- o 'Off we \go, then.
- o 'Here's little Ve\ronica.
- o En\/joy yourselves.
- o My 'new com\/puter | is a \godsend.

- o I 'think you \know the way | to /Oxford.
- o 'See you next \Monday.
- o He'll 'want to see my I\D.
- o 'What about the re\ceipt?
- o The 'children are \ready for you.

• He's /pleased with you, is he?
• You're 'quite /ready, are you?
• She's 'got her /teddy-bear, has she?
• We can 'take the /car, can we?
• You're /pleased with it, are you?

• I 'take the M/40, do I?
• We'll 'leave it till /then, shall we?
• You'll 'bring it /with you, will you?
• I'll 'leave it with /Nora, shall I?
• They've 'had their /dinner, have they?

E4.10.3 Pair-work practice: command, constant-polarity tag in tail.

- o /Yes? | 'What /is it?
- o 'Anything I can /do for you?
- o 'All /set then?
- o 'Are you /comfortable in here?
- o 'Here's the ad/dress.

• 'Keep the /noise down, would you, please?
• 'Let me have the /Johnson files, could you?
• 'Tell me the /number again, would you?
• \Open | the /window a bit, would you?
• \Lend me | your /pen, would you?

See 2.14 and 3.16 for other exercises on tag questions.

5 Beyond the three Ts

PRENUCLEAR PATTERNS

5.1 The anatomy of the prenuclear part of the IP

Up to now we have concentrated on identifying the nucleus and its tone. We turn now to the prenuclear part of the IP. What items, other than the nucleus, get accented? And what is the pragmatic effect of this accentuation?

Recall that the accenting of an item is achieved by accenting its lexically stressed syllable(s). To accent a syllable we make it stand out by a combination of rhythmic and pitch features.

Words before the nucleus may be accented. In unemphatic speech, only the *first* content word in the prenuclear part of the IP receives an accent (= a rhythmic stress plus intonational prominence on its lexically stressed syllable). In more emphatic speech, *all* content words may receive an accent. Function words, too, may receive an accent if contrastive.

If there are any accents before the nucleus, the first such accent (= the **onset**) constitutes the beginning of the **head** of the intonation pattern. The head extends from the onset up to the last syllable before the nucleus:

'Why didn't you 'tell me?	*onset* = Why; *head* = Why didn't you
The 'manager was an'noyed.	*onset* = man-; *head* = manager was an-
I re'member your 'mother.	*onset* = -mem-; *head* = -member your
A'nother mistake!	*no onset, no head*

The head does not necessarily consist of complete words. In the second example it includes the first syllable of *annoyed*, but not the second; in the third it includes the second and third syllables of *remember*, but not the first. If we use the term 'foot' to denote the rhythmic unit consisting of a syllable bearing a rhythmic stress (beat) plus the unstressed (off-beat) syllables that follow it, we can say that the head consists of one or more whole feet.

Depending on the length of the IP, there may be several words between the onset and the nucleus:

I'd 'rather we discussed this matter more 'fully.
It's an 'awfully long distance to have to 'walk.

The syllables (if any) before the first accented syllable are called the **prehead**. In the examples just given, the preheads are *I'd* and *it's an* respectively.

> It's 'really very 'simple.   *prehead* = It's
> She's de'termined to try it a'gain.   *prehead* = She's de-

In the following examples there is no onset, and the entire prenuclear part is a prehead:

> They a'gree with me.   *prehead* = They a-
> We've got 'hundreds of them.   *prehead* = We've got

Depending on the words available, it follows that before the nucleus we may have a prehead and a head, or a prehead and no head, or a head and no prehead, or nothing. Formulaically, the structure of the IP is:

> (prehead) (head) nucleus (tail)

The reason we recognize prehead, head and nucleus as separate parts of the IP is that the speaker makes separate tonal choices at each of these points. The choice of prehead tone (high or low), the choice of head tone (high or low), and the choice of nuclear tone (rise, fall, fall–rise) are all independent of one another. There is, however, no such choice in the tail. The pitch characteristics of the tail are determined by the choice of nuclear tone.

EXERCISES

E5.1.1 Identify the parts of the prenuclear pattern (prehead, head) in the following:

> It's dis'gusting.
> 'What a 'pity.
> I've for'gotten your 'name.
> There are 'three kinds of gi'raffe.
> I think it's ex'tremely up'setting.

E5.1.2 True or false?

(a)   The prehead is always followed by the head.
(b)   Every IP contains a nucleus.
(c)   The head always contains at least one accented syllable.
(d)   The pitch characteristics of the head are determined by those of the nucleus.
(e)   Every nucleus is preceded by an onset.

5.2   Simple heads

A **simple** head is one that contains only one accented syllable. We shall consider simple heads first, before looking at **complex** heads (= heads that contain two or more accented syllables).

We recognize four typical pitch patterns to be found in simple heads. We distinguish them as **high** and **low**, depending on the pitch of the onset. We distinguish them further according to whether the pitch remains steady (= level) or changes. Thus we have our four types: **high level** ['], **high falling** [`], **low level** [,] and **low rising** [,].

The high level head is the default type, and we shall continue to write it [']. For the other types of head we shall use, where relevant, the special symbols shown. (Elsewhere in this book, where the type of head is not relevant, we write them all ['].)

In a simple **high level** head [`], the onset and all the remaining syllables of the head are uttered on a high level pitch:

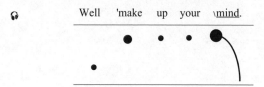

In a simple **high falling** head [`], the onset starts on a high pitch. There is then a gradual fall from a high pitch to a mid pitch, spread over all the syllables of the head:

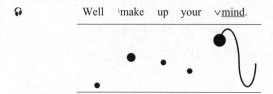

In this book, the high falling head is used only before a fall–rise nuclear tone. The high level head is used before all other nuclear tones.[1]

In a simple **low level** head [,], the onset and all the remaining syllables of the head are uttered on a low pitch:

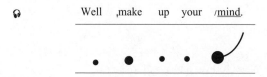

In a simple **low rising** head [,], the onset starts on a low pitch. There is then a gradual rise from low to mid pitch, spread over all the syllables of the head:

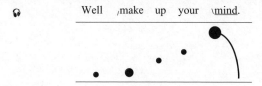

In this book, the low level head is used only before a rising tone. The low rising head is used only before a falling tone.[2]

EXERCISES

E5.2.1 Performance practice: simple high level head followed by a fall.

  'Better than ˎever.
  'Fast and ˎfurious.
  'Glorious ˎweather!
  'Seventy ˎdollars.
  'Central ˎEurope.

  It's 'nearly ˎready.
  They've 'all sucˎceeded.
  I've 'never felt ˎbetter.
  Ri'diculously ˎcheap.
  In'credible ˎvalue.

E5.2.2 Pair-work practice.

 o 'What did you think of the ˎconcert? • 'First ˎrate.
 o 'When will you be ˎhere? • 'Half past ˎsix.
 o 'Where's my ˎmousepad? • I 'lent it to ˎMichael.
 o 'Where shall I send the ˎbill? • 'Send it to my acˎcountant.
 o We 'ought to have asked Doˎlores. • That's 'just what I ˎtold you.

E5.2.3 Performance practice: simple high level head followed by a rise.

  'First in ˊline?
  'Sure that's what you ˊmeant?
  'Got all your ˊcases?
  'Feeling Oˊ K?
  'Raring to ˊgo?

  Is 'that your ˊpartner?
  Does 'everyone aˊgree?
  Do the 'plugs need reˊplacing?
  Have you 'brought all the ˊdocuments?
  Can we be 'sure she'll acˊcept?

E5.2.4 Performance practice: simple high falling head followed by a fall–rise.

  ˋNot at the ᵛmoment.
  ˋOnly in Decᵛember.
  ˋNever on a ᵛSunday.
  ˋLike your ᵛjacket.
  ˋGlorious ᵛweather!

  It's ˋnot very ᵛgood.
  I'm ˋawfully ᵛsorry.

I `don't like the ˯vegetables you've chosen.
She's `not going to ˯like it.
You've `only got your˯self to blame.

E5.2.5 Pair-work practice.

○ 'Who let the \cat out?

- It `wasn't ˯me.
- `Not ˯me.
- I `don't think ˯I did.
- I `don't think it was ˯me.
- I `don't think ˯I was the one who let her out

○ But I'm \sure he said to turn left.
○ And 'fruit juice is \alkaline.
○ So we'll 'all be \winners.
○ And 'you can pay the \fees.
○ I 'can't find anyone who \sells them.

- I `don't think he ˯did.
- I `don't think you're ˯right.
- Well I'm `not sure about ˯that.
- Well I `don't know about ˯that.
- You could `always go on the ˯internet.

E5.2.6 Performance practice: simple low level head followed by a rise.

🎧 ˌDon't ⁄worry.
ˌNot very ⁄much.
ˌQuite ⁄good.
ˌFifty ⁄pounds.
ˌLast ⁄Saturday.

🎧 It ˌdoesn't ⁄matter.
You ˌcan't do ⁄that.
I ˌtrust you're ⁄well.
You're ˌhome ⁄early.
You're ˌlooking very ⁄smart.

E5.2.7 Performance practice: simple low rising head followed by a fall. These sound protesting (see 5.8).

⁄Not at \all.
⁄Number \five.
⁄No I \can't.
⁄That's not e\nough.
🎧 ⁄Saturday's \hopeless.

But I ⁄told them my\self.
I ⁄don't be\lieve it.
I ⁄haven't the \foggiest.
The ⁄food was \terrible.
🎧 We've ⁄only just be\gun.

E5.2.8 Listening practice: identify the head tone and nuclear tone in each of the following.

🎧 ˀSeventy ˀeight. (*five versions*)
🎧 It's ˀnearly ˀready. (*five versions*)

E5.2.9 Performance practice: use high level heads.

D'you 'really /mean that, | or are you 'just being ＼nice about it?
'Either you change your /ways, | or I'm 'simply going to ＼leave you.
D'you have 'change for a /twenty, | or 'had I better ＼owe it to you?
'Was that a knock at the /door, | or 'am I i＼magining things?
Would you 'rather watch a /video, | or 'just sit here and ＼talk?

E5.2.10 Performance practice: use a high falling head before the fall–rise.

Be＼fore you jump to con＼clusions, | 'listen to what I have to ＼say.
Un＼less you ob˅ject, | I'm going to 'book the ＼Florida holiday.
＼This ˅wine | is 'too ＼dry.
＼If you're so ˅keen on it, | 'pay for it your＼self.
What with ＼one thing and a˅nother, | we 'felt a bit let ＼down.

5.3   Complex heads

Corresponding to the four simple head patterns, there are also four **complex** head patterns. Each of them enables the speaker to accent more than one syllable in the prenuclear material. In terms of intonational meaning, they can be seen as adding emphasis or weightiness to the IP as a whole (rather than to particular words). Naturally, this device is available only in IPs in which the head is long enough to accommodate two or more accented syllables.

We symbolize a complex head by writing the accent mark (', ＼, ‚, ⁄) before each accented syllable.

In a **complex high level head**, successive accented syllables form a series of level steps, each one lower pitched than the preceding. Any unaccented syllables are at the same pitch height as the accented syllable they follow. For this reason, this is sometimes known as a 'stepping head' (O'Connor & Arnold, 1973). There are as many steps as there are accented syllables in the head.

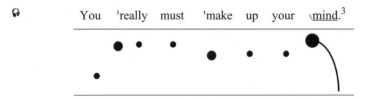

In a **complex falling head**, there is a series of falls, one from each accented syllable, and each one starting at a slightly lower pitch than the preceding one. Each fall is spread over the accented syllable and any unaccented syllables that may follow. The complex falling head is sometimes known as a 'sliding head' (O'Connor & Arnold, 1973).

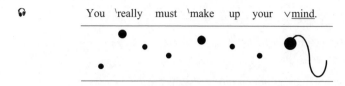

You ˈreally must ˈmake up your ᵛmind.

There is no complex low level head.[4]

In a **complex low rising head**, there is a series of rises, one from each accented syllable. Each may start at a slightly higher pitch than the preceding one; or each may start again at the same low pitch. Each rise is spread over the accented syllable and any unaccented syllables that may follow. The complex rising head is sometimes known as a 'climbing head' (O'Connor & Arnold, 1973).

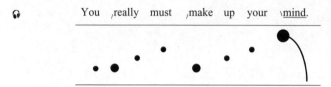

You ˌreally must ˌmake up your ˎmind.

Mixed complex heads (= a combination of different types within the same IP) are occasionally heard, but are outside the scope of this book.

EXERCISES

E5.3.1 Performance practice: complex high level head followed by a fall.

ˈDon't ˈinterˎrupt!
ˈDo as ˈmuch as you ˎcan.
ˈWhere did you ˈput the ˎscrewdriver?
ˈPut some ˈmore ˎmilk in it.
ˈHow d'you ˈthink we ˈought to ˎstart?

I'm ˈgetting ˈrather imˎpatient.
Comˈpletely and ˈutterly ˎuseless.
It's an ˈawfully ˈlong ˎway.
I ˈcan't ˈsee the ˎpoint in all this rigmarole.
So ˈwhen do they exˈpect to give us an ˎanswer to our question?

E5.3.2 Performance practice: complex high level (stepping) head followed by a rise.

ˈSure you're ˈquite ˊready?
ˈGot all the ˈbits and ˊpieces?
ˈTraining the ˈteam ˊhard?
ˈWhen is ˈGodfrey ˊcoming?
ˈWhat do I ˈwant to ˊorder? (‖ ˎCoffee, | I ˊthink.)

Does ˈeveryone ˈwant ˊcoffee?
You must ˈcome and ˈvisit us aˊgain.

That's 'not the 'style I /asked for.
Did 'Mrs 'Thatcher suc/ceed in her campaign?
You're 'planning to 'stay /where?

E5.3.3 Performance practice: complex high falling head followed by a fall–rise.

`Lovely `piece of vporcelain.
`Only on `Wednesdays and vFridays.
`Don't `drop the vglass.
`Three hundred and `forty-vnine.
`Awful `news from vTuscany.

I'm `quite sure it `isn't vmine.
She `never `really vliked it.
I `hardly `think it's vlikely.
I `don't think we can ac`cept a vsubstitute.
You `might at `least have vphoned me.

E5.3.4 Performance practice: complex low rising (climbing) head followed by a fall.

/Try and con/trol your \temper.
/Where have you /put the \files?
/When are they /going to be \ready?
I /really /don't \mind.
I /haven't the /slightest i\dea.

E5.3.5 Listening practice: identify the head tone and nuclear tone in each of the following.

?Fifty ?three ?thousand. (*four versions*)
I ?asked for ?smoked ?salmon. (*four versions*)

5.4   Preheads

If there is any material at the beginning of the IP before the onset, it constitutes the **prehead** of the intonation pattern (see 5.1).

Usually preheads are spoken with a fairly low level pitch, the speaker's neutral or unmarked pitch, indicating the absence of any particular intonational meaning:

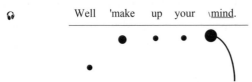

Preheads usually consist of nothing but lexically unstressed syllables. Sometimes, however, they may include a syllable that is lexically stressed but that the speaker chooses not to accent – i.e. in a word that the speaker chooses not to accent. Such syllables usually carry a rhythmic stress (beat):

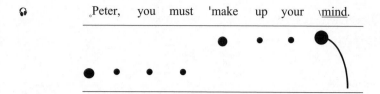

.Peter, you must 'make up your \mind.

Speakers can add emphasis to an IP by using a 'marked' (= distinctive) prehead. In a **high prehead** all the syllables are said on the same high pitch, usually higher than any pitch within the rest of the IP – sometimes up in the falsetto range. (Thus the high prehead is higher pitched than the onset at the start of a high head.) Nevertheless, these syllables are not accented. High preheads are usually quite short: not more than two or three syllables. The symbol [⁻] shows that everything between this mark and the next intonation mark belongs to the high prehead. (If we need to show explicitly that a prehead is low, we can use the symbol [_].)[5]

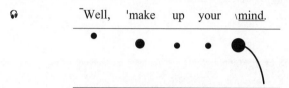

⁻Well, 'make up your \mind.

Whereas accenting a word by accenting its stressed syllable(s) adds emphasis to that word, using a high prehead adds emphasis to the whole IP.

Thus there are two ways of adding emphasis to the whole IP:

- by accenting more than one syllable in the head, thus making it a complex head;
- or by using a high prehead.

It is also possible to combine both methods:

> I was 'very disap\pointed with it. (*unemphatic*)
> I was 'very 'disap\pointed with it. (*emphasis by complex head*)
> ⁻I was 'very disap\pointed with it. (*emphasis by high prehead*)

EXERCISES

E5.4.1 Listen to the difference between low and high prehead. Then say whether the prehead is low or high in the test items.

You ,mustn't /worry.	⁻You ,mustn't /worry.
I /simply don't be\lieve it.	⁻I /simply don't be\lieve it.
She ˅wasn't.	⁻She ˅wasn't.
I \will.	⁻I \will.
A /handbag?	⁻A /handbag?

○ ?The train was ⁄absolutely ⟍packed.
○ ?It was in⟍credible!
○ ?I ⌄didn't.
○ ?In the ⁄garden?
○ ?I 'can't be ⟍bothered.

E5.4.2 Pair-work practice.

○ o You're just a 'sad ⟍loser.
○ o I ⟍clocked him one.
    o 'When can we ⟍meet?
    o You've 'missed the ⟍turn.
    o I'm 'not going to be able to ⟍do it.

• ˉYou ,can't speak to me like ⁄that!
• ˉYou ⟍didn't!
• ˉWould ⁄Friday be a good day?
• ˉI'm ⁄sorry.
• ˉWell ⌄try.

E5.4.3 Show how the following could be made emphatic:

And 'how would you like your ⟍eggs, sir?
What a 'really marvellous ⟍sunset!
I was 'absolutely ⟍furious.
Did you 'really expect me to be⁄lieve that?
I 'can't believe he meant what he ⌄said.

FINER DISTINCTIONS OF TONE

5.5   Varieties of fall

In chapter 2 we identified the fall as one of the three primary tones, and saw that it has a range of tone meanings: definitive, often complete (independent), insistent (in the case of a yes–no question) and reinforcing (in the case of an adverbial). These meanings apply to all types of falling nuclear tone. We go on now to discuss the **additional** tone meaning associated with the choice of a particular variety of fall.

We recognize three such particular varieties of fall: a **high fall**, a **low fall** and a **rise–fall**. Both the high fall and the low fall are **simple** falls. There may be a slight kick up in pitch at the start of the nuclear syllable, but apart from that the pitch movement is all in one direction, namely downwards. The rise–fall, on the other hand, is a **complex** fall, since there is a significant upward (rising) movement before the downward (falling) movement.

A **high fall** (⟍) involves a falling pitch movement from a relatively high pitch to a low pitch:

○   ⟍Wonderful!

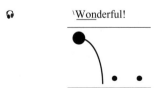

If there is material before the nucleus, then there is a **step up** from it to the beginning of the fall (see 2.2).

A **low fall** (˯) involves a falling pitch movement from a mid pitch to a low pitch:

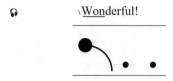

If there is material before the nucleus, then there is typically a **step down** from it to the beginning of the fall.

If there is a tail after a simple fall nuclear tone, the pitch of the tail is all low and level. The falling movement takes place at the nuclear syllable, so that the entire tail is low pitched.

A **rise–fall** (∧) involves a complex pitch movement, starting with a rise from a mid pitch to a high pitch and then a fall from high to low, finishing on a low pitch. The initial mid pitch may be somewhat prolonged before the start of the upward–downward movement. The most prominent part is the initial rise:

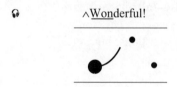

If there is a tail after a rise–fall nucleus, the rise–fall pitch movement is spread over the nuclear syllable and the first or first two syllables of the tail. Low level pitch may not be reached until the second syllable of the tail.

As can be seen, the first syllable in a polysyllabic tail after a rise–fall nucleus (here, -*der*-) may well be the highest-pitched syllable in the whole IP. Nevertheless, it is unaccented, as can be seen from the fact that its vowel may be weak.[6]

The difference between different kinds of fall depends on the pitch height or movement at the start of the fall. If it starts above mid pitch, and particularly if it involves a step up from the last prenuclear syllable, it is a high fall. If it starts below mid pitch, and particularly if it involves a step down from the last prenuclear syllable, it is a low fall. If it starts around mid pitch and then first rises before falling, it is a rise–fall. There may also be cases that are intermediate between these possibilities.

We shall continue to use the basic symbol [˘] when we choose not to identify any subtype of fall.

All falling nuclear tones finish low; the final tendency in the tail after a falling nuclear tone is always low level.

The difference of tone meaning between high fall and low fall is the **degree of emotional involvement**. The high fall implies greater interest on the part of the speaker, greater excitement, greater passion, more involvement. The low fall implies relative lack of interest, less excitement, a dispassionate attitude, less involvement. The higher the starting point of a simple fall, the greater the degree of emotional involvement; the lower the starting point, the less the emotional involvement:

🎧 I'll be 'staying for a ˋmonth. (*excited, enthusiastic*)
🎧 I'll be 'staying for a ˎmonth. (*factual, objective*)

We're 'going on an ˎouting | to⁄day.   • 'Where ˋto? (*bright, interested*)
🎧 I 'need you to give me a ˎlift.   • 'Where ˎto? (*serious*)
🎧 'Why don't you want to ˎgo?   • Well it's ˋraining, | ˋisn't it? (*indignant*)
🎧 'Why don't you want to ˎgo?   • Well it's ˎraining, | ˎisn't it? (*discouraged*)

🎧 I 'don't know what to ˎdo.   • Can I ˋhelp you at all? (*light*)
🎧 I 'don't know what to ˎdo.   • Can I ˎhelp you at all? (*urgent*)

🎧 'Come and have ˋdinner with us. (*warm, an invitation not an order*)
🎧 'Come and have ˎdinner with us. (*serious, expects to be obeyed*)

There are two special tone meanings associated with the **rise–fall**. One is that the speaker is **impressed** (or expects the listener to be impressed). This tone meaning is found with statements, exclamations and yes–no questions, but not with wh questions or commands:

It cost 'twenty ∧thousand!
Have you 'heard about ⁄Bill? | He's been ∧fired!
I'll be 'staying for a ∧month. (*very excited*)
'What a di∧saster!

This meaning is sometimes reinforced by using breathy voice. The result can sound gossipy:

🎧 She came 'top of the ˎclass.   • ∧Did she just! | 'Well ∧well!
🎧 I paid 'fifty ˎdollars for it.   • ∧Fifty!
🎧 'Jane's left her ˎhusband.   • ∧Terrible, | ∧isn't it?
🎧 'Sally's just had ˎtriplets.   • My ∧goodness!
I'm 'not wearing anything under∧neath. (*flirtatious*)

Native speakers of English often react to a demonstration of the rise–fall tone by giggling.

The other special element of tone meaning associated with the rise–fall is that of **challenge**, even disapproval. This meaning is found with all clause types, including wh questions:

🎧   I 'don't want to anˇtagonize her.   • But you've 'got to be ∧firm.
            I 'can't find any \dinnerplates.   • But we've got ∧lots of them.
            They're 'going to be \late again.   • They always ∧are late, | ∧aren't they?
🎧   'I need a \break.   • 'Don't we ∧all!
            He's behaving 'very \badly.   • 'Why not ∧tell him?

Compare two intonation patterns for the same words:

(i)   Exˇcuse me.
(ii)   Ex'cuse ∧me!

Pattern (i) is the way person A might politely ask person B to move so that he, A, could get past. Pattern (ii) is the way B might ironically react if A pushed in front of her without saying anything. The tonicity is ironic because it suggests that B is to blame; the tone meaning of the rise–fall is a challenge.

   With commands, the rise–fall suggests that the speaker refuses responsibility, refuses to be involved:

🎧   What \colour shall I choose?   • Please your∧self.
🎧   I 'don't want to take ˇchemistry.   • Take ∧physics, then.
🎧   'May I take this /newspaper?   • ∧Do.

EXERCISES

E5.5.1 Revisit the exercises in 2.5. Perform them with high fall, low fall and rise–fall in turn. What is the effect on intonational meaning? Think of circumstances in which each might be used.

Model:	I 'think it's \great.	
→I 'think it's `great.	*enthusiastic . . .*	
I 'think it's \great.	*could be a put-down*	
I 'think it's ∧great.	*impressed, could be flirtatious*	

E5.5.2 Do the same with the exercises on wh questions in 2.12.
E5.5.3 Do the same with the exercises on exclamations in 2.17.
E5.5.4 Do the same with the exercises on commands in 2.18.

5.6   Varieties of fall–rise

   The tone meanings of the fall–rise nuclear tone were discussed in chapter 2 (particularly sections 2.6–7, 2.18, 2.20): as an independent tone, implication (including polite correction partial correction, and negation, and in commands warning); as a dependent tone, non-finality.

We now make finer distinctions among fall–rise tones, recognizing three particular varieties: the mid fall–rise, the rise–fall–rise and the high fall–rise.

A **mid fall–rise** involves a pitch movement that first falls from a high pitch to a low pitch and then rises, ending on a mid pitch. This is the default type, and we continue to write it [ᵥ]:

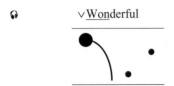

If there is material before the nucleus, then there is a **step up** from it to the beginning of the fall, though the pitch of the onset is typically higher than that of the start of the fall–rise.

A **rise–fall–rise** (ᷱ), like a rise–fall, starts with a rise from a mid pitch to a high pitch; but this is followed by a fall from high to low and then a rise back to a mid pitch. The initial mid pitch may be somewhat prolonged before the start of the upward–downward–upward movement. The most prominent part is the initial rise. The pitch of the voice changes more rapidly during the fall than during the rises:

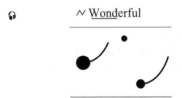

A **high fall–rise** (ᵛ) involves a pitch movement that falls from a mid pitch to a low pitch and then rises back up to a high pitch:

The difference between the mid fall–rise and the rise–fall–rise depends on the pitch movement at the start. If it is mainly downwards, we have a mid fall–rise. If it is emphatically upward, then we have a rise–fall–rise. The difference between the mid fall–rise and the high fall–rise depends on the pitch movement or level at the **end**. If the pitch does not rise above mid, we have a mid fall–rise. If the pitch goes higher, and seems to point indefinitely upwards rather than towards any level pitch, then we have a high fall–rise.

The default (= neutral) fall–rise pattern is the mid fall–rise. It has the implicational tone meaning described in 2.5–6.

⏽	Is 'that your /scarf?	• I ⌄think so.
⏽	Could 'I write a /novel?	• You could ⌄try.
⏽	Are the 'children /ready now?	• Well ⌄some of them are.
	'How shall we pro⌄ceed?	• 'First choose the ⌄colour, │ then the ⌄size.

The rise–fall–rise keeps the same implicational tone meaning, but adds in the 'impressed' meaning of the rise–fall (see 5.5).[7]

⏽	Could 'I write a /novel?	• You could /⌄try.
⏽	Are the 'children /ready now?	• Well /⌄some of them are.

   As a dependent tone (see 2.20–3), the only variety of fall–rise used is the mid fall–rise.

   Neither the mid fall–rise nor the rise–fall–rise is used with questions.
The high fall–rise (ˇ) is similar to the other varieties of fall–rise in terms of pitch movement but rather different in terms of tone meaning. Its tone meaning is similar to that of the high rise. It is used only with questions (particularly echo questions), where it adds animation or intensity and has the effect of making the question more specific. It can suggest astonishment, 'as if the speaker can hardly believe his ears' (O'Connor & Arnold, 1973: 71).[8]

⏽	You'll 'have to do it a⌄gain.	• 'Do it aˇgain?
	'Where's the ⌄bathroom?	• The ˇbathroom?
⏽	He's the 'MP for ⌄Runcorn.	• ˇWho did you say he was?
	We can 'put them in the ⌄lounge.	• ˇWhere d'you want to put them?

EXERCISES

E5.6.1 Revisit the exercises in 2.6–7. Perform them with mid fall–rise, a rise–fall–rise and a high fall–rise in turn. What is the effect on intonational meaning? Think of circumstances in which each might be used.

Model:	It 'wasn't really ⌄bad.	
	→It 'wasn't really ⌄bad.	*implicational*
	It 'wasn't really /⌄bad.	*impressed as well as implicational*
	It 'wasn't really ˇbad?	*checking, or echo question*

E5.6.2 Do the same with the commands in E2.18.3.

E5.6.3 Revisit the declarative questions in E2.8.1 and the exercises on checking questions in 2.16. Perform them with a high fall–rise instead of a rise.

5.7   Varieties of rise

The tone meanings of the rise nuclear tone were discussed in chapter 2: as a dependent tone, incomplete or open, or (in the case of an adverbial) limiting (2.20–3); as an independent tone, either interested, perhaps soothing, or alternatively signalling non-solidarity, indignation, truculence or perfunctoriness (2.9); in yes–no questions, neutral, or signalling pardon questions or uptalk (2.10–6). This is a wide range of different tone meanings, and in fact some of them are distinguished by differences in the range or height of the rise. Others are distinguished by particular prenuclear patterns (see 5.8).

We now make finer distinctions among rising tones, recognizing three particular varieties: the high rise, the low rise and the wide rise. There is also the mid level nuclear tone, which shares one intonational meaning with the low rise.

The **high rise** (ˊ) involves a rising pitch movement from a mid pitch to a high pitch. The movement seems to point indefinitely upwards rather than towards a high level point:

The **low rise** (ˏ) involves a rising pitch movement from a low pitch to a mid pitch:

The **wide rise** (ˏˊ) combines the special characteristics of the low rise and the high rise, since it has a rising pitch movement that starts from a low pitch and moves to a high pitch:[9]

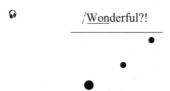

For the **mid level** (ˉ) the voice maintains a level pitch between high and low, and neither rises nor falls:

🎧   ˃Wonderful!

![symbol]

In analysing running speech by ear or by machine it may be sometimes difficult or impossible to distinguish with certainty between these different varieties of rise; but they do appear to have distinct tone meanings.

The **high rise** is the tone associated with checking, pardon questions and echo questions. It is also the tone of uptalk statements:

🎧   ꞌMartin's lost his ∖cat.   🎧 • ´Who's lost his cat?
                                       🎧 • ꞌMartin's lost his ´what?
                                            • ꞌMartin's done ´what to his cat?

The **wide rise** is associated with the non-solidarity of indignant or truculent disagreement:

🎧   It was an ꞌutter di∖saster.   • It ⟋wasn't!
🎧   She's ∖not going to ∨finish it. • She ⟋is.
            He's a buf∖foon.   • ∖No, | he's ⟋not!

In yes–no questions and greetings it signals surprise:

🎧   Is ⟋that what you think?! (| You must be ∖crazy!)
            Hel⟋lo! (| I ꞌdidn't expect to see ∨you here!)

The **low rise** is associated with the remaining independent uses of the rise nuclear tone, in particular the supportive rise showing interest or routinely encouraging further conversation:

🎧   I've ꞌgot something to ∖tell you. • Go ⟋on.
🎧   Have you ꞌheard about ⟋Jeff?   • ⟋No.

Compare the high rise of query, the wide rise of indignant disagreement, and the low rise of interest or routine:

🎧   You've forꞌgotten your ∖gloves.   • I ´have? (*query*)
🎧   You ꞌhaven't paid for the ∖coffee.   • I ⟋have! (*disagreement*)
🎧   ꞌHave you got the ⟋details?   • I ⟋have. (*interest*)

The low rise is found particularly with responses consisting of a 'limiting' adverb or adverbial (see 2.23).

🎧   ꞌCould I borrow your ⟋pen?   • If you ⟋must.
🎧   Do you ꞌever eat in the can⟋teen?   • ⟋Sometimes.

In a greeting, compare the low rise of routine, the high rise of query, and the wide rise of surprise. (Imagine that it is just before midnight.)

🎧   Good ⁄morning.   • Good ´morning? (| But it's ＼nighttime!)

🎧   Good ⁄´morning! (| What a 'pleasant surprise to ＼see you!)

In the case of **yes–no questions**, the differences between these possibilities are more subtle. A high rise signals informality; a low rise signals polite interest (at least in British English; Americans may perceive it as patronizing); a wide rise adds a note of surprise:

🎧   'Would you like some ´tea? (*casual, airy*)

🎧   'Would you like some ⁄tea? (*polite*)

🎧   'Would you like some ⁄´tea? (*surprised*)

Both the low rise and high rise can be used as **leading dependent** tones. This is also the main use of the **mid level**.

🎧   'First we have ⁄one thing, | 'then we have a＼nother.

🎧   'First we have ´one thing, | 'then we have a＼nother.

🎧   'First we have ＞one thing, | 'then we have a＼nother.

Except for some interjections, the mid level is not used as an independent nuclear tone.

The difference in tone meaning between these four tone varieties is not great. Sometimes speakers just seem to ring the changes between them to avoid repetition. The low rise is perhaps more formal, more oratorical; the high rise is more casual; and the mid level has no special tone meaning except non-finality. The fall–rise may factor in its usual tone meaning of implication or contrast:

🎧   (i) ˌThat's the end of the ⁄weather forecast; | 'now we go on to the ＼news.

🎧   (ii) ˌThat's the end of the ´weather forecast; | 'now we go on to the ＼news.

🎧   (iii) ˌThat's the end of the ＞weather forecast; | 'now we go on to the ＼news.

🎧   (iv) 'That's the end of the ᵛweather forecast; | 'now we go on to the ＼news.

Version (i) sounds slightly more serious, version (ii) rather more airy. Version (iv) could include the implication 'the end of the weather forecast, but not of everything'.

American English differs from British in making little or no use of the low rise as a leading dependent tone – one of the reasons, perhaps, that British English may strike Americans as stuffy and formal.

For a **trailing dependent** rise, the usual variety is a low rise:

      I'm going to ＼Edinburgh | on ⁄Tuesday.

      We could in'vite the ＼Robertsons | if you ⁄like.

EXERCISES

E5.7.1 Revisit the declarative questions in E2.8.1 and the queries in E2.16.1–8. Perform them, making sure that the rise is a high rise (or a high fall–rise).

E5.7.2 Revisit the alternative questions E2.22.4–5. Perform them with a mid level tone instead of the rise.

> *Model:*
> Would you prefer /coffee | or \tea?
>> → Would you prefer ⌐coffee | or \tea?

E5.7.3 Revisit the trailing adverbials in E2.23.3 and the fall-plus-rise examples in E2.24.1–8. Perform them, making sure that the final rise is a low rise.

5.8   Prenuclear and nuclear tone meaning

In certain combinations, the tone meaning depends not on the nuclear tone alone but on a particular combination of prenuclear pattern and tone. This applies particularly in the case of the head before (i) a fall and (ii) a low rise.

The default head before a fall is the high head. Using a **low rising head** adds a special tone meaning, namely that of **protest**:

🎧   We've been /waiting for \hours.
🎧   You /shouldn't keep on com\plaining like that.
🎧   What on /earth does she think she's \doing?

Compare the tone meanings in the following:

🎧   'Where are your \essays?   🎧   (i) • We 'handed them in ⌐yesterday.
                                      🎧 (ii) • We 'handed them in \yesterday.
                                      🎧 (iii) • We /handed them in ⌐yesterday.
                                      🎧 (iv) • ⌐We /handed them /in ⌐yesterday.

The high head and high fall of (i) show emotional involvement. The high head and low fall of (ii) makes it factual and unemotional. The low rising head of (iii) turns it into a protest. In (iv) the high prehead and complex head make the protest very emphatic.

The head with a **leading dependent low rise** may be high or low, at least in British English:

🎧   I 'opened the /door | and 'looked \in. *or*
          I ,opened the /door | and 'looked \in.
          In 'central /London | there's a con\gestion charge. *or*
          In ,central /London | there's a con\gestion charge.

In American English, however, a rising head is sometimes used, but not a high level head:

> I ˏopened the ˏ<u>door</u> | and 'looked ˎ<u>in</u>.

With a **trailing dependent rise**, the prenuclear pattern is always low:

ᕦ   You can 'do what you ˎ<u>like</u>, | as ˌfar as ˏ<u>I'm</u> concerned.

With an **independent rise**, the choice of prenuclear pattern may affect the tone meaning. In a statement or command, a high head or prehead with a low rise creates a **soothing** and reassuring effect:

> Now 'don't ˏ<u>worry</u>. | I'm 'not going to ˏ<u>hurt</u> you.
> 'Could I make a sugˏ<u>gestion</u>?

This soothing rise is often used when talking to children, and if used to adults can sound patronizing:

> It's 'all ˏ<u>right</u>. ‖ I'll be 'back ˏ<u>soon</u>.
> Now you must 'take it ˏ<u>easy</u>. | 'Don't eˏ<u>xert</u> yourself.
> I'll be 'back in a ˏ<u>moment</u>.

(This does not apply in short responses and greetings, where there is no particular soothing effect:

ᕦ   'Right you ˏ<u>are</u>.
         'Oˏ<u>K</u>.
ᕦ   ¯Helˏ<u>lo</u>.
         ¯Goodˏ<u>bye</u> then.)

A **low level head** before a rise, on the other hand, may sound defensive, grudging, or generally non-supportive of the other person:

ᕦ   The ˎ<u>top's</u> fallen off.   • I ˌdon't suppose it ˏ<u>matters</u>.
ᕦ   Her per'formance was ˄<u>dire</u>!   • Oh it ˌwasn't as bad as ˏ<u>that</u>.

We can see the two possibilities and the difference between them in the following exchange:

> I'm 'not looking forward to my   (i) • There's 'no need to ˏ<u>worry</u>.
> vˎ<u>dental</u> appointment.
>   (ii) • There's ˌno need to ˏ<u>worry</u>.

The high head of (i) makes it kindly and soothing. The low head of (ii) makes it sound brusque, dismissive of the first speaker's anxiety.

ᕦ   'Are the ˏ<u>figures</u> ready?   ᕦ (i) • ¯They ˏ<u>are</u>.
                                           ᕦ (ii) • They ˏ<u>are</u>.

Here the high prehead in (i) can make it cheerful and encouraging, while the low prehead in (ii) can sound guarded and resentful.

With **yes–no questions**, a high head plus low rise is the usual one in RP and similar kinds of British English (BrE). To Americans it sounds formal. A low prenuclear pattern plus high rise suggests informality:

ᴖ   D'you 'come here ˌ/o̲f̲t̲e̲n̲? (*only BrE, can sound formal*)
ᴖ   D'you ˌcome here ′o̲f̲t̲e̲n̲? (*casual*)

A **wide rise** may have either a low or (BrE) a high prenuclear pattern:

ᴖ   D'you ˌcome here ⁄o̲f̲t̲e̲n̲? (*surprised*)
ᴖ   D'you 'come here ⁄o̲f̲t̲e̲n̲? (*surprised, only BrE*)

Before a **high fall–rise**, on the other hand, the usual head is a high (i.e. level) head. The head pattern is thus the same as for the high rise, just as the tone meaning is similar to that of the high rise:

ᴖ   You 'think he's doing ᵛw̲h̲a̲t̲?
           'No one's blaming ᵛy̲o̲u̲.
ᴖ   That's 'not what I ᵛs̲a̲i̲d̲. (*indignant*)
           'Don't start till they're ᵛr̲e̲a̲d̲y̲. (*warning*)

EXERCISES

E5.8.1 Pair-work practice: declarative questions. High level head, high rise nucleus.

ᴖ
- o 'Alan's not \h̲e̲r̲e̲, I'm afraid.
- o We're 'going to the \s̲u̲p̲e̲r̲m̲a̲r̲k̲e̲t̲.
- o 'Where's my \p̲a̲p̲e̲r̲?
- o We've 'been together a \y̲e̲a̲r̲ now.
- o It's 'number \t̲w̲e̲n̲t̲y̲.

- • He's 'gone ′h̲o̲m̲e̲?
- • 'Straighta′w̲a̲y̲?
- • You 'want it ′b̲a̲c̲k̲?
- • You 'don't re′g̲r̲e̲t̲ it?
- • It's 'number ′h̲o̲w̲ many?

E5.8.2 Pair-work practice: guarded, tentative, non-supportive responses. Low level head (if present), low rise nuclear tone.

ᴖ
- o 'Could I have the afternoon ˌ/o̲f̲f̲?
- o 'How much have they \s̲e̲n̲t̲?
- o Oh I've \l̲e̲f̲t̲ | ⁄t̲h̲a̲t̲ job.
- o 'How \c̲l̲u̲m̲s̲y̲ of you, | to 'break the \t̲e̲a̲p̲o̲t̲.
- o I'm 'not properly pre\p̲a̲r̲e̲d̲.

- • I supˌpose I can manage withˌ/o̲u̲t̲ you.
- • The ˌsame as beˌ/f̲o̲r̲e̲.
- • You ˌnever ˌ/t̲o̲l̲d̲ me.
- • I ˌdidn't do it on ˌ/p̲u̲r̲p̲o̲s̲e̲.
- • ˌNo one will ˌ/n̲o̲t̲i̲c̲e̲.

- o Will U'nited win the ⁄c̲u̲p̲?
- o 'Could you have made a mi\s̲t̲a̲k̲e̲?
- o Have we 'reached the ⁄t̲a̲r̲g̲e̲t̲?
- o Will you be 'singing in the ⁄c̲h̲o̲i̲r̲?
- o Have you 'sold your ⁄h̲o̲u̲s̲e̲?

- • They ˌ/m̲i̲g̲h̲t̲.
- • It's ˌjust about ˌ/p̲o̲s̲s̲i̲b̲l̲e̲.
- • ˌMore or ˌ/l̲e̲s̲s̲.
- • I ˌ/c̲o̲u̲l̲d̲, I suppose.
- • Perˌ/h̲a̲p̲s̲.

- o 'When did you get \b̲a̲c̲k̲?
- o You 'keep making mi\s̲t̲a̲k̲e̲s̲.

- • A ˌfew ˌ/d̲a̲y̲s̲ ago.
- • ˌSo do ˌ/y̲o̲u̲.

o Oh I'm 'not \seeing her any more.
o 'What did she \say?
o I'll 'never suc∨ceed.

• You ˌnever told /me that.
• The ˌsame as be/fore.
• But you could /try.

E5.8.3 Pair-work practice: soothing responses. High head, low rise.

o 'Where are you \going?

• 'Just to get some /milk.
• I 'won't be /long.
• 'You can come /with me.
• 'Not /far.
• I'll be 'back /soon.

o 'Hurry /up.
o I just 'daren't pick it \up.
o 'Call your \dog off!
o 'Will I be all /right?
o I'm \sorry | I let you /down.

• I'm 'just /coming.
• You 'won't /break it.
• He's 'not going to /bite you.
• \Yes, | it's 'quite /safe.
• It 'doesn't /matter. | We 'all make mi/stakes.

E5.8.4 Revisit the drills in E2.18.7–8. To get the soothing or patronizing effect, ensure that the head is high level and that the rise is a low rise.

E5.8.5 Discuss the possible tone meaning of *They're certainly not going to cheat you* in the following conversational exchange. How would it be affected by the pitch used for the head?

o D'you 'think they'll pay /up?

• Of \course they will. | They're 'certainly not going to /cheat you.

NON-NUCLEAR ACCENTING

5.9   Lexical stress and downgrading

Every content word has at least one lexically stressed syllable. Some of these syllables, but not all, are accented when the word is said aloud. We have seen how the location of the first accent (the onset) and the last accent (the nucleus) is determined. Any lexically stressed syllables that do not receive an accent may bear just a rhythmic stress. In this book we ignore non-accent rhythmic stresses, since they are irrelevant for intonation. If desired, however, they can be symbolized with the ring symbol °. Following O'Connor & Arnold (1973), some may wish to distinguish those that are high pitched, [°], from those that are not, [ₒ].[10]

Basic markup
Does Peter /really want me to tell him?
Andrew was ˌquite sure he'd \lost it.
The ∨first exam paper | and the \second exam paper.

Possible comprehensive markup
⁻Does °Peter /really °want me to °tell him?
ₒAndrew was /quite °sure he'd \lost it.
The ∨first eₒxam ₒpaper | and the \second eₒxam ₒpaper.

Another way of approaching the relationship between lexical stress and accentuation is to start by recognizing all the **potential** accents in an IP. They comprise all the lexically stressed syllables from the onset to the nucleus inclusive. The speaker then has the option to **deaccent** (= downgrade, weaken or remove) some of them.

The option to downgrade potential accents is a pervasive characteristic of English rhythm. It tends to operate whenever an accent is located between two other accents in the same IP.

We can illustrate downgrading with the phrase *Thank you very much*. Basically it has three **accentable syllables**: *thank*, *ver-*, *much*. It is possible to accent them all. More usually, though, we downgrade the accent on *ver-*. In this example we show as (°) the potential rhythmic stress that is left:

> 'Thank you 'very 'much.   (*three accents*)
> 'Thank you (°)very 'much.   (*middle accent downgraded*)

The onset accent remains; the nuclear accent remains; but the accent between them disappears. The effect is to change a complex head into a simple head.

The faster we speak, the more familiar the words we use, the more likely we are to downgrade.

🎧	I 'really 'don't 'like it.	→	I 'really don't 'like it.
	It's an 'awfully 'good i'dea.	→	It's an 'awfully good i'dea.
	It's a 'very 'difficult 'problem.	→	It's a 'very difficult 'problem.

The downgrading principle is sometimes known as the **rule of three**, since it weakens the middle accent or stress of three. It applies very obviously in strings of letter names or numbers:

	'A 'B 'C	→	'A B 'C
🎧	'one 'two 'three	→	'one two 'three

But it also applies to any kind of material:

	the 'big 'bad 'wolf	→	the 'big bad 'wolf
	I 'can't be'lieve you 'mean it.	→	I 'can't believe you 'mean it.
🎧	They're 'trying to cre'ate a di'version.	→	They're 'trying to create a di'version.

With longer strings of potential accents, the speaker has considerable freedom over which ones to downgrade. But the onset accent and the nuclear accent are always unaffected. (In the following examples we ignore potential °.)

> 'A 'B 'C 'D → 'A B 'C 'D *or* 'A 'B C 'D → 'A B C 'D
> 'three 'six 'five 'seven → 'three six five 'seven
> 'A 'B 'C 'D 'E → 'A B 'C D 'E → 'A B C D 'E
> I 'want to 'ask you 'something con'cerning my 'taxes. → I 'want to ask you 'something concerning my 'taxes. → I 'want to ask you something concerning my 'taxes.

The two main reasons for a lexical stress *not* to be reflected in the utterance as an accent are (i) that it precedes the onset or follows the nucleus, and (ii) because of downgrading.

EXERCISES

E5.9.1 Identify the accentable syllables in the following. Place the mark ' before each such syllable. Then place brackets round those accents that can be downgraded.

> *Model:*   She's trying to finish her essay.
> → She's 'trying to 'finish her 'essay.
> → She's 'trying to (')finish her 'essay.

I want to borrow some books.
They've ordered some fish and chips.
I'm determined to visit Paris.
I've just returned from Athens.
Do you like my new hairstyle?

5.10   Two or more lexical stresses

Every word – more generally, every lexical item – has a lexical stress pattern involving a **primary** (= main) stress. The primary-stressed syllable is the one that bears the nuclear accent if the nuclear accent is on that word:

> re'markable →
> It was re\markable. (*the nuclear syllable is* -mark-)

In some words or multi-word lexical items, the primary stress is followed by a **post-primary stress** (also sometimes called a **secondary** or **tertiary** stress). This is shown in dictionary entries by the mark ˌ. Examples include compounds such as 'washˌbasin, 'baby-ˌsitter, 'telephone ˌnumber. (See the discussion in 3.4.) These syllables are not accentable, although they may have a rhythmic stress:

> 'telephone ˌnumber →
> I'm 'looking for her \telephone number.
> Her 'telephone number's in the \book.[11]

Some words, however, have a lexical stress that **precedes** the primary stress, or indeed more than one such stress. These lexical stresses are important for intonation, since they are accentable.

Items that have a pre-primary stress (for example, ˌunder'stand, ˌchicken 'sandwich) are referred to as **double-stressed**. Items that have more than one pre-primary stress (for example, ˌmisapˌpropriˈation) are **multiple-stressed**. Many longer English words are double-stressed or multiple-stressed. We have already met double-stressed compounds (3.5). Further examples of double-stressed items include ˌsixˈteen, ˌcontroˈversial, ˌacaˈdemic, ˌunˈknown; examples of multiple-stressed items include ˌinterˌcontiˈnental, iˌdentiˌfiaˈbility.

Pre-primary stresses can be reflected as accents:

> ˌunderˈstand →
> We ˈunderˈstand.
>
> I ˈunderˈstand your anˈxiety. → I ˈunderstand your anˈxiety.
>
> ˌchicken ˈsandwich →
> A ˈchicken ˈsandwich!
> A ˈchicken ˈsandwich with ˈsalad. → A ˈchicken sandwich with ˈsalad.

If a double-stressed word, such as *understand*, is accented, there will be an accent on at least one of the lexically stressed syllables, and possibly on both. But either of them may be deaccented – an accent may be downgraded – by the rule of three.

In the examples just given the onset is on the first syllable (*un-*) of *understand* and on the first syllable of *chicken sandwich* – syllables which do not bear a lexical primary stress.

If a double-stressed or multiple-stressed item is the *only* accented item in an intonation phrase, then it usually bears both the onset and the nucleus. Thus the word has two intonation accents:

> We ˈunderˈstand.
> There were ˈsixˈteen of them.
> It's ˈcontroˈversial.
> Through ˈmisappropriˈation.

> ˈWhere are you ˈstaying?   • At the ˈIntercontiˈnental.

If the onset is located on a double-stressed or multiple-stressed item, but the nucleus comes somewhere later in the IP, then the onset accent usually still goes on the *first* available lexically stressed syllable:

> I ˈunderstand ˈclearly.
> A ˈchicken sandwich with ˈsalad.

Downgrading may have the effect of removing the potential accent from the syllable with the lexical primary stress. Compare the following examples:

> I can ˈhardly ˈunderˈstand. (*three accents, emphatic*)
> I can ˈhardly underˈstand. (un- *deaccented by downgrading*)
>
> I ˈunderˈstand ˈclearly. (*three accents, emphatic*)
> I ˈunderstand ˈclearly. (-stand *deaccented by downgrading*)
>
> I ˈdon't understand at ˈall. (*both accents of* understand *downgraded*)

'Bring me a 'chicken 'sandwich. (*three accents, emphatic*)
'Bring me a chicken 'sandwich. (chick- *deaccented by downgrading*)

a 'chicken 'sandwich with 'salad (*three accents, emphatic*)
a 'chicken sandwich with 'salad (sand- *deaccented by downgrading*)

The result of accenting the first stressed syllable, but not the last, in a multiple-stressed item is that the stress pattern of the word appears to change. This is the phenomenon sometimes known as **stress shift** or 'iambic reversal'. It is merely a special case of downgrading.

    ₍six'teen
    She's 'aged six'teen.
    There were 'sixteen 'people there.

    ₍contro'versial
    It's 'rather contro'versial.
    It's a 'controversial de'cision.

'Stress shift' contributes towards a natural alternation of the strong and the weak, the accented and the unaccented, the stressed and the unstressed, and towards the avoidance of the clash of adjacent strong, accented, or stressed syllables.

Although 'stress shift' is usual, it is not categorical. Speakers do sometimes choose not apply it, downgrading an initial accent instead:

    (*less commonly*) I under'stand 'clearly.

Nevertheless, EFL learners are recommended to treat stress shift as a rule that should be applied. An accent pattern of the type *I under'stand 'clearly* is rarely heard from core native speakers of English. Rather, it is typical of EFL.

Where there are four or more potential accents, patterns of downgrading are more variable and often irregular. Where there are two successive double-stressed items, implying four potential accents, stress shift tends not to occur:

    ₍oppo'sition, ₍poli'tician
    'oppo'sition 'poli'ticians →
    'opposition poli'ticians (*or, equally possibly*) oppo'sition poli'ticians

The accent pattern of a double-stressed word is obviously affected by decisions about tonality. In (i) below, we have the usual stress shift on the double-stressed word *seventeenth*, with the downgrading of the accent on *-teenth*. But in (ii) the intonation break causes *-teenth* to bear the nuclear accent:

    ₍seven'teenth
    (i) It'll be her 'seventeenth ⟍birthday.
    (ii) It'll be her 'sevenᵥteenth | ⟍birthday.

EXERCISES

E5.10.1 With the tonicity as shown, where is the onset likely to be in each IP?

in nineteen 'fifty
some independent ad'vice
association 'football
your undivided at'tention
misappropriation and cor'ruption

There were seventeen 'people there.
It's a controversial 'issue.
It was a fundamental mi'stake.
We can understand your 'problems.
There are thirteen 'paths | to en'lightenment.

5.11 The focus domain

Does the onset *always* go on the first lexically stressed syllable of the first content word in the IP? Often, but not always.

We have seen (3.9–15) that in **broad** focus everything is brought into focus, while in **narrow** focus (including **contrastive** focus) only part of what we say is. We call the part that is in focus the **focus domain**.

It is tempting to claim that just as the nucleus marks the end of the focus domain, so the onset marks its beginning. There are many cases where this is the case; but in practice not always. Take this example:

'What happened \next?　　• Lor'raine 'kissed \Steve.

Here, the whole of *Lorraine kissed Steve* is new and in focus. All three words are likely to be accented. The onset is on the lexically stressed syllable of the first item, *Lorraine*, and the nucleus is on the lexically stressed syllable (the only syllable) of *Steve*. The focus domain is coextensive with the utterance.

/Really?　　　　　• \Yes, | she placed an e'normous \smacker on his lips.

Here, the focus domain is just *an enormous smacker*. The words *she placed* and *on his lips* are out of focus. This is signalled by the facts that the onset is on *-norm-* and the nucleus on *smack-*. Because *she placed* is out of focus, there is no accent on *placed*. So the location of the onset may depend on the speaker's decisions about focus.

Quite often the focus domain does not coincide in extent with intonational elements (prehead, head, nucleus, tail). In our example the *e-* of *enormous* and the *-er* of *smacker* are unstressed, and form part of the prehead and the tail respectively, even though the words *enormous* and *smacker* are in focus and accented. Indeed, arguably *an*, too, is in focus, because the entire noun phrase (*an enormous smacker*) of which it forms a part is in focus. Thus the **phonetic** domain from onset to nucleus (from one accented syllable to another) does not necessarily quite coincide with the **pragmatic** domain of focus.

Another metaphor sometimes used to convey the same idea as focus is that of **background** and **foreground**. We would say that the phrase *an enormous smacker* is in the foreground – like the part of a photograph that is nearest to you as you look at it, the part you notice first – while *she placed* and *on his lips* are in the background. The onset and nucleus signal to the hearer where the foreground begins and ends.

Compare the next two exchanges. The same words are used in reply to two differently worded invitations:

☊	(i) 'Care for a /drink?	• \Thanks. | A 'gin and \tonic, |/please.
☊	(ii) 'Care for a /gin?	• \Thanks. | A gin and \tonic, | /please.

In response (i), the whole phrase *a gin and tonic* has to be put in focus (foregrounded), since it contains all-new information. In (ii), *gin* is already given, so does not have to be accented (it gets backgrounded); only *and tonic* needs to be put in focus by accentuation.

In practice, the distinction between cases such as (i) and (ii) is not always clear-cut, since (a) the speaker always has the option of reaccenting the repeated item (here *gin*), and (b) the speaker may treat the whole of *gin and tonic* as a single item, double-stressed, and therefore put the onset on its first lexically stressed syllable, which is *gin*. Hence in practice we are very likely to get:

(ii′) 'Care for a /gin?	• ˌ\Thanks. | A 'gin and \tonic, | /please.

Further examples:

(i) What happened to Jim?	• He 'hurt his left 'leg.
(ii) Was Bill injured?	• He hurt his 'left 'leg.

Response (i) has broad focus. Response (ii) has narrow focus, *hurt* being given since it is a synonym of *injured*. So you would expect *hurt* not to be accented. But in practice we often get:

(ii′) Was Bill injured?	• He 'hurt his (')left 'leg.

And again:

☊	A: What does Deirdre do?	B: She 'writes 'novels. (i)
☊	A: And does she write plays?	B: 'No, | she writes 'novels. (ii)
☊	A: Does she read novels?	B: I 'don't 'know, | but she 'certainly 'writes novels. (iii)

Here, the successive responses have respectively (i) broad focus, (ii) contrastive focus on *novels* and (iii) contrastive focus on *writes*. In (i), all of *writes novels* is in focus, and all the content words are accented accordingly. In (ii), *writes* is old information and can therefore be deaccented. In (iii), *novels* is old information and therefore deaccented. But in practice there is a strong tendency in (ii) to place the onset on *writes* despite its being a repeated item:

> A: And does she write plays?   B: 'No, | she 'writes 'novels. (ii′)

The response in the next example seems logically to demand a very long prehead, since the first item of new information is *office*:

> Did you say he lost the key to his car?   • 'No, | I said he lost the key to his 'office. (?)

But it would feel awkward to have such a long prehead. The usual way of pronouncing this response would be to put the onset on *key* or *lost* or even on *said*.

So we can say that in practice the onset does indeed usually go on the **first lexical item** of the IP, whether or not it would be expected to be in focus. We discuss certain exceptions in the next two sections.

EXERCISES

E5.11.1 Devise questions which might elicit the following responses, in (a) narrow and (b) broad focus.

> *Model:*   A 'prawn ⟍sandwich, | ⟋please.
>   →(a) D'you want a prawn baguette or a prawn sandwich?
>   (b) What can I get you, sir?

> She's 'broken her 'right ⟍ankle.
> He's into ba'roque ⟍music.
> We're going on a 'pub crawl in ⟍Manchester.
> I want to 'travel around 'Asia.
> I was 'watching T'V.

5.12   Major and minor focus

Imagine you have just been given an excellent meal, and at the end, as you take your leave, you want to thank your hosts. You will use the words *That was an excellent meal*. Logically, you will accent the two items *excellent* and *meal*. So one possibility, with neutral tonicity, is:

(i)   That was an 'excellent 'meal.

You might well say this. In the context, however, *meal* is not exactly new. So it would also be possible to remove the accenting on *meal* and say:

(ii)   That was an 'excellent meal.

But in the discourse *meal* might indeed be new: you have been talking about other matters, and now finally talk about the meal. So you still want to accent the word *meal*. One way of resolving this problem is to divide the material into two IPs (even though you will not pause between them):

(iii)   That was an 'excellent | 'meal.

You can signal that the first is to be treated as having greater importance than the second by using a less salient tone on the latter. You can achieve this by using a less emphatic tone for the second IP. For example, we might have a high fall or a rise–fall for the first IP, followed by a low fall or, very typically, a low rise for the second.

   Crystal (1975: 27) regards the second tone as **subordinated** to the first:

(iii) (a)   That was an ˋexcellent | ˎmeal.
   (b)   That was an ∧excellent | ˎmeal.
   (c)   That was an ˋexcellent | ˏmeal.
   (d)   That was an ∧excellent | ˏmeal.

The sequence of tones in (iii c) is the fall-plus-rise pattern discussed in 2.24 above. Both *excellent* and *meal* are in focus. We could say that there is a major focus on the first and a minor focus on the second.

EXERCISES

E5.12.1 Revisit the exercises in 2.24. Identify the major and minor focus in each example.

E5.12.2 Suggest suitable intonation patterns for the following:

   It's awfully embarrassing.
   I'm so relieved you managed to make it.
   He was terribly ashamed of what he'd done.
   They're fascinating, these new gadgets.
   I do enjoy choral singing.

5.13   Unimportant words at the beginning

        There are various words and phrases that are regularly left unaccented at the beginning of an utterance. That is to say, they form part of the prehead.
   This applies, obviously, to function words such as articles, pronouns, conjunctions and modal or auxiliary verbs:

   I was 'just going to 'call you.
   It was a 'terrible 'shock.
   And the 'sad thing 'was | that . . .
   She's 'only 'ten, | yet she 'sings 'brilliantly.

It also applies, optionally, to introductory interjections such as *well*, *so*, *yes*, *no*:

> Well I'm 'not 'sure.
> Yes I'll 'do it to'morrow.
> No I 'can't ac'cept.

It applies to short introductory phrases such as *I think*, *I mean*, *I suppose*, *you know*. It also applies to reporting clauses that precede the quoted words:

> I think we've 'all got to try to co'operate.
> I mean I'm 'not trying to 'criticize, | but . . .
> I said, 'It's 'quite 'wrong.'
> She was like ''Get 'stuffed!'
> I found it 'very 'interesting.

Alternatively and exceptionally, most of these 'unimportant' words and phrases can be accented and given their own IP. But this is likely to be done only if there is some pragmatic reason (for example, if the speaker is hesitating or is talking with great emphasis, deliberation, or pathos):

> 'Well, | I'm 'not 'sure.
> 'And | the 'sad thing 'was | that . . .

EXERCISES

E5.13.1 Which syllables are likely to form the prehead?

> I was on the point of phoning you.
> There'll be another train soon.
> It was a remarkably interesting programme.
> No, I'd have told you if she was.
> You know, we're only human.

5.14 Onset on a function word

Against the general rule, certain function words do nevertheless regularly get accented (see 3.17, 3.19). If they are at the beginning of an intonation phrase they bear the onset accent.

Among those regularly accented are **interrogative wh words**:

> 'Who wrote the re'port?
> 'How do you 'feel?
> 'Where are you 'going?
> 'What does 'sus'ceptible' mean?
> 'Which one do you 'want?
> What'ever is she going to do 'next?

Relative wh words, however, are usually not accented:

> When 'planning a 'meal, | 'first you must . . .
> 'This is the 'officer | who 'wrote the re'port.
> He'd for'gotten her 'name, | which was 'rather em'barrassing.

Demonstratives (*this*, *that*, *these*, *those*) are accented to draw attention to a new topic:

> 'That's an interesting 'point.
> 'This is the girl I'm going to 'marry.
> 'This 'boyfriend of yours, | 'what does he do for a 'living?

The demonstrative *that* (pronoun or determiner) is readily accented, but the conjunction *that* (complementizer or relative) is not:

> 'That 'boy | 'needs to learn some 'manners.
> That 'anyone should for'get | was un'thinkable.

As an adverb of place, initial *there* is accented. As a pronoun ('existential *there*'), it is not:

> 'There he 'sat, | 'drinking his 'beer.
> There's 'nothing we can 'do.

In yes–no questions, accentuation of an initial **auxiliary** or **modal** verb is optional:

'Are you 'ready? *or*	Are you 'ready?
'Did you re'member? *or*	Did you re'member?
'Can you 'swim? *or*	Can you 'swim?
'Have you cleaned your 'teeth? *or*	Have you 'cleaned your 'teeth?

The modals *ought*, *used*, *need*, *dare* are usually accented even in statements:

> We 'ought to be making 'tracks.
> I 'used to live in San Di'ego.

An initial contracted **negative** verb is almost always accented, so too is the word *not*.

> 'Haven't we been here be'fore?
> 'Didn't you hear what I 'said?
> I'm 'not really 'sure.

Even in statements, we often accent auxiliaries and modals if by doing so we avoid an awkwardly long prehead (5.11).

> They're going to be 'late for 'work. *or*
> They're 'going to be late for 'work.

Other modals that are usually accented include *may*, *might* and *should* in most senses. *Must* is accented to express an inference, but usually not when it expresses an obligation:

> He 'may have for'gotten.
> It 'should be ready on 'Thursday.
> She 'must be nearly 'sixty by now.
> You must re'member to brush your 'teeth.

Pronouns are accented not only when contrastive, but also when coordinated, or to signal a change of grammatical subject or object:

> 'You and 'I | could 'sort it out 'quickly.
> 'Bill told 'Mary, | and then 'she told 'Jennifer.

When *you* is used as the overt subject of an imperative, it is implicitly contrastive and therefore accented:

> 'You do the 'ironing | and 'I'll wash the 'floor.
> 'Peter can buy the 'food, | and 'you get the 'drinks.

In the following examples, the reference of the pronoun *he* depends on whether or not it is accented:

> Bill threatened Jim, | and then he 'hit him. (= Bill hit Jim.)
> Bill threatened Jim, | and then 'he 'hit him. (= Jim hit Bill.)
> Bill threatened Jim, | and then 'he hit 'him. (= Jim hit Bill.)

The words *even* and *only* are accented when they point forward to the item that bears the nucleus:

> I've 'even bought you a new 'bike! (= not only other gifts)
> I've 'even bought you a 'new bike! (= not a second-hand one)
> She 'only likes 'tea with her toast. (= not coffee)

When used as a synonym of 'but', *only* is not accented:

> I'd 'love to 'come, | only un'fortunately I 'can't.

Prepositions (e.g. *in*, *on*, *by*, *from*) and **subordinating conjunctions** (e.g. *if*, *when*, *although*) can go either way. If they have considerable semantic content, or are polysyllabic, then they may well be accented; otherwise they are not accented.

> (')On the 'table | you'll find a . . .
> By a re'markable co'incidence, | . . .
> If you 'really can't 'wait, | . . .
> Al'though I tried my 'best, | . . .

When prepositions or other grammatical items are **coordinated** they are usually accented (although the second accent may then be downgraded):

> I 'go by 'bus | 'to and (')from 'work.
> 'If and (')when he re'turns, | we'll 'ask him to ex'plain.

EXERCISES

E5.14.1 Locate the onset.

> When leaving the 'bus, | don't forget your be'longings.
> When do you plan to re'turn?
> That money talks is not in dis'pute.
> That 'lad you were talking to – | what's his 'name?
> There's 'Mary. | You could ask 'her. (*two meanings*)

E5.14.2 Identify the pronoun references.

(i)   ∨Jennifer | was 'talking to An∕nette, | and then she ∖turned on her.
(ii)   ∨Jennifer | was 'talking to An∕nette, | and then 'she turned on ∖her.

FURTHER CONSIDERATIONS

5.15   Stylization

As well as the intonation patterns described so far, English also has a few special, **stylized** patterns. These patterns are used only rather rarely, and their pitch and rhythmic characteristics differ from ordinary patterns. They are used for short utterances in circumstances that are routine and predictable, typically to repeat something you have said many times before. (For new, unexpected circumstances we use a regular non-stylized pattern.) Furthermore, a stylized pattern never forms part of a longer intonation structure: the IP that bears it stands alone. In this book we deal with only one such stylized pattern, the high-mid.

The **stylized high-mid** pattern consists of a high level pitch followed by a mid level pitch:

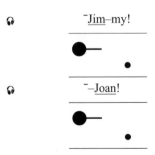

Unlike an ordinary falling tone, the stylized high-mid has an abrupt step down between the two level syllables. The first of the two level pitches (the high level)

goes on the nuclear syllable. The step down to the second level pitch (the mid level) takes place towards the end of the tail, if there is one, and continues to the end of the IP:

I'll be in the ˉlecture –theatre.
We're ˉwaiting –for you.
We're ˉwait–ing.
We'll have to ˉ–wait.

ˉAli–son!

ˉ–John!

If there are prenuclear syllables, they constitute a prehead. There can be no accented syllables before the nucleus:

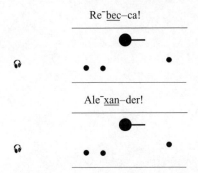

Reˉbec–ca!

Aleˉxan–der!

The above examples show the stylized high-mid pattern as used for vocatives (often called from a distance). It can also be used for certain other short routine utterances:

Come and ˉget –it! (= the food is ready)
ˉThank –you.
(*answering the phone*) Can I ˉhelp –you?
(*answering the phone*) Five four six ˉ–three.
(*during a phone call*) Hold the ˉ–line!

Scholars disagree as to whether the stylized high-mid should be regarded as a variant of the fall or of the fall–rise. In meaning it is probably closest to the fall–rise. Stylization then consists in the suppression of the final rising part. This analysis is supported by the fact that the final syllable is sometimes low-rising rather than low level (House, 1995), and by the fact that the location of the second level pitch is identical with the location of the rise in a fall–rise.

EXERCISES

E5.15.1 Performance practice: nucleus plus monosyllabic tail.

> ⁻Mer–vyn!
> ⁻Jan–ice!
> ⁻Wil–liam!
> ⁻Grub's –up!
> ⁻Go–ing!

> I can't ⁻hear –you.
> Good ⁻morn–ing.
> Don't forget your ⁻tick–ets.
> I'm getting ⁻an–gry.
> Smokers are ⁻los–ers!

E5.15.2 Performance practice: no tail.

> ⁻–Jane!
> ⁻–Food!
> Hel⁻–lo!
> We're ⁻–here.
> She's ⁻–gone.

> Good after⁻–noon!
> Seven three seven ⁻–five.
> Hold on to your ⁻–hats!
> It's time to ⁻–go.
> I don't⁻–care.

E5.15.3 Performance practice: with longer tail.

> ⁻Mela–nie!
> ⁻Jenni–fer!
> Pe⁻nelo–pe!
> I'm⁻talking –to you.
> I don't⁻like –cornflakes.

E5.15.4 Dialogue practice.

> A: ⁻–Jim! | Where ⁻are –you?
> B: I'm ⁻–here!
> A: I can't ⁻see –you.
> B: That's cos I'm ⁻hid–ing.
> A: Oh 'come /on now. ‖ We \must stop playing games.

5.16 Key

As well as the pitch movement within each IP, we need also to consider the general pitch characteristics of longer stretches of speech. The pitch range – the distance between the top pitch and the baseline – is not fixed, but changes as we speak. We constantly readjust our pitch range, and in doing so convey information about the structure of the discourse.

High key involves an abrupt upward shift of the pitch range. **Low key** involves an abrupt downward shift. Where relevant, high key can be symbolized by an up-arrow, ↑, and low key by a down-arrow, ↓.[12]

One use of key is to signal the structure of spoken material. If we listen to a newsreader, for example, we can tell from the use of key where one item ends and another begins. A new item is signalled by high key: the first accent is relatively high pitched in comparison with the end of the item that preceded it. There is then a descent in general pitch level, with a low-pitched finish to the item. Just as a written passage can be divided into paragraphs, so a passage of speech can be divided into **paratones**.

The universal tendency of gradual pitch **downdrift** (or 'declination') affects not only successive high points within an IP, but also successive IPs within a paratone.

You can hear paratone structure in any kind of monologue, in a lecture for example, or a sermon. Each time the speaker starts a new section – to embark on a new topic or make a new point – the new paratone is signalled by high key:

↑ My ∨first point | concerns . . .
↑ Let's look ∕now | at the matter of . . .
↑ You may be ∨wondering | how this relates to . . .
↑ ∨Lastly, | we must consider the . . .
↑ ∖So, | that's ∖it. || We've seen . . .

In conversation you might use high key in the same way, to start on a new topic. Or you might use it when turning to a different listener, or to signal that what you are saying is particularly important. Conversely, low key can signal that something is perfunctory or unimportant.

Another use of low key is to signal that something is **parenthetical** (= separate from the main flow of what we are saying). Both the pitch range and the loudness may be lowered for a fairly short stretch of speech – one IP or at most two – in the middle of an otherwise consistent paratone. This signals that the material involved is not part of the main subject that you are talking about, or perhaps not intended for all your listeners:

Thank ∨goodness, |↓ I keep ∕thinking, | that I live in the ∖country!
The ∨teachers |↓ (and I'm quite ∨sure of this) | will not ac∖cept it.

A parenthetical can even be located inside an IP, for example between the prehead and the head:

🎧   There must have been, ↓ \what, 'fifty or sixty \people there.

Notes

1. Native speakers do not always fully respect this principle. Nevertheless, EFL learners are advised to adopt it. The high level head and the high falling head can then be seen as positional variants ('allotones') of the high head, the choice between them being determined by the choice of nuclear tone.
2. Given this restriction, the low level head and the low rising head can be seen as positional variants (allotones) of the low head, the choice between them being determined by the choice of nuclear tone.

   A low level prenuclear pattern preceding a rising nuclear tone raises a dilemma of analysis. There may be rhythmic stresses among the prenuclear syllables; but if they are all low pitched it may not be clear whether they are accented (= low level head) or not (= low prehead):

   (i)   And (ᵢ)did you a⁄gree?

   The situation becomes clear only if there is a high prehead followed by a low level head:

   (ii)   ⁻And ᵢdid you a⁄gree?

3. Less commonly, there may be a step up rather than a step down. This throws extra emphasis on the word in which the upstepped accent is found.
4. There seems to be no reliable phonetic way to distinguish accented syllables within a low level head from those that are merely said with a rhythmic stress. Pragmatically, we may be able to argue that the former are accented, the latter not; but the distinction is not audibly signalled within a low level head.
5. Pedagogically it seems inadvisable to go into any greater detail about types of prehead. However, for a very full classification, including the possibility of 'homosyllabic' (= non-syllabic) preheads, see Kingdon (1958: 50–6).
6. It can sometimes be difficult to hear the difference between a rise–fall plus poly-syllabic tail and a low or rising head plus high fall plus tail, although the two

differ in tonicity and thus correspond to clearly different pragmatic situations. Compare:

'Why are you looking sur\prised?   • Well /\George is ready.
and vMary isn't ready.   • Well /George \is ready.

7. The rise–fall–rise tone was well described by Kingdon (1958), but has been ignored by recent scholars.

8. It seems that the use of a fall–rise for a question is rather new. Kingdon (1958: 10) says firmly, 'it is not used on questions'. A quarter of a century later, I characterized it as a 'near-RP or local pattern' (Wells 1982: 373). In the first edition of O'Connor & Arnold (1961), it is mentioned in passing as 'an intensified variant of [the low rise] in certain questions' but ignored in the drills chapter; in the second edition (1973), it is described and drilled like other patterns.

9. The name **full rise**, sometimes encountered, is to be avoided because of the likelihood of confusion in speech between 'full rise' and fall–rise.

10. For pedagogical purposes, at least for teaching EFL/ESL, it seems best not to mark non-accent rhythmic stress. Many learners of English find it difficult to pronounce words in the tail without an accent (= without pitch prominence), and the use of any intonation mark at all is likely only to confuse.

11. Some dictionaries also show post-primary stress in cases where the second element of a compound has only one syllable, e.g. '*table ˌlamp*, '*credit ˌcard*; other dictionaries show no post-primary stress here. Some dictionaries (particularly American ones) also show post-primary stress in simple words such as '*eduˌcate*, '*broadˌcast*; the usual British practice is to write simply '*educate*, '*broadcast*. An alternative method of showing lexical stresses, used in some dictionaries, is with acute (primary) and grave (secondary) accent marks, thus *télephone nùmber, táble làmp, crédit càrd, éducàte, bróadcàst*. This is a mere difference of notation, with no different implications for pronunciation. For intonation purposes, all post-primary stresses should be ignored.

'credit (ˌ)card →
I 'want to see her \credit card.
Her 'credit card's out of \date.

The only exceptions to the principle that a post-primary stress is not reflected as an accent are rare cases of contrastive focus:

I 'don't want to see her credit vrating, | I want to see her credit \card.

12. The term **key** is used in somewhat different senses by different authors. For Halliday (1967, 1970) it refers to the subvarieties of each tone, including the associated prenuclear pattern: thus neutral fall, high fall, low fall, and low rising head plus fall are all his Tone 1, but in different keys. For Allan (1986) it is 'relative pitch level', e.g. high fall vs mid fall vs low fall. For Brazil (1985) it refers to the height of the first accent, i.e. in our terms, of the onset if there is one, otherwise of the nucleus.

Putting it all together

6.1 Describing an intonation pattern: the oral examination

In many universities in Britain, and perhaps elsewhere, the practical oral examination in phonetics includes an intonation test. It goes as follows. A short written sentence is put before the candidate. The first task is for the candidate to say the sentence aloud and then to describe the intonation pattern used. After that the examiner says the same sentence with a different pattern, and the candidate's second task is to describe the pattern the examiner used.

For example, the test sentence (written on a piece of paper or card) might be:

But how do you want to pay for it?

The candidate might say this aloud as:

𝛀   But 'how do you want to \pay for it?

– and correctly describe the pattern used by saying 'I used one intonation phrase, I put the nucleus on *pay*, and the tone was a fall. The onset accent was on *how*.'

Depending on the level of detail required by the examiners, the candidate might also need to go on to say: 'The nuclear fall was a high fall, the prehead *but* was low, there was an onset accent on *how* with a high level head extending from *how* to *to*. There was a further rhythmic stress on *want*.'

The examiner might then say aloud the alternative version:

𝛀   ¯But /how do \you want to pay for it?

– which the candidate would correctly describe by saying: 'There was one IP, still with a falling nuclear tone, but the nucleus was now on *you*. The onset accent was still on *how*.'

Depending on the level of detail required, the candidate might also need to say: 'There was a high prehead on *but*, a rising head comprising the words *how do*, and a rhythmic stress on *pay*.'

Other plausible ways of saying this sentence that might well be produced by either the candidate or the examiner include the following. (All are given with comprehensive mark-up.)

𝛀   But 'how do you want to ∧pay for it?

🎧   But 'how do you want to /<u>pay</u> for it?
🎧   But 'how do you ˎ<u>want</u> to pay for it?
🎧   But ˎ<u>how</u> do you want to pay for it?
🎧   But /how do you /want to ˎ<u>pay</u> for it?
🎧   But ˎhow do vˌ<u>you</u> | 'want to ˎ<u>pay</u> for it?

What advice can be given to candidates facing a test of this kind? The best advice seems to be to keep things simple and natural. It is not wise to enter the examination room determined to use some predetermined pattern: if you do that, and the wording of the sentence is not suitable for that pattern, you are unlikely to be able to stick to your plan. The other big danger is that of inadvertently breaking the material into several IPs and failing to recognize this fact. For example, if your sentence is:

          The weather will probably be awful again.

– you might well be tempted to say it as:

🎧   The v<u>weather</u> | will v<u>prob</u>ably | be ˎ<u>aw</u>ful again.

or:

🎧   The 'weather will probably be v<u>aw</u>ful | aˎ<u>gain</u>.

These versions are fine, but do mean that you must describe a pattern for each IP into which you have broken the material. Correspondingly, you must be on the lookout for unkind examiners who use more than one IP in their version.

It is safer for the candidate to avoid theatrical, animated renditions of the test sentence (which are likely to have a complicated intonation pattern), and opt rather for an unemphatic, throwaway version:

🎧   The 'weather will probably be ˎ<u>aw</u>ful again.

Other general points to remember are that:

*   the head always starts with an accented syllable (the onset); you must not mistake the onset accent for the nucleus;
*   words are often split between the prehead and the head, or between the head and the nucleus; so you will have to refer to 'the second syllable of the word' and so on as necessary;
*   if you want to produce a plausible pattern involving a nucleus in the early part of the IP, you will have to imagine an appropriate scenario (i.e. one in which the content of the later part of the IP is already 'given'). If you fail to perform this mental feat, you will probably utter an intonation break and then a second nucleus in another IP. This is fine, but only if you can recognize what you are doing.

EXERCISES

E6.1.1 Pair work. One person takes the role of examiner, the other person the role of candidate. The examiner asks the candidate to say one of the following sentences aloud, and to identify the intonation pattern used. Then the examiner produces a different version, and the candidate has to identify the intonation pattern of the examiner's version.

1	Would you like another orange?
2	I think she'll return tomorrow.
3	But where can we put the new sofa?
4	You haven't finished printing your essay.
5	My cat doesn't like squirrels.

E6.1.2 Instructions as for E6.1.1. (These sentences are more difficult for a weak examination candidate than those in E6.1.1. Why?)

1	The washing machine has flooded the kitchen floor.
2	She found some interesting flowers in Hyde Park.
3	My brother has taken up long-distance running.
4	The car wash was closed again on Monday.
5	It won't be possible to repair your computer.

6.2   Analysing spoken material

Analysing the intonation patterns of a passage of recorded speech, or indeed of speech overheard in real life, is not always easy.

In a sense, your task is the same as that of the participant in a conversation: the important thing is not to detect intonation patterns as an end in itself, but to infer the pragmatic effects intended by the speaker. You have to get inside the speaker's head: what parts of the message did the speaker make into a topic and therefore accent? what was the discourse effect the speaker aimed to achieve? how did the speaker signal in intonation the grammatical structures chosen to convey the message?

Some possible analyses that might be plausible on physical grounds must be rejected because they conflict with what we know about the speaker's intention. (This is one of the main reasons why a competent human analyst is more reliable than a computer analysing physical parameters alone.)

For example, we know that a lexically unstressed syllable is not a candidate for bearing the nucleus. Therefore, faced with the one-word utterance *Absurd!* bearing a pitch pattern starting high and falling to low, we must reject the possibility of there being a falling nuclear tone located on the first syllable. Rather, there must be a high prehead (or head) on the first syllable and a falling nuclear tone on the second – no matter how great the fall over the first syllable or between the first and second syllable, no matter how great the duration of its vowel, no matter how slight the falling movement on the low second syllable. The analysis cannot be (i), it must be (ii) or conceivably (iii).

(i)   ×\Absurd!
(ii)   ⁻Ab\surd!
(iii)   'Ab\surd!

In an utterance *I do!* with an overall falling pitch the pragmatics might tell us that the speaker has no reason to treat *I* as a topic, but might plausibly be emphasizing the tense or polarity of the verb *do* (see 3.14). If so, the analysis must be (i). If, however, the context is such that the speaker might be accenting the pronoun, then (ii) is a plausible candidate. If the physical signal is ambiguous, we must carefully weigh the two possibilities in the light of the pragmatics.

☊   (i) ⁻I \do.
☊   (ii) \I do.

Some of the most readily confused patterns are as follows.

1 **Tone**. The pitch movement may sometimes be insufficient for the analyst to come to a firm conclusion. Sometimes there seems to be hardly any pitch movement on or after the nucleus; not all such cases are the mid level variant of the (low) rise. This applies particularly to non-final IPs.

2 **Finer distinctions of tone**. There is not always a clear-cut line between a rise–fall on the one hand and a high fall with a precursory rising movement on the other. Decisions about high vs. low variants of tones are sometimes difficult, indeed may be arbitrary.

3 **Tonality**. It is notoriously difficult to decide between a single fall–rise spread over nucleus plus tail, on the one hand, and a fall followed by a rise on the other (which in the analysis presented in this book necessarily involves an IP boundary between them). See 2.24. It is sometimes difficult to decide whether a falling pitch movement represents an accent in the head (high falling head) or a separate nucleus (fall tone); likewise, whether a rising pitch movement represents a low rising head or a rise tone. A high (level) head and a barely moving fall–rise nucleus may also be very hard to tell apart:

☊   1 (a) I ˅wish I was rich. (. . . but I'm not.)
              (b) I \wish | I was /rich. (That's what I wish.)

☊   2 (a) We ˋneed some more ˅rain.
              (b)We \need | some more ˅rain.

☊   3 (a) My /wife was \furious.
              (b) My /wife | was \furious.

☊   4 (a) I'm 'nearly \ready.
              (b) I'm ˅nearly | \ready.

4 **Tonicity**. The main problem is that of mistaking a high-pitched syllable elsewhere in the IP for the nucleus. High preheads were mentioned above. Beginners in intonation analysis often mistake a high-pitched onset syllable (high head) for the nucleus. A long tail following a rising nucleus may make it difficult to identify the nucleus (low-pitched), particularly for those in whose language accent is always associated with high pitch. Thus correct identification of the place of the nucleus may be difficult in all the following:

ᖜ   ‾I'm ˎreally annoyed.
ᖜ   I'm 'really anˎnoyed.
ᖜ   ˏYou're really annoyed?
ᖜ   You're ˏreally annoyed?
ᖜ   So ˯will you do it?

EXERCISES

E6.2.1 Listen and identify the pattern used (including possible prehead).

ᖜ   a. (i) I'm going.
              (ii) I'm going.
ᖜ   b. (i) She did it.
              (ii) She did it.
ᖜ   c. (i) They have a marathon in London.
              (ii) They have a marathon in London.
ᖜ   d. (i) I'm sure he's wrong.
              (ii) I'm sure he's wrong.
ᖜ   e. (i) Your notebooks are excellent.
              (ii) Your notebooks are excellent.
ᖜ   f. (i) They're virtually indistinguishable.
              (ii) They're virtually indistinguishable.
ᖜ   g. (i) I'm hoping to succeed.
              (ii) I'm hoping to succeed.
ᖜ   h. (i) How are you going to do it?
              (ii) How are you going to do it?

6.3   Passages for analysis

A typical task in a written examination on English phonetics is a passage in orthography that must be phonetically transcribed. That is outside the scope of this book. Sometimes, however, the candidate is asked to transcribe not only the segments (= vowel and consonant sounds) but also the intonation. In this section we tackle the question of how to do this.

For each of the following passages we supply a model answer, with a reasoned explanation of why the intonation patterns suggested are appropriate. The analysis and markup are at the basic level of chapters 2–4, rather than the comprehensive level developed in chapter 5.

General instructions:

- Start with **tonality** (chunking). Put a boundary mark (|) at the end of each IP. Put a double mark (||) at the end of each sentence. Number the IPs for convenience of reference.
- Next, decide on **accentuation**. Place a mark before each accented syllable. Underline the last one in each IP: this is the nucleus.
- Then decide on the nuclear **tone** in each IP: fall, rise, or fall–rise. Replace the accent mark by the appropriate tone mark.

6.3.1   Towels

Notice in a hotel bathroom

> If you're staying more than one night and are happy to use your towels again, please hang them on the towel rail.
> If you'd like us to replace your towels, please put them in the bath.
> OK, it may not save the world, but it will certainly help.

Tonality (chunking)

The only uncertainty in this passage is the interjection *OK*. It will probably have its own IP (though it might alternatively be treated as a prehead).

> [1] If you're staying more than one night | [2] and are happy to use your towels again, | [3] please hang them on the towel rail. ||
> [4] If you'd like us to replace your towels, | [5] please put them in the bath. ||
> [6] OK, | [7] it may not save the world, | [8] but it will certainly help. ||

Accentuation

In IP 2, *again* means 'one more time', in which sense it is usually accented (see 3.24). (It would alternatively be possible to put the nucleus on *towels*.) In IP 3, *towel rail* is a regular single-stressed compound noun. In IP 4, *towels* have already been mentioned. This word is therefore not accented. Instead, there is narrow focus on *replace*. (In IP 7, it might alternatively be possible to treat *the world* as given, with narrow focus on *save*, which would therefore bear the nucleus.)

Onset accents go as usual on the first lexical item in each IP. This includes the interjection *please*. In IP 7, there is likely to be an accent on *may* (see 5.14).

> [1] If you're 'staying more than one 'night | [2] and are 'happy to use your towels a'gain, | [3] 'please hang them on the 'towel rail. ||
>   [4] If you'd 'like us to re'place your towels, | [5] 'please put them in the 'bath. ||
>   [6] O'K, | [7] it 'may not save the 'world, | [8] but it will 'certainly 'help. ||

Tone

IPs 1 and 2 are leading dependent elements, and therefore take a fall–rise (or rise). IP 3 is an independent element and takes a definitive fall. IP 4 is a leading dependent element, so takes a fall–rise or rise. IP 5 is independent and takes a definitive fall. In IP 6, any tone is possible. *OK* here means something like 'I admit the force of your unstated objection', and thus has the force of a statement. We have chosen to give it a definitive fall. The statement in IP 7 leads up to a *but*. It is therefore most appropriately said with an implicational fall–rise (see 2.6). IP 8 finishes the passage with a definitive fall (although alternatively another implicational fall–rise would also be possible).

> [1] If you're 'staying more than one ˅night | [2] and are 'happy to use your towels a˅gain, | [3] 'please hang them on the ˎtowel rail. ||
>   [4] If you'd 'like us to re˅place your towels, | [5] 'please put them in the ˎbath. ||
>   [6] O˅K, | [7] it 'may not save the ˅world, | [8] but it will 'certainly ˎhelp. ||

6.3.2   Getting breakfast

In a hotel lobby

Hotel guest:	Excuse me, where do I get breakfast?
Receptionist:	In the Panorama Restaurant, sir.
Hotel guest:	Where's that?
Receptionist:	Twenty-seventh floor, sir. Use the lift, over there.
Hotel guest:	But the lift only goes to the twenty-fourth floor.
Receptionist:	Ah. Use lift number five, sir. That one goes to the twenty-seventh floor.
Hotel guest:	I see. Thanks.

Tonality

In IPs 3 and 5, *sir* is a vocative, which does not need its own IP. The comma after *use the lift* in IP 6 implies that *over there* does not modify the noun, but is presented as a separate piece of information, with its own IP. (There might additionally be an intonation break in IP 8, after *lift*. The intonation break between IPs 11 and 12 is optional.)

Hotel guest:	[1] Excuse me, | [2] where do I get breakfast?
Receptionist:	[3] In the Panorama Restaurant, sir.
Hotel guest:	[4] Where's that?
Receptionist:	[5] Twenty-seventh floor, sir. || [6] Use the lift, | [7] over there.
Hotel guest:	[8] But the lift only goes to the twenty-fourth floor.
Receptionist:	[9] Ah. || [10] Use lift number five, sir. || [11] That one | [12] goes to the twenty-seventh floor.
Hotel guest:	[13] I see. | [14] Thanks.

Accentuation

In IP 3, *Panorama Restaurant* is double-stressed, being the name of an institution (see 3.5). Here and in IP 5, the final vocative *sir* is unaccented. The first mention of a floor number, in IP 5, has the nucleus on the last lexical item, *floor*. In IP 7, the demonstrative *there* adds new information, and takes the nucleus. In IPs 8 and 12, however, *floor* is old information, while the number of the floor is contrastive, so the number word takes the nucleus. The onsets in IPs 2 and 4 go on the interrogative wh word. In IP 3, the double-stressed *Panorama* takes the onset on its first stressed syllable (see 5.9 on stress shift). The same applies to *twenty-seventh* in IP 5. In IP 12, the floor number is again contrastive: both the onset and the nucleus are on *twenty-seventh*. (In IP 10, it would also be possible to deaccent *use*, as unimportant in the context, and to place the onset on *lift* or even to deaccent that too and have no onset.) In IP 11, the demonstrative *that* must be accented, but not *one* (see 3.20).

Hotel guest:	[1] Ex'cuse me, | [2] 'where do I get 'breakfast?
Receptionist:	[3] In the 'Panorama 'Restaurant, sir.
Hotel guest:	[4] 'Where's 'that?
Receptionist:	[5] 'Twenty-seventh 'floor, sir. || [6] 'Use the 'lift, | [7] 'over 'there.
Hotel guest:	[8] But the 'lift only goes to the twenty-'fourth floor.
Receptionist:	[9] 'Ah. || [10] 'Use lift number 'five, sir. || [11] 'That one | [12] goes to the 'twenty-'seventh floor.
Hotel guest:	[13] I 'see. | [14] 'Thanks.

Tone

In IP 1, a fall–rise is polite. (A fall would sound like a command that must be obeyed.) In IP 2, the wh question takes a fall. In IP 3, the tone is a definitive fall. Falls are also appropriate in IP 4, a wh question, and in IP 5, a definitive answer. IP 6 could have been complete in itself, so takes a definitive fall, as does IP 7, presented as a separate point.

In IP 8, the protesting statement needs a fall (namely, probably a rising head plus high fall). In IP 9 the interjection *ah*, showing surprise as the receptionist realizes the reason for the guest's difficulty, requires a fall (which might well be a rise–fall). In IP 10, the tone is again a definitive fall. In IP 11, *that* (lift) is contrasted with other lifts, so needs an implicational fall–rise. IP 12, the final part of the sentence, takes a definitive fall. There is a definitive fall in IP 13 (though alternatively there might be an idiomatic pattern accenting both words, with a rising tone, thus '*I* /*see*), and another one at the end of the conversation, IP 14.

☎	*Hotel guest:*	¹ Exˇcuse me, | ² 'where do I get ˌbreakfast?
	Receptionist:	³ In the 'Panorama ˌRestaurant, sir.
	Hotel guest:	⁴ 'Where's ˌthat?
	Receptionist:	⁵ 'Twenty-seventh ˌfloor, sir. ‖ ⁶ 'Use the ˌlift, | ⁷ 'over ˌthere.
	Hotel guest:	⁸ But the 'lift only goes to the twenty-ˌfourth floor.
	Receptionist:	⁹ ˌAh. ‖ ¹⁰ 'Use lift number ˌfive, sir. ‖ ¹¹ ˇThat one | ¹² goes to the 'twenty-ˌseventh floor.
	Hotel guest:	¹³ I ˌsee. | ¹⁴ ˌThanks.

6.3.3   Books

Two friends, fellow-students

A:	Hey, are you going to return those books of mine you borrowed?
B:	Which books? I can't remember borrowing any.
A:	The ones about biology and language.
B:	Oh, those books. Er – could I keep them a few more days?
A:	Why?
B:	Because I need them for my essay.
A:	But you've had them for a month already.
B:	Just give me until Monday, and then you can have them back. OK?
A:	I suppose so.

Tonality

The interjection *hey* receives its own IP. In IP 2, the defining relative clause *you borrowed* does not. In IP 5, an intonation break after *biology* would tend to imply that some of the books were about biology, others about language; but the intended meaning is that each book related to both subjects. (It would be possible to treat the interjection *oh* as a prehead to IP 7 instead of as a separate IP.) (There could be an intonation break in IP 9 after *them*, making *a few more days* a separate IP. There could be a further break within IP 11 after *them*, making *for my essay* a separate IP. The intonation break between IPs 12 and 13 might be absent. So might that between IPs 14 and 15.)

A: [1] Hey, | [2] are you going to return those books of mine you borrowed?

B: [3] Which books? | [4] I can't remember borrowing any.

A: [5] The ones about biology and language.

B: [6] Oh, | [7] those books. | [8] Er – | [9] could I keep them a few more days?

A: [10] Why?

B: [11] Because I need them for my essay.

A: [12] But you've had them for a month | [13] already.

B: [14] Just give me until Monday, | [15] and then you can have them back. || [16] OK?

A: [17] I suppose so.

Accentuation

In IP 2, the nucleus goes on the last noun. Both the defining relative clause that follows it (see 3.29) and the postmodifier *of mine* (see 3.11) go in the tail. In IP 3, *books* is old information. In IP 4, the most likely place of the nucleus is the subject *I*, since there is evidently a discrepancy between what this speaker believes and what the other speaker believes. (Alternatively, the nucleus might be on *remember*.) In IP 7, *books* is again old information. IP 8 is a hesitation noise (= AmE *uh*), with no meaningful intonation. (In IP 9, the nucleus might alternatively be on *more*.) In IP 17, *so* is a pro-form (see 3.20), therefore unaccented. The most likely onset locations are as shown (although in IP 2 the onset might alternatively be on *are* or *return*, in IP 5 on *biology*, in IP 9 on *keep*).

A: [1] 'Hey, | [2] are you 'going to return those 'books of mine you borrowed?

B: [3] 'Which books? | [4] 'I can't remember borrowing any.

A: [5] The 'ones about biology and 'language.

B: [6] 'Oh, | [7] 'those books. | [8] Er – | [9] 'could I keep them a few more 'days?

A: [10] 'Why?

B: [11] Because I 'need them for my 'essay.

A: [12] But you've 'had them for a 'month | [13] al'ready.

B: [14] 'Just give me until 'Monday, | [15] and 'then you can have them 'back. || [16] 'O'K?

A: [17] I sup'pose so.

Tone

In IP 1, *hey* must have a fall (see 2.19). IP 2 is a yes–no question, thus most likely to have a rise. IP 3 is a wh question, requiring a definitive fall. In IP 4, the implication is *but you evidently can remember my borrowing them*, so the tone is an implicational fall–rise. IP 5 takes a definitive fall. (Speakers of uptalk, 2.9, could use a rise here.) IPs 6 and 7 also take a fall, which might well be a rise–fall. IP 8 takes a level pitch: we do not treat this as a nuclear tone. IP 9 is a yes–no question, with a rise. IP 10 is a wh question, most likely with a fall (though a fall–rise is also possible). IP 11 takes a definitive fall (or perhaps an uptalk rise). IP 12 takes an implicational fall–rise, drawing attention to the contrast between *days* and *month*. IP 13 is a reinforcing final adverb (see 2.23), said with a fall. (In IP 14, any tone is possible.) IP 16 has a checking rise (see 2.16). In IP 17, the fall–rise signals the speaker's reservations (see 2.6).

A: ¹ \Hey, | ² are you 'going to return those /books of mine you borrowed?
B: ³ \Which books? | ⁴ vI can't remember borrowing any.
A: ⁵ The 'ones about biology and \language.
B: ⁶ \Oh, | ⁷ \those books. | ⁸ Er – | ⁹ 'could I keep them a few more /days?
A: ¹⁰ \Why?
B: ¹¹ Because I 'need them for my \essay.
A: ¹² But you've 'had them for a vmonth | ¹³ al\ready.
B: ¹⁴ 'Just give me until \Monday, | ¹⁵ and 'then you can have them \back. ‖ ¹⁶ 'O/K?
A: ¹⁷ I supvpose so.

6.3.4   Cornwall

Two colleagues talking

A: Are you planning to go away this year?
B: We've just been away! We had a week in Cornwall.
A: And how was it?
B: Oh, we had a marvellous time. The only problem was the weather. Unfortunately it rained most of the time.
A: So what did you do during all this rain?
B: Well the best thing we did was to go to the Eden Project.
A: What's that?
B: It's a kind of museum of ecology. I found it utterly fascinating. It's more like a theme park, really. There's lots to do, and the children loved it, too.

Tonality

The break after IP 6 could be omitted, since the subject NP is not particularly heavy. The break after IP 8 could also be omitted. The break after IP 11 is less likely to be omitted. (It would also be possible to accent *well* and give it its own IP.) In rapid speech IPs 14 and 15 could be combined into a single IP; but since the subject matter is new they are more likely to be separate, each covering one chunk of information (*museum, ecology*). IP 18, consisting of the adverb *really*, could alternatively be made the tail of IP 17. In IP 21, final *too* tends to be given its own IP (see 3.19), but could alternatively be combined with IP 20.

A: ^{1}Are you planning to go away this year?
B: ^{2}We've just been away! ‖ ^{3}We had a week in Cornwall.
A: ^{4}And how was it?
B: ^{5}Oh, we had a marvellous time. ‖ ^{6}The only problem | ^{7}was the weather. ‖ ^{8}Unfortunately | ^{9}it rained most of the time.
A: ^{10}So what did you do during all this rain?
B: ^{11}Well the best thing we did | ^{12}was to go to the Eden Project.
A: ^{13}What's that?
B: ^{14}It's a kind of museum | ^{15}of ecology. ‖ ^{16}I found it utterly fascinating. ‖ ^{17}It's more like a theme park, | ^{18}really. ‖ ^{19}There's lots to do, | ^{20}and the children loved it, | ^{21}too.

Accentuation

In IP 1 the onset could alternatively be on *are*. The final *this year* is a time adverbial, therefore by default deaccented (see 3.23). In IP 2, *away* is repeated; the nucleus goes on the verb as the bearer of positive polarity. *Just* might alternatively be unaccented and therefore part of the prehead. In IP 3, *had* might be accented; but since it has little semantic content it is more likely to be unaccented. In IP 4, a wh + *be* construction, the nucleus goes on the verb *to be* (see 3.18). In IP 5, *had*, semantically empty, is unlikely to be accented. *Time* is a hypernym of *week* and therefore unaccented (see 3.7). In IP 9, the nucleus will probably be on *rained*, since this is the important new idea; *most of the time* is a time adverbial. In IP 10, *all this rain* is a restatement of *rained most of the time* and so counts as given. In IP 11, *best* is the only new lexical item. In IP 12, *Eden Project* has compound stress. The accent on *go* is optional. In IP 14, there could be an accent on *kind*. In IP 16, the introductory *I found* is likely to be unaccented (5.13). In IP 17, *theme park* has compound stress. By the time we get to IP 20 it is clear that the adults *loved* it, so the focus is now on the *children*, not on *loved*.

A: [1]Are you 'planning to go a'<u>way</u> this year?
B: [2]We've 'just '<u>been</u> away! || [3]We had a 'week in '<u>Cornwall</u>.
A: [4]And 'how '<u>was</u> it?
B: [5]Oh, we had a '<u>mar</u>vellous time. || [6]The 'only '<u>problem</u> | [7]was the '<u>weather</u>. || [8]Un'<u>fortunately</u> | [9]it '<u>rained</u> most of the time.
A: [10]So 'what did you '<u>do</u> during all this rain?
B: [11]Well the '<u>best</u> thing we did | [12]was to 'go to the '<u>Eden</u> Project.
A: [13]'What's '<u>that</u>?
B: [14]It's a kind of mu'<u>seum</u> | [15]of e'<u>cology</u>. || [16]I found it 'utterly '<u>fascinating</u>. || [17]It's 'more like a '<u>theme</u> park, | [18]<u>really</u>. || [19]There's 'lots to '<u>do</u>, | [20]and the '<u>children</u> loved it, | [21]'<u>too</u>.

Tone

IP 1 is a friendly yes–no question, so has a rise. The answer in IP 2 takes an exclamatory (definitive) fall, as does its continuation in IP 3. The wh question in IP 4 is most likely to take a fall; the answer in IP 5 certainly will. IP 6 has a leading dependent non-fall, most likely a fall–rise; IP 7 has a definitive fall. The same pattern is repeated in IPs 8 and 9. (Uptalk speakers could use a rise in IPs 7 and 9.) IPs 10 and 13 are wh questions, with a fall. IP 11 is a leading dependent clause, and takes a contrastive fall–rise. IP 12 has a definitive fall. In IP 14 we could have any tone; I have chosen a leading dependent fall–rise, followed by the definitive fall in IP 15. IP 16 certainly needs a fall (perhaps actually a rise–fall showing that the speaker was impressed). IP 17 has a definitive fall, with a rise for the limiting adverb (2.23) in IP 18. IP 19 probably has a fall–rise, leading to the falls in IPs 20 and 21. Final *too* exhibits tone concord (see 2.25).

A: [1]Are you 'planning to go a/<u>way</u> this year?
B: [2]We've 'just \<u>been</u> away! || [3]We had a 'week in \<u>Cornwall</u>.
A: [4]And 'how \<u>was</u> it?
B: [5]Oh, we had a \<u>mar</u>vellous time. || [6]The 'only v<u>problem</u> | [7]was the \<u>weather</u>. || [8]Unv<u>fortunately</u> | [9]it \<u>rained</u> most of the time.
A: [10]So 'what did you \<u>do</u> during all this rain?
B: [11]Well the v<u>best</u> thing we did | [12]was to 'go to the \<u>Eden</u> Project.
A: [13]'What's \<u>that</u>?
B: [14]It's a kind of muv<u>seum</u> | [15]of e\<u>cology</u>. || [16]I found it 'utterly \<u>fascinating</u>. || [17]It's 'more like a \<u>theme</u> park, | [18]/<u>really</u>. || [19]There's 'lots to v<u>do</u>, | [20]and the \<u>children</u> loved it, | [21]\<u>too</u>.

Appendix: Notation

A1 The intonation symbols used in this book

The intonation marking system used in this book is designed to bring out the nature of the choices the speaker makes. It can also be made more or less detailed, depending on how fine an analysis we wish to make.

In the **basic** markup:

- **tonality** is shown by placing vertical bars between successive IPs, like this: | or ||. This is one intonation phrase, | this is another.
- **tonicity** is shown by underlining, like <u>this</u>.
- **tone** is shown by the symbols ◟, ◞, and ◡, placed before the nuclear syllable, to show fall, rise and fall–rise tone respectively.
- **accent** is shown by a stress mark, (').

To show finer distinctions, the following additional symbols are used:

- The symbols ◟ and ◞ are raised and lowered to symbolize ˋhigh fall, ◟low fall, ´high rise, ◞low rise. Additionally, we recognize ⌃rise–fall, 'wide rise, ◡rise–fall–rise, ◡high fall–rise, and >mid level nuclear tones.
- The symbol sequence ˉ – is also used to show a stylized tone.
- Types of head are distinguished as 'high level, ˋhigh falling, ˌlow level, and ◞low rising.
- Rhythmic stress (with no fresh pitch implications) can be shown by the degree sign, thus ° (or ₒ if low).

This notation system has several useful characteristics.

It is based on **supplementing** (or ornamenting) ordinary text rather than changing it. It calls for adding marks to ordinary spelling (or to phonetic transcription) rather than altering it, e.g. by using capitals. This makes our notation system more convenient than the one used by Brazil (1985, 1994), which requires accented syllables to be changed from lower case to upper case. This means that Brazil's notation system cannot be combined with phonetic transcription. The system used by Wennerstrom (2001) is typographically even more complex, including not just plain capitals but also subscripted capitals.

Table A1 *Intonation symbols used in this book*

A **nuclear tone** is shown by <u>underlining</u> the nuclear syllable, and placing one of the following tone marks before it.

Basic markup	Symbol	Finer distinctions	Symbol
fall	\	high fall	ˋ
		low fall	ˎ
		rise-fall	‿\
rise	/	high rise	ˊ
		low rise	ˏ
		wide rise	⁄
		mid level	>
fall-rise	v	mid fall–rise	v
		rise–fall–rise	‿v
		high fall–rise	˅
Other symbols			
accent	'	high head	'
		high falling head	ˋ
		low level head	ˌ
		low rising head	ˏ
prehead	(no mark)	high	ˉ
		low	ˍ
rhythmic stress	(no mark)		°, ₒ

Our notation system is **iconic**. The shape of the marks is suggestive of the pitch movement they refer to. In a left-to-right writing system, \ clearly suggests a fall and ∕ a rise. Underlining is a familiar way of indicating emphasis. Raising a symbol, thus ˋ, denotes a higher start. The symbol ˉ obviously suggests high pitch. The mark ° is like a zero, indicating no change in pitch specification. This makes our notation system easier to interpret than the H, L,%, etc. of the ToBI system (Pierrehumbert, 1987).

It is **non-exotic**: it uses only six intonation marks at the basic level (| ‖ \ ∕ v '), plus underlining. In principle, they require no special character set: there are easy surrogates for those that are not ASCII or Latin-1 characters.

The accent mark (') can be replaced by a straight apostrophe ('). The low mark (ˌ) could be represented as a comma (,) or inverted exclamation mark (¡).

If superscripting and subscripting are not available, ˋ can be replaced by H\, ∕ by L∕, etc. Where underlining is not available, the letter span can be surrounded by underscores, e.g. a_noth_er for <u>another</u>.

This makes our notation system more convenient than that used by O'Connor & Arnold (1961, 1973), which requires many special symbols not available in conventional fonts.

A2   Comparison with other notation systems

Many different intonation notation systems have been devised over the years. Some can be seen as mere notational variants of ours; others are based on different theoretical assumptions.

Not all scholars apply the concepts of IP and nucleus. Kingdon (1958), for example, despite his many interesting insights, operates only in terms of 'static tones' and 'kinetic tones'. He recognizes a very large number of different tones, including for example eight varieties of rise–fall–rise, and uses a correspondingly large set of tone marks.

Those whose analysis does include a concept of nucleus (or tonic) indicate this status in different ways. Underlining dates back to Halliday (1967). Brazil et al. (1980) not only underline the tonic but also capitalize it. However, O'Connor & Arnold (1961, 1973) leave the status of the nucleus to be inferred from the use of tone marks which denote only nuclear tones.

In our notation, we place the mark indicating tone immediately before the syllable in question. In this we follow Kingdon and O'Connor & Arnold. Halliday, however, places it at the beginning of the entire IP, as do Brazil and his followers.

Halliday's tone marks are numerical (1 = fall, 2 = rise, 3 = fall–rise, etc.) rather than iconic. Brazil uses letters as tone marks (p = proclaiming, i.e. fall, r = referring, i.e. fall–rise, etc.); but his more recent followers, e.g. Cauldwell (2003), make the notation iconic by using chunky sloping arrows instead.

Cauldwell's intonation notation system can be straightforwardly converted into our basic system, and vice versa. Underlining is the same. His sloping arrows ↘, ↗, ↘↗ correspond to our tone marks ˎ, ˊ, ˇ. His capitals (showing 'prominence') are redundant for the nucleus, but otherwise correspond to our '. For our | he writes //.

A3   The ToBI system

The ToBI (Tones and Break Indices) system of intonation analysis and notation is rather different from the system described in this book. Rather than analyse intonation patterns in terms of pitch **contours** (rise, fall, fall–rise, etc.), it breaks them down into **components**, basically High and Low in various combinations.

It is described in Beckman & Elam (1997), and summarized rather more readably in Cruttenden (1997: 59ff, 110ff). The current model is based on earlier work by Pierrehumbert & her colleagues (Pierrehumbert, 1987; Pierrehumbert & Hirschberg, 1990). It was devised and standardized particularly for work in speech technology and annotating speech corpora, rather than for language teaching. It has been applied particularly to American English, though it can be modified or adapted to apply to any language or variety. Grabe & Nolan (2003) have adapted it to various kinds of British English, and apply it to a corpus covering nine urban varieties.

A ToBI analysis of intonation consists of a tone tier, an orthographic tier, a break index tier and a miscellaneous tier.

The tone tier is the part that represents an utterance's intonation pattern. It consists of 'labels for distinctive pitch events, transcribed as a sequence of high (H) and low (L) tones marked with diacritics indicating their intonational function as parts of pitch accents or as phrase tones marking the edges of two types of intonationally marked prosodic units' (Beckman & Elam, 1997: 8). Pitch accents (whether nuclear or not, in our analysis), are marked with an asterisk, thus L*, H*. Additional 'phrase tones' are marked with a hyphen diacritic, thus L-, H-. 'Bitonal' pitch accents are shown as L+H*. Each IP ends with a 'boundary tone', shown thus L%, H%. A 'downstep' is shown by the symbol !, thus !H.

The break index tier relates to tonality, and involves various types of intonation break (corresponding to our | and ‖). Here is a pair of examples from Pierrehumbert & Hirschberg (1990):

George	ate chicken	soup and	got	sick.
H*	H*	H*L /	H*	H*L-L%
George	ate chicken	soup and	got	sick.
H*	H*	H*H- /	H*	H*L-L%

which correspond in our notation to:

'George 'ate chicken \ soup | and 'got \sick.
'George 'ate chicken /soup | and 'got \sick.

Falls are analysed as having an L% boundary tone, whereas rises and fall–rises have an H% boundary tone.

Key to exercises

Chapter 2

E2.1.7

1. \Who?   2. /Who?   3. /Who?   4. \Who?   5. \Who?
6. /Who?   7. \Who?   8. \Who?   9. /Who?   10. /Who?

E2.3.3

A: 'Who's \that over there?
B: It's \Jim, | I /think.
A: 'What's he \like?
B: Oh he's 'one of our best \students.
A: 'What's he \studying?
B: 'Modern \languages.
A: \Which languages?
B: /English, | /French, | and \Spanish.
A: \That | sounds /interesting.

E2.4.4

A: I'm 'not really ∨sure, | but I 'think I may have to \cancel our meeting.
B: Oh I'm 'sorry about ∨that. ‖ 'What's the \trouble? Has 'something come /up?
A: Well ∨actually | it's my \mother. ‖ She 'needs to go into \hospital | and she 'wants ∨me | to \take her there.

E2.6.5

A: 'Planning to go a/way this year?
B: We've 'just \been away. ‖ We had a 'week in \Cornwall.
A: And 'how \was it?
B: Oh we had a \marvellous time. ‖ The 'only ∨problem | was the \weather. ‖ Un∨fortunately | it \rained most of the time.
A: So 'what did you \do during all this rain?
B: Well the 'great at∨traction | was the \Eden Project. ‖ I found it 'utterly \fascinating.

E2.7.5

(i)   v polite   (ii)\ brusque   (iii) \ brusque
(iv)   v polite   (v) v polite

E2.11.3 for example, as a response to:

1   They 'visit her every \week. *(polarity is positive; response is an agreement)*
2   They 'don't like the vteacher. *(polarity is negative; response is a contradiction)*
3   They 'don't eat \meat. *(polarity is negative; response is an agreement)*
4   They 'always finish on \time. *(polarity is positive; response is a contradiction)*
5   You're 'not \strong enough. *(polarity is negative; response is a contradiction)*
6   You're a \fool. *(polarity is positive; response is a contradiction)*

E2.11.4

\No, | she /hasn't.   *or*   \Oh no, | she /hasn't.
\Yes, | I /have.   *or*   \Oh yes, | I /have.
\No, | they /haven't.   *or*   \Oh no, | they /haven't.

E2.21.5

1   (a) (i),   (b) (ii).
2   (a) (i),   (b) (ii).
3   (a) (ii),   (b) (i).
4   (a) (ii),   (b) (i).
5   (a) (i),   (b) (ii).

E2.21.6 Possible contexts:

1 (i)   Is Linda your secretary?
  (ii)   Are you married to Penny, then?
2 (i)   I don't think much of Jeff.
  (ii)   Does anyone admire Jeff?
3 (i)   Is that short man over there Peter Sudbury?
  (ii)   So the bigger of the two must be Jim.
4 (i)   What about your family? Are they all in Manchester?
  (ii)   I have a lot of relatives in the West Midlands.
5 (i)   Tell me about your grandchildren.
  (ii)   I'm a lecturer in the Pharmacology Department.

E2.26.2 One set of possible scenarios:

(i)	'What have your ﹨family been doing recently?	• My ∨parents | have 'been to ﹨China.
(ii)	Has 'anyone you know 'ever been outside ⁄Europe?	• My ﹨parents | have 'been to ∨China.
(iii)	I was 'wondering whether to visit ﹨China.	• My ﹨parents | have been to ⁄China.
(iv)	'Who's been to ﹨China?	• My ﹨parents have been to China.
(v)	'Where have your ﹨parents been?	• My 'parents have been to ﹨China.

Versions (i) and (v) are neutral, in that they make no presuppositions. They might be a narrow-focus reply to 'Where have your parents been?': version (v) is straight-forward, while version (i) involves a refocusing on *my parents*. Or they might be a broad-focus reply to 'What's new?' or 'Is there any news of your family?'. Or they might be used at the start of a new conversation or a new topic of conversation. They differ in that (i) makes the subject *my parents* into a separate intonation phrase, while (v) does not. So (i) is more likely in slower, more deliberate speech, while (v) is more likely in rapidly spoken conversation. Both use a definitive fall, in Brazil's terms 'proclaiming'.

In versions (ii), (iii) and (iv) the fall nucleus is in the phrase *my parents*, so focusing on it and marking it as the main part of the statement. This means that the topic 'going to China' must have been mentioned already. In (iv) *have been to China* is left unaccented, out of focus, and so forms the tail of the only IP: the whole utterance is 'proclaimed' as a single unit. This would be a likely narrow-focused response to 'Who's been to China?'.

In (ii) and (iii) *have been to China* is treated as a separate IP with its own non-falling nucleus: that is to say, the speaker refocuses upon this material. This referring is more emphatic if done with a fall–rise, (ii), more routine if done with a rise, (iii).

Version (iii) might be uttered in response to someone else having said 'I'm thinking of visiting China.' Version (ii) is also possible under those circumstances, but more plausibly would be a response to 'Has anyone you know ever been outside Europe?' or to 'No one seems prepared to travel far these days' (assuming we are a long way from China).

Chapter 3

E3.1.1

'football, 'vegetables, 'stripes, 'clothes, to'morrow.
'square, 'oblong, tri'angular, 'circular, 'L-shaped.
an'noyed, 'happy, ec'static, dis'gruntled, o'kay.

E3.1.2 The 'traps' are '*promise* and *con'trol*, which do not change their lexical stress. All the other words here are like *digest*.

E.3.1.3

'Moscow, Pa'cific, 'Germany, To'ronto, Ja'pan.
'coffee, Coca-'Cola, 'bitter, 'water, lemo'nade.

E3.4.11

eating apple (compound), exciting event (phrase), charming house (phrase), wishing well (compound), tuning fork (compound).

E3.4.12

'fishing, 'horse, 'writing, 'gambling, i'dea.

E3.5.3 (Here and elsewhere the instructions ask only for the location of the
nucleus. For completeness, however, we show all likely accents.)

'Call the 'fire brigade.   'Over the garden 'fence.
'Go to the po'lice station.   'Let's watch the ballroom 'dancing.
'Wait for the 'Morden train.   I 'love winter 'sports.
'What are the exami'nation dates?   'Come to my country 'cottage.
'Get some plastic 'bags.   'What's the weather forecast?

E3.5.5

'Euston, | 'Warren Street, | 'Goodge Street, | 'Tottenham Court 'Road, |
    'Leicester 'Square, | 'Charing 'Cross.
'Paddington, | 'Edgware 'Road, | 'Baker Street, | 'Great 'Portland Street, |
    'Euston 'Square, | 'King's 'Cross.
'Finchley 'Road, | 'Swiss 'Cottage, | St 'John's 'Wood, | 'Baker Street, | 'Bond
    Street, | 'Green 'Park, | Vic'toria.
'Harrison, | 'Journal 'Square, | 'Grove St, | Pa'vonia, | 'Christopher St, | 'Ninth
    St, | 'Four'teenth St.
'Bedford 'Avenue, | 'Lorimer St, | 'Graham 'Avenue, | 'Grand St, | Mont'rose
    'Avenue.

E3.5.6

'Pea 'Soup, | 'Chicken 'Pie, | 'Green 'Peas, | 'Mashed Po'tatoes, | 'Fruit Cake.
'Orange Juice, | 'Mushroom 'Omelette, | 'Green 'Salad, | Ba'nana 'Fritters, |
    Dun'dee Cake.
'Won Ton 'Soup, | 'Beef in Black Bean 'Sauce, | 'Prawn and 'Bean Shoots, |
    'Special Fried 'Rice, | 'Chinese 'Tea.
'Chef's 'Salad, | 'Chicken Club 'Sandwich, | 'Grapefruit Juice, | 'Coffee
    'Latte.
'Fruit Juice, | 'Veal Esca'lope, | 'Boiled 'Rice, | 'Mushy 'Peas, | 'Strawberry
    Pav'lova.

E3.5.9

coming, govern<u>ment</u>, un<u>ed</u>ucated, coll<u>eagues</u>, any<u>thing</u>: wrong lexical stress.
   <u>of</u>, <u>at</u>: prepositions. <u>the</u>: article. <u>can</u>: modal verb (also old information, 3.8).
   <u>it</u>: pronoun.

E3.6.3

'May I intro'<u>duce</u> | 'Catherine '<u>Hughes</u> | and her 'husband '<u>Jim</u> Hughes.
I'd 'like you to meet 'Danny Ale'<u>xan</u>der | and his 'wife '<u>Jen</u>ny Alexander.
'Do you know Shaun '<u>Pro</u>theroe | and his 'wife Lucy '<u>Jo</u>sephs?
This is Pro'fessor Mc'<u>Call</u> (*or* Pro'<u>fes</u>sor McCall) | and '<u>Mrs</u> McCall.
'Over '<u>there</u> | are 'Shaun Mc'<u>Cleod</u> | and his 'brother '<u>Ru</u>di McCleod.

In the foregoing it is assumed that the speaker plans each IP separately. If they were preplanned together (3.8), we might get:

'May I intro'<u>duce</u> | 'Catherine Hughes | and her 'husband '<u>Jim</u> Hughes.

etc.

No I 'don't \<u>want</u> to become a member. (. . .| to become a ⁄<u>mem</u>ber.)
Oh I \<u>hate</u> doing housework. (. . . | doing ⁄<u>house</u>work.)
No I 'never \<u>use</u> public transport. (. . . | public ⁄<u>trans</u>port.)
No I've 'never \<u>vis</u>ited South America. (. . . | South A⁄<u>mer</u>ica.)
I'm 'not \<u>in</u>terested in footballers. (. . . | in ⁄<u>foot</u>ballers.)

studying pho'<u>net</u>ics | and '<u>oth</u>er useful subjects
showing '<u>span</u>iels | and '<u>oth</u>er breeds of dog
looking after '<u>cats</u> | and '<u>oth</u>er similar animals
bring along '<u>Wayne</u> | and the '<u>rest</u> of the boys
buying and selling '<u>phones</u> | and '<u>oth</u>er electronic equipment

E3.8.1

a 'big book and a '<u>small</u> book
the 'first exam paper and the '<u>sec</u>ond exam paper
'Andrew got drunk and '<u>Tom</u> got drunk.
'Monica fell over and then '<u>Lu</u>cy fell over.
The 'second edition was better than the '<u>first</u> edition.

E3.8.2

a '<u>big</u> book | and a '<u>small</u> book
the '<u>first</u> exam paper | and the '<u>sec</u>ond exam paper
'Andrew got drunk | and '<u>Tom</u> got drunk.
'<u>Mon</u>ica fell over | and then '<u>Lu</u>cy fell over.
The '<u>sec</u>ond edition | was 'better than the '<u>first</u> edition.

E3.16.9

    A: I've 'just bought some new \shoes.
    B: ⁄Have you?
    A: \Yes, | and ∨Anna says | she thinks they're 'very \smart. (*or:* \very)
    B: Oh ⁄does she? (*or* \does)
    A: \Look, | I'm 'wearing them \now. ‖ 'What do you \think? (*or:* \you)
    B: I 'don't think I'd have chosen them my∨self.
    A: Oh ⁄wouldn't you?
    B: ∨Sorry, | \no.

E3.24.6

'Could you try a'gain
'all over a'gain
back to 'health again
have you 'home again
told you a'gain and a'gain

E3.26.5

be a'way for, get 'on with, look 'up to, go 'through with, get a'way with.

E3.27.2

'come from, 'go with, 'looking for, stand 'back, drew 'back.
drawn 'off, 'sorry for, an 'eye on, be a'way for, to 'deal with.

E3.27.3

(i) to pay 'in: to deposit funds, so this could be paraphrased 'what currency did you deposit?';

(ii) to 'pay (in a currency = using a currency), so this could be paraphrased 'with what currency did you pay?'.

E3.28.3

'handkerchief, 'pencil, 'details (AmE: de'tails), 'plates, 'meeting.
'out, 'up, 'down, a'way, 'forward.
'form, 'chairs, re'port, mo'mentum, 'bottles.
'up, 'essays, 'sitting (*or:* 'chair), led 'in, 'run.

Chapter 4

E4.1.1 There are several possibilities. The following version seems the most likely:

When we got to the top | we paused for a rest. || Fortunately | we had some chocolate with us | and some bottles of water, | and Nell had some raisins, | which were very welcome. || After we'd rested there for a few minutes | we were ready to continue our journey, | which we did | with a new spring in our steps.

E4.2.1 Suggested tonalities for (i) reading aloud and (ii) unscripted speech.

(i) The first thing we have to consider | is the earthworm and its relation to the condition of the soil. || In autumn, | falling leaves cascade onto the ground | and accumulate there. || If there were no earthworms | the leaves would rot down into a solid viscous mass | which would suffocate the soil beneath. || But what the earthworms do | is to drag down pieces of decomposing leaf into the soil, | bringing with them air and moisture, | so that the soil is rendered lighter and less compact. || The result is a good friable tilth | which is the gardener's delight | and in which plants grow well. || Without the earthworm | nothing much would grow at all.

   (ii) The first thing we have to consider | is the earthworm | and its relation | to the condition of the soil. || In autumn, | falling leaves | cascade onto the ground | and accumulate there. || If there were no earthworms | the leaves | would rot down | into a solid viscous mass | which would suffocate | the soil beneath. || But what the earthworms do | is to drag down | pieces of decomposing leaf | into the soil, | bringing with them | air and moisture, | so that the soil | is rendered lighter | and less compact. || The result | is a good friable tilth | which is the gardener's delight | and in which plants grow well. || Without the earthworm | nothing much | would grow at all.

E4.4.1 Only the third line.

'Here, colleagues,| . . .
. . . the 'flowers, Mrs Jeffers.
Mr 'Kenyon, | . . .
'You, Ms Sanderson, | . . .
. . . the po'lice, Andrew.

E4.5.2

We'd 'better consider them indi\vidually.
They've 'all \vanished, | un/fortunately. (or . . .| un∨fortunately.)
We'll finish them to\morrow, | /hopefully. (or . . .| ∨hopefully.)
a. The 'water evaporated \naturally.
b. The 'water e\vaporated, | \naturally. (or The 'water ev∨vaporated | . . .)

E4.9.1 All can (to some extent) be disambiguated by appropriate location of intonation breaks, except possibly:

red and blue shirts (= (i) red shirts and blue shirts; (ii) shirts, each of which is both red and blue)

Chapter 5

E5.1.2 (a) false, (b) true, (c) true, (d) false, (e) false

E5.2.8

'seventy \eight, seventy /eight, `seventy ˅eight, 'seventy /eight, ˌseventy \eight

it's 'nearly /ready, it's `nearly ˅ready, it's /nearly \ready, it's `nearly \ready, it's ˌnearly /ready

E5.3.5

`fifty `three ˅thousand, /fifty /three \thousand, 'fifty 'three \thousand, 'fifty 'three /thousand

I 'asked for 'smoked \salmon, I /asked for /smoked \salmon, I 'asked for 'smoked /salmon, I `asked for `smoked ˅salmon

E5.4.1

‾The train was /absolutely \packed.
_It was in\credible!
‾I ˅didn't.
_In the /garden?
‾I 'can't be \bothered.

E5.10.1

'nineteen, 'independent, as'sociation, 'undivided, 'misappropriation; 'seventeen, 'controversial, 'fundamental, 'understand, 'thirteen

Chapter 6

E6.2.1

a.   (i) \I'm going. (ii) ‾I'm \going.
b.   (i) ‾She \did it. (ii) \She did it.
c.   (i) They have a ˅marathon in London. (ii) They have a \marathon | in /London.
d.   (i) I'm `sure he's ˅wrong. (ii) I'm \sure, | he's ˅wrong.
e.   (i) Your /notebooks | are \excellent. (ii) Your /notebooks are \excellent.
f.   (i) They're ˅virtually | 'indi\stinguishable. (ii) They're 'virtually 'indi\stinguishable.
g.   (i) I'm 'hoping to suc\ceed. (ii) I'm \hoping to succeed.
h.   (i) How are you going to /do it? (ii) /How are you going to do it?

References

Allan, K., 1986. *Linguistic meaning*. London and New York: Routledge & Kegan Paul.

Altenberg, B., 1987. *Prosodic patterns in spoken English*. Lund: Lund University Press.

Beckman, M. E. & Elam, G. A., 1997. *Guidelines for ToBI labelling*. Version 3.0. Ohio State University Research Foundation. www.ling.ohio-state.edu/~tobi/

Bolinger, D., 1986. *Intonation and its parts: melody in spoken English*. London: Edward Arnold.

Bolinger, D., 1989. *Intonation and its uses: melody in grammar and discourse*. London: Edward Arnold.

Bradford, B., 1988. *Intonation in context*. Student's book; teacher's book. Cambridge: Cambridge University Press.

Bradford, B., 1997. Upspeak in British English. *English Today* 51. 13.3: 29–36.

Brazil, D., 1975. *Discourse intonation*. Birmingham: English Language Research, University of Birmingham.

Brazil, D., 1978. *Discourse intonation II*. Birmingham: English Language Research, University of Birmingham.

Brazil, D., 1985. *The communicative value of intonation in English*. Birmingham: Bleak House and ELR. Republished 1997, Cambridge: Cambridge University Press.

Brazil, D., 1994. *Pronunciation for advanced learners of English*. Student's book; teacher's book. Cambridge: Cambridge University Press.

Brazil, D., Coulthard, M. & Johns, C., 1980. *Discourse intonation and language teaching*. Harlow: Longman.

Britain, D., 1992. Linguistic change in intonation: the use of high rising terminals in New Zealand English. *Language Variation and Change* 4.1: 77–104.

Cauldwell, R., 2002. *Streaming Speech: Listening and Pronunciation for Advanced Learners of English*. CD-ROM, ISBN 0-9543447-0-7. Birmingham: Speech in Action.

[Cauldwell, R., 2003.] *Discourse intonation*. Centre for Discourse Intonation Studies. www.speechinaction. pwp.blueyonder.co.uk/CDIS_DiscourseIntonation_a.htm

Celik, M., 2001. Teaching English intonation to EFL/ESL students. *Internet TESL Jl* vii.12. http://iteslj.org/Techniques/Celik-Intonation.html

Collins, B. & Mees, I. M., 2003. *Practical phonetics and phonology: a resource book for students*. London: Routledge.

Couper-Kuhlen, E., 1986. *An introduction to English prosody*. London: Edward Arnold.

Cruttenden, A., 1986[1], 1997[2]. *Intonation*. Cambridge: Cambridge University Press.

Cruttenden, A., 1990. Nucleus placement and three classes of exception. In Ramsaran, 1990: 9–18.

Crystal, D., 1975. *The English tone of voice: essays in intonation, prosody, and paralanguage*. London: Edward Arnold.

Dehé, N., 2002. *Particle verbs in English*. Amsterdam: John Benjamins.

Diresta, D., 2001. Does uptalk make you upchuck? http://www.appearfirst.com/language/w_and_s_99.html and http://ezinearticles.com/?Does-Uptalk-Make-you-Upchuck?&id=959 (accessed Nov 2004)

Grabe, E. & Nolan, F., 2003. *English intonation in the British Isles*. The IViE corpus. http://www.phon.ox.ac.uk/~esther/ivyweb

Gussenhoven, C., 1984. *On the grammar and semantics of sentence accents*. Dordrecht: Foris.

Gussenhoven, C., 2004. *The phonology of tone and intonation*. Cambridge: Cambridge University Press.

Halliday, M. A. K., 1967. *Intonation and grammar in British English*. The Hague: Mouton.

Halliday, M. A. K., 1970. *A course in spoken English: intonation*. The Hague: Mouton.

House, Jill, 1990. Intonation structures and pragmatic interpretation. In Ramsaran, 1990: 38–57.

House, Jill, 1995. Intonational stereotype: a re-analysis. In Windsor Lewis, 1995: 211–29.

Kingdon, R., 1958. *The groundwork of English intonation*. London: Longmans, Green.

Knowles, G., Wichmann, A. & Alderson, P. (eds.), 1996. *Working with speech: perspectives on research into the Lancaster/IBM Spoken English Corpus*. Harlow: Longman.

Knowles, G., Williams, B. & Taylor, L. (eds.), 1996. *A corpus of formal British English speech: the Lancaster/IBM Spoken English Corpus*. Harlow: Longman.

Ladd, D. Robert, 1978. Stylized intonation. *Language* 54.3: 517–40.

Ladd, D. Robert, 1980. *The structure of intonational meaning: evidence from English*. Bloomington: Indiana University Press.

Ladd, D. Robert, 1996. *Intonational phonology*. Cambridge: Cambridge University Press.

Maidment, J., 1990. Focus and tone in English intonation. In Ramsaran 1990: 19–26.

McLemore, Cynthia, 1991. The interpretation of L*H in English. *Texas Linguistic Forum* 32: Discourse: 175–96.

O'Connor, J. D. & Arnold, G. F., 1961[1], 1973[2]. *Intonation of colloquial English*: *a practical handbook*. London: Longman.

O'Connor, J. D., 1980. *Better English pronunciation*. Second edition. Cambridge: Cambridge University Press.

Ortiz-Lira, H., 1995. Nucleus placement in English and Spanish: a pilot study of patterns of interference. In Windsor Lewis, 1995: 255–65.

Ortiz-Lira, H., 2000. *Word stress and sentence accent*. [Santiago de Chile:] Universidad Metropolitana de Ciencias de la Educación, Facultad de Historia, Geografía y Letras.

Pierrehumbert, J. B., 1987. *The phonology and phonetics of English intonation* (PhD thesis, 1980). Indiana University Linguistics Club.

Pierrehumbert. J. B. & Hirschberg, J., 1990. The meaning of intonation contours in the interpretation of discourse. In P. R. Cohen, J. Morgan & M. E. Pollack (eds.), *Plans and intentions in communication and discourse*, SDF Benchmark series in computational linguistics, Cambridge, MA: MIT Press, 271–311.

Quirk, R., Greenbaum, S., Leech, G. & Svartvik, J., 1985. *A comprehensive grammar of the English language*. London: Longman.

Ramsaran, Susan (ed.), 1990. *Studies in the pronunciation of English: a commemorative volume in honour of A. C. Gimson*. London and New York: Routledge.

Schmerling, Susan F., 1976. *Aspects of English sentence stress*. Austin: University of Texas Press.

Seaton, Matt, 2001. Word Up. *The Guardian* 21 Sep. http://www.guardian.co.uk/g2/story/
    0,3604,555379,00.html (accessed Nov 2004)

Tench, P., 1996. *The intonation systems of English*. London: Cassell.

Wells, J. C., 1982. *Accents of English*. Cambridge: Cambridge University Press.

Wennerstrom, A., 2001. *The music of everyday speech*. Oxford: Oxford University Press.

Wichmann, A., 2000. *Intonation in text and discourse: beginnings, middles and ends*.
    Harlow: Longman.

Windsor Lewis, J. (ed.), 1995. *Studies in general and English phonetics: essays in honour
    of Prof. J. D. O'Connor*. London and New York: Routledge.

Index